To Dad
Love From
Julia
Apr 202

PROMOTION-WINNING
CANARIES

PROMOTION-WINNING
CANARIES

THE MEMORIES, PLAYERS, FACTS AND FIGURES BEHIND ALL TEN NORWICH CITY POST-WAR PROMOTIONS

PETER ROGERS

First published by Pitch Publishing, 2019

Pitch Publishing
A2 Yeoman Gate
Yeoman Way
Worthing
Sussex
BN13 3QZ
www.pitchpublishing.co.uk
info@pitchpublishing.co.uk

ISBN 978 1 78531 565 7

Typesetting and origination by Pitch Publishing
Printed and bound in India by Replika Press Pvt. Ltd.

CONTENTS

ACKNOWLEDGEMENTS

Norwich City Football Club has played a huge part in my life, and I have cherished every step of my involvement with the club. From initially attending my first game with my dad in 1983, I subsequently spent three seasons as a senior ball boy; from there I progressed to an 11-year stint as a member of match-day staff in the Canary Store – followed by 15 memorable years as the club's programme editor.

Many of my most enjoyable times have centred around the club's promotion-winning successes, so my initial round of thanks must go the sterling efforts of the 213 players – all of whom are featured in this book – who have helped provide so many happy times for the club and its supporters to cherish.

My particular thanks go to Bill Punton, David Cross, Dave Stringer, Mark Barham, Kevin Drinkell, Iwan Roberts, Simon Lappin, Andrew Crofts and Russell Martin for giving so generously of their time to share their promotion tales with me for this publication. Nine true gentlemen who were all outstanding servants to Norwich City Football Club.

On the subject of true gentlemen, I would like to place on record my sincere thanks to Chris Lakey, head of sport at Archant. Following confirmation of City's 2018/19 promotion – and with it the need for an additional season review! – Chris very kindly granted permission for the reproduction of quotes from Tim Krul, which had appeared on various Archant platforms, to be used in this publication.

Many thanks to former boss Nigel Worthington for kindly providing the foreword. Oh, and also for signing Darren Huckerby and for my place on the open-top bus parade in 2004! Incredible memories for which I remain eternally grateful.

Sincere thanks too to Paul Camillin, Jane Camillin and all at Pitch Publishing for their assistance, advice and professionalism throughout this project.

I would like to place on record my appreciation and thanks to James Woodrow, from the Norwich City Football Club Historical Trust, for his statistical knowledge and input, and for all the time spent checking facts and figures relating to appearances and goalscorers. And when it came to checking and double-checking the text, the support of former *Eastern Daily Press* Norwich City reporter and general Canary aficionado Trevor Burton proved simply priceless.

The help of Dan Brigham at Norwich City has also been gratefully appreciated.

Finally, I must thank my long-suffering partner Jenny for her never-ending patience whilst I have spent far too long with my head in a laptop working on this latest book. Now we can book that holiday ...

Peter Rogers
June 2019

FOREWORD

Leading Norwich City to the First Division title in 2003/04 was certainly the highlight of my time as manager at Carrow Road.

When I reflect on my own playing career, as both a promotion winner and a cup winner, the promotion campaigns always tend to be more satisfying as your success is the culmination of a long season's work. The league is your bread and butter, and if you end up winning promotion it has been achieved over a gruelling season and you've established yourselves as one of the best three teams in your respective division.

So, the essence of this book is the celebration of promotion-winning campaigns – but for players, managers and staff the real prize is being able to test yourself at a higher level the following season. As a professional in the game you always want to be able to compete at the highest level and pit your wits against the best.

After coming so close to promotion in 2001/02, when we lost the play-off final against Birmingham on penalties, it was a tremendous feeling to win promotion as champions two seasons later. That success really was a fitting reward for an outstanding group of players. It was particularly satisfying that so many of the side, which came so close that afternoon in Cardiff's Millennium Stadium, then stuck together and went on to form the backbone of the team that reached the Premier League in 2004.

Eight of the promotion campaigns in this book relate to Norwich City winning promotion to the top flight of English football, today's Premier League. The club's 2018/19 success has propelled them back to that level and I congratulate everyone involved in the latest triumph.

Towards the end of the 2018/19 campaign, I was invited back to the Colney training ground by the club's sporting director, Stuart

Webber, to present Alex Tettey with a shirt to commemorate his 200th appearance for the club. That trip to Colney also offered me an opportunity to see the excellent work that has taken place to improve the training ground, and to meet Daniel Farke. I was extremely impressed by both Daniel and Stuart, and having sensed the atmosphere amongst the group it came as little surprise to me that they went on to achieve their aim.

So far as this celebration of promotions is concerned, Peter Rogers was the club's programme editor throughout my tenure as Norwich City manager, and I know he always took great pride in producing an excellent publication that the club were rightly proud of. I therefore have no doubt that this book, too, will provide an enjoyable and entertaining read for all Norwich City supporters.

Nigel Worthington

INTRODUCTION

The 2018/19 campaign has just seen Norwich City celebrate their fourth promotion in ten seasons – it may be that current members of the yellow army have been somewhat spoilt in recent times!

Delighted to have attended City's League Cup Final victory at Wembley with my dad in 1985, I also carried my inflatable canary with pride during the 1988/89 FA Cup run, and was reduced to tears following the semi-final defeat at Hillsborough three years later. My timing was perfect in 1992/93 as I attended every game, home and away – completing my first ever-present season as City took the inaugural Premier League by storm. I was then thrilled to witness all six UEFA Cup ties in 1993/94 – and, after all, who knows when that opportunity will come around again?

But despite all the great memories listed above, in my eyes there really is no season quite like a promotion season.

City's return to the Premier League via the 2014/15 play-off final victory over Middlesbrough at Wembley was a wonderful occasion, and as a single one-off day it rates for many fans as their fondest moment following the Canaries' fortunes.

For me, and for many thousands of other City fans, being able to share that Wembley triumph with friends and family was the icing on the cake. The hands of time had moved on inexorably since my first visit to the old Wembley some 30 years earlier. Back in 1985, I was perched on a bench seat with my dad and peering through mesh fencing to see Dave Watson hoist the Milk Cup. Fast forward to 2015 and I was now the dad, and my sons were sitting with me – but now in a breathtaking modern stadium, light years removed from its ageing predecessor. So many generations of City fans flocked to the national stadium that day in May 2015, and they were treated to a day they'll never forget. I guess it was that 'Wembley glow' that gave me the inspiration to get this project under way. However, it was not until the following season was in full flow that you appreciated just how good the actual 'going up' bit really was. At Wembley we celebrated our promotion to the Premier League, but what was there to top that Wembley experience during the subsequent 2015/16 campaign? Answer, absolutely nothing ...

From the dizzy heights of an excellent 2-1 win over Manchester United at Old Trafford to the downright miserable depths of a 3-0 defeat at Bournemouth – nothing in 2015/16 held a candle to Wembley.

Perhaps some of those feelings come from the extreme difficulties that smaller promoted clubs (such as Norwich City) face when trying to compete and survive in the modern-day Premier League. I just happen to believe that the journey can often be more thrilling than the destination.

It is similar even when reflecting on City's historic promotion as Second Division champions in 1971/72, when Ron Saunders's team brought First Division football to Norfolk for the first time. Supporters who watched games in that period will rarely talk about Jimmy Bone scoring Norwich's first-ever top-flight goal against Everton – yet they'll still give you chapter and verse on the previous season's never-to-be-forgotten trips to Orient and Watford.

So the essence of this book is to revel in my belief that promotion seasons are often the best seasons, memorable campaigns that are there to be enjoyed and cherished by those watching and, of course, by those playing.

On the subject of the wonderful players who made these ten great seasons possible, no matter how large or small their contribution, I felt it vital to profile all those who entered the field of play during a league fixture across the ten promotion-winning campaigns. I also made the decision to detail only their playing statistics from those promotion seasons rather than for their full Norwich City careers. I hope this gives readers a chance to reflect on each individual player's offering to these fantastic campaigns.

All supporters will have their favourite promotion campaigns and this book reflects on all ten of Norwich City's post-war promotions. So whether it's Archie Macaulay's 1959/60 promotion winners, Ron Saunders's history makers, Ken Brown's boys of the 80s or something from more recent times – whatever gets the green-and-yellow promotion blood pumping through your veins, I'm sure you'll find something to enjoy!

On the ball, City!

Season Reviews

1959/60 DIVISION THREE RUNNERS-UP

Speedy winger Bill Punton's debut season at Carrow Road saw the Canaries build on their FA Cup heroics of the previous campaign by winning promotion from the Third Division in 1959/60.

The 1959/60 campaign proved to be a landmark season for both Norwich City and Southampton as both clubs won promotion from the old Third Division and remained within the top-two tiers of the English league set-up for almost half a century, until they were both relegated to the third tier in 2009.

Recollections of the Canaries' success in 1959/60 were thrust back into the spotlight in the spring of 2019 as City's class of 2018/19 closed in on promotion to the Premier League. Despite Norwich City winning promotion on eight occasions between 1960 and 2019, it was only Archie Macaulay's men and Daniel Farke's side that actually secured promotion on home soil at Carrow Road.

If the promotion of Farke's Norwich team in 2018/19 came as something of a surprise, then the achievements of Macaulay's men in 1959/60 were perhaps the polar opposite.

A no-nonsense, straight-talking Scot, Macaulay replaced Tom Parker as Norwich boss in April 1957. He began building Norwich City from ground zero – there was nowhere else to start. The team had just finished their 1956/57 campaign rooted to the foot of the Third Division (South) table following a financial crisis which had almost brought the club to the very brink of extinction, and they were now faced with applying for re-election to the Football League.

A smart operator, Macaulay soon plotted the way forward and in his first full season in charge, in 1957/58, he guided the club to an eighth-place finish in Division Three (South). Under Macaulay's watch, City had increased their points haul from 31 to 53 and their league standing by 16 places. All in all, an impressive season's work by all concerned at Carrow Road.

The progress made in Macaulay's first season was built upon again in 1958/59. The Canaries' league progress was of course totally overshadowed that season as Norwich City shocked the football world with a gallant run to the semi-finals of the FA Cup – a phenomenal achievement for a then Third Division team. The heroics of the club's famed '59ers, who recorded never-to-be-forgotten victories over Manchester United, Cardiff City, Tottenham Hotspur and Sheffield United before bowing out in a semi-final replay to Luton Town, saw them widely recognised as the men who put Norwich on the map in footballing terms.

While the cup run grabbed all the attention, headlines and focus, the side once again crept their way up the Third Division table. They ended the 1958/59 season in fourth place, just four points shy of second-place Hull City, who won promotion with champions Plymouth Argyle. City's cup exploits resulted in the Canaries facing a major fixture backlog, so much so that they had to play 11 games in 26 days in April 1959 to complete their fixture programme.

Everyone associated with Norwich City cherished the unforgettable excitement of the FA Cup run, particularly all the national attention it brought to the city, but one has to wonder if it also hampered what could have been a promotion-winning campaign.

Following all the drama of 1958/59, Macaulay had his men ready to go again come August 1959, and he possessed a group of players fully focused on winning promotion to the Second Division.

One of that group of players, geared for a promotion push, was new signing Bill Punton, who had joined the Canary ranks in July 1959. A pacey Scottish winger, 25-year-old Punton had been signed from Southend United and was delighted to be reunited with his former Roots Hall team-mate Errol Crossan, who had made the identical move some ten months earlier.

'Errol and I both played for Southend in a game against Norwich right at the start of the 58/59 season – it was just after I'd joined Southend. We beat Norwich and it was then that Archie Macaulay wanted to sign both of us,' recalled Punton, who turned 85 in May 2019. 'Southend would only sell one of us and it was Errol who got the move and I had to wait until the end of the season.'

Macaulay's interest in Punton certainly never waned despite the delay in getting his man. Come the summer of 1959 and the City boss made Punton his number-one target. 'He came up to Scotland to see me and talked me into making the move. I'll always remember that; he certainly went out of his way to make sure I signed for Norwich City.

'He explained that he wanted me to take over from Bobby Brennan. He felt time was starting to catch up with Bobby and he was losing a bit of his pace and they needed someone really quick on the wing.

'The conversation we had centred around my role in the team and his plan to win promotion. Errol was a really quick player and he wanted to use our pace to help the team get up.'

Once Punton arrived in Norfolk and began training with his new team-mates, he soon got the impression that this was a group of players with unfinished business. After falling at the semi-final hurdle in the cup, the team were really looking to make their move up to the Second Division.

'It was a good side, as they had shown the year before in the cup. I was certainly joining a good team, there was no doubting that,' confirmed Punton. 'They all wanted promotion and certainly didn't lack any belief. As a group of players they never thought they were beat; going behind wasn't a problem.'

Norwich's 1959/60 league campaign started away to Southampton on Saturday, 22 August 1959 with Terry Bly and Jimmy Hill on target for City in a 2-2 draw at The Dell. A hard-fought meeting with the Saints certainly set the tone for what would unfold throughout the season as both clubs slogged it out at the top of the table for the majority of the campaign.

The Canaries followed up their point on the south coast with home wins over Tranmere Rovers and Reading. A swift return meeting with Tranmere saw Punton make his Canary debut in place of Brennan as the teams drew 0-0 at Prenton Park on Monday, 31 August 1959. However, the new man had to wait until mid-October before cementing himself a regular place in the team.

'At first I couldn't get in the side because Brennan was a very, very good player and a big crowd favourite. Plus the crowd didn't really take to me to start with because Brennan was such a favourite and I had been bought to take his place.

'In those days they used to play a pre-season practice match at Carrow Road between the first team and reserves which used to pull in thousands of people. I played for the reserves, and we lost 3-2, but I scored both the goals so that helped!'

With 20 games played, Norwich had won 11, drawn four and lost five. It meant their tussle at the top with Southampton was well and truly under way.

'We had a real battle with Southampton – they had a cracking side. Every side in those days had two fast wingers. We had Crossan and myself, Southampton had Terry Paine and John Sydenham.'

Crossan and Punton could both run 100 yards in 10.2 seconds wearing spikes, and the manager often put the two speed merchants through their paces around the Carrow Road perimeter track. Eventually it was the tactical awareness of Macaulay, coupled with Punton's natural pace, that added another dimension to the player's game.

'Archie Macaulay was the best manager I ever played under. He was such a shrewd tactician – he'd look at a defender and say, "Don't try to beat him on the outside – he can't tackle on his left foot, come inside him." I'd do that and just walk past the fellow, but I'd never have noticed it myself.'

Punton netted his first goal for City in a surprise 4-1 defeat at home to Coventry City on 21 November 1959 and he was on target again in the big match with Southampton on 19 December. Sadly, the free-scoring Saints ran out victors in this top-of-the-table clash at Carrow Road, winning what was certainly Division Three's 'Match of the Day' 2-1.

After suffering back-to-back home defeats, City then turned on the style to get their promotion push back on track when

Mansfield Town provided the opposition at Carrow Road on 28 December.

'I remember the Mansfield game. We played really well – they weren't a bad side, they had beaten us at their place on Boxing Day but we absolutely hammered them that day.'

That victory over the Stags saw a rare goal for defender Barry Butler, a player whom Punton had the greatest respect for.

'Barry Butler, he was the best centre-half I ever played with. Great footballer, really strong and boy he could play; very comfortable on the ball but just so brave and so strong. I played four years at Newcastle, before I went to Southend, and they had some really good players at centre-half – but none as good as he was.'

Another player on the score sheet in that morale-boosting victory over Mansfield was Jimmy Hill. The Irishman ended the season as joint top scorer with 16 league goals and his skills were nothing new to Punton.

'I played with Jimmy Hill at Newcastle. He then came down to Norwich around the same time that I went to Southend. I'd liken him to Wes Hoolahan in terms of some of the recent players. Jimmy was really clever on the ball and could always make things happen for us.'

Boosted by their resounding victory over Mansfield Town, City began the calendar year of 1960 with two excellent wins away from home. A Terry Bly brace sealed a 2-0 win away to Reading before Errol Crossan's first-half goal secured both points from a trip to Halifax Town on 9 January.

The big difference now from 12 months earlier was that City were not distracted by the FA Cup – there was to be no repeat of the previous season's incredible adventure as City bowed out of the competition to Reading. After a first-round tie ended 1-1 at Carrow Road, the Royals triumphed in the Elm Park replay.

Superb form throughout February and March saw Norwich and Southampton break further away from the chasing pack. Macaulay strengthened the City squad with the signings of Bunny Larkin and Brian Whitehouse, who were bought just before the transfer deadline in March 1960, and their arrival helped City's drive towards the finish line.

April saw Carrow Road victories over York City and Halifax Town and, after a point was secured from a goalless draw away to Queens Park Rangers, City went into their penultimate game of the season with promotion in their grasp.

It was Punton's former club, Southend United, who stood between City and a place in the Second Division. The Canaries had slipped to a narrow 1-0 defeat in Essex when the two sides had met back in October 1959, so Norwich now had both revenge and promotion in their sights.

In front of a bumper Carrow Road crowd of 34,905 on Wednesday, 27 April 1960, promotion was finally clinched following a thrilling 4-3 victory. This memorable midweek promotion clincher certainly saw ex-Shrimpers Punton and Crossan use a little inside knowledge to see off their former employers. Both men were fired up and in top form, with Crossan netting twice, Punton once, and Whitehouse also on target.

'It was probably one of the best games I ever had,' says Punton. 'I made two goals and scored one, the crowd really got behind me and I never looked back from there.

'The funny thing is that because Errol Crossan and I had both played for Southend we knew that their goalkeeper, Harry Threadgold, was as blind as a bat under floodlights so we just kept putting high balls in and he kept missing them!

'There was a tremendous atmosphere, the whole place was really tingling. We knew we had to get a result from that game and the crowd – they went bananas when we won!'

'On the Ball, City' was sung throughout the game, and at the final whistle thousands of fans ran across the pitch to celebrate City's return to Division Two just three years after having to apply for re-election in the summer of 1957.

Southampton finished the season with 61 points to pip the Canaries to the title by two points, but both sides finished comfortably clear of third-placed Shrewsbury, who managed a 52-point return.

Incredibly, Southampton's 46-match league programme featured no fewer than 181 goals – 106 for, and 75 against, with Derek Reeves netting 39 league goals. The Canaries were no goalscoring slouches either, their 82 strikes including notable contributions from Terry Allcock (16), Jimmy Hill (16), and Errol Crossan (13).

Ron Ashman, Barry Butler, Roy McCrohan and Bryan Thurlow played in every game that season, and Matt Crowe, Sandy Kennon, Terry Allcock, Errol Crossan and Jimmy Hill missed only a handful of matches between them. Many of them were, of course, already Canary legends following their great FA Cup heroics the previous season, but now they had a promotion on their CV and Second Division football to look forward to. They were a great group of players – some of whom were a little underrated, according to team-mate Punton.

'Matt Crowe, he was certainly one of our best players. A great left-half, he would say, "Get on your bike, Punty" and he would hit balls over full-backs' heads and leave the full-back thinking that the ball's going to run into touch, but he would have put back-spin on the ball and I'd keep going and run to it and be in from there.

'Terry Allcock used to score a lot of goals, mostly in and around the six-yard box. He was like Martin Peters – he'd drift in last minute and people never saw him. He was certainly an intelligent striker.'

Mention the name of ever-present Bryan Thurlow and a big grin appears on Punton's face:

'Bryan, he was tough you know. We'd often play first team against reserves in training and whenever I came up against Bryan in attack v defence he kicked the shit out of me! Archie Macaulay would say, "What are you doing Bryan?" and he'd reply, "It's the only way I can play!"'

This promotion-winning team were a close-knit group who certainly enjoyed one another's company both on and off the pitch. Unsurprisingly, Punton has fond memories of the celebrations that followed:

'We all went to the University Arms pub after the match for a supper and some drinks. We all had our wives up there too – it was really nice.'

21

1971/72 DIVISION TWO CHAMPIONS

There is no forgetting the first time, and Canary fans will always remember the thrilling 1971/72 season as Norwich City finally achieved their dream of promotion to the top tier of English football. Former striker David Cross reflects on a memorable campaign at Carrow Road.

Norwich City's historic first-ever promotion to the top flight in 1971/72 elevated the club into the big time and ended more than a decade mired in mid-table Second Division obscurity.

Following his arrival at Carrow Road in July 1969, manager Ron Saunders had step-by-step been piecing together his Norwich City team. The City boss always had promotion to the First Division as his aim, and he made some astute purchases while also extracting every last ounce of ability from the players he had inherited.

Goalkeeper Kevin Keelan; central-defenders Duncan Forbes and Dave Stringer; full-backs Alan Black, Clive Payne and Geoff Butler; midfielders Max Briggs, Trevor Howard and Terry Anderson; and forward Ken Foggo – all were City players when Saunders arrived from Oxford United, and all played major roles in helping the Canaries fulfil their top-flight dream.

Saunders wisely blended the players already at his disposal with a number of new faces to create a side that could move the Canaries to the next level.

In September 1969 the Canaries paid £20,000 to Reading for striker Peter Silvester, and a month later they paid Coventry

City around £25,000 for teenager Graham Paddon. Another key signing was made in November 1970 when creative midfielder Doug Livermore arrived from Liverpool.

Under Saunders's management, City had finished 11th in Division Two in 1969/70, and tenth in 1970/71. So on the back of two mid-table finishes, there was no great level of expectancy among supporters ahead of the 1971/72 campaign.

The season kicked off with a twice-taken Paddon penalty that gave City a 1-1 draw at Luton Town on the first day of the season, and then Silvester, Foggo and Malcolm Darling were on target in a 3-1 home win over Portsmouth. Goalless draws against Fulham and Orient were far from inspiring, but an unlikely run of five successive victories over Carlisle United, Blackpool, Oxford United – who were beaten 3-2 at Carrow Road despite taking the lead after 20 seconds – Bristol City and Preston North End forced even the most sceptical to sit up and take notice.

City were far from easy on the eye – Saunders being a greater believer in hard work than creative flair. The Canaries were, however, proving highly effective. A goalless draw at home to Queens Park Rangers at the start of October attracted a crowd of 22,000 – the biggest for four years – and put unbeaten City three points clear (these were in the days of two points for a win) after ten league games.

The Canaries' appetite to capitalise on their good start was made clear in October 1971 when they paid a club-record fee of £40,000 to sign striker David Cross from Rochdale. Saunders had not even seen Cross play – but he was happy to act on the advice of chief coach Terry Allcock, who had been impressed when he watched the 20-year-old.

While modern-day managers frequently treat 'promotion' as a dirty 'P' word, often preferring to play down their team's ambitions, new signing Cross recalls City boss Saunders as a man untroubled by any kind of cautious approach:

'What struck me was the determination and conviction that we were going up,' said Cross. 'There was no question about it. The first thing I noticed in the dressing room was that Ron Saunders had put up a sheet splitting the season into a series of six-game blocks with points targets. He was probably looking for something like nine points from each block, and that became something we focussed on. It broke the season into little bite-sized pieces, and when we finished one block of six we moved on to the next one.

'This was the season when Norwich were going to be promoted, and Ron Saunders was prepared to state that, and to live or die by it. A lot of people didn't like him but that didn't bother him – he was very forthright, and he would tell the press where to go if he didn't like something that had been written.'

Meanwhile it was only after arriving in Norfolk that 20-year-old Cross realised the weighty burden on his own shoulders:

'They were already top of the league when I arrived so I didn't realise the history,' says Cross, who went on to score eight goals in the 1971/72 campaign.

'What had happened was that Ron Saunders was building the team he felt would get promotion, but was always short of a striker to partner Peter Silvester, who was scoring a lot of goals but needed some support. It transpired that Ron Saunders had been promising the crowd "the final piece in the jigsaw", so that was quite a big thing for a rookie striker who had scored 20-odd goals for Rochdale over the past two-and-a-half years.

'Peter Silvester and I became good friends – he looked after me. I was a single lad, he was married and settled. You're always conscious, as a striker, that if another striker comes in they might potentially take your place, but he didn't view me as a threat – he was glad to have a big lad to play alongside.'

Cross made his debut in a 1-1 draw at Sunderland, and City maintained their momentum with two thrilling Carrow Road victories in four days – beating Burnley 3-0 and Luton 3-1.

Saunders's 4-3-3 line-up was by now fairly settled, with Keelan in goal; Payne, Forbes, Stringer and Butler forming the back four; Anderson, Livermore and Paddon in midfield; and Silvester, Foggo and Cross – who took over from Trevor Howard – in attack.

Saunders's men suffered their first defeat of the season in their 14th league game – a top-of-the-table clash away to second-place Millwall in the ferocious atmosphere of the Den. City went into the game three points ahead of the Lions, and as the only unbeaten side in all four divisions. Furthermore, they had conceded only seven goals in 13 games. But Stringer conceded an own goal after five minutes, and although Silvester levelled it was Millwall who ran out 2-1 winners.

With just two promotion places and no play-offs, the Canaries were embroiled in a titanic struggle with Millwall and Birmingham City – although both Queens Park Rangers and Sunderland also posed a threat.

'It was a great set of lads,' recalls Cross, whose later career as a powerful target man included spells at Coventry City, West Bromwich Albion and West Ham United, for whom he played in the 1980 FA Cup Final success over Arsenal.

'Peter Silvester had come in from Reading, and a few other lads had come from smaller clubs, and we were seeking to prove ourselves. Others, like Graham Paddon and Doug Livermore, had come from the reserves at bigger clubs and had something to prove from another angle. Then you had the older hands like Duncan Forbes, Dave Stringer and Kevin Keelan.

'We were basically a young team, and there was no jealousy. Ron Saunders was as interested in your character as your ability – he wanted decent people – what he termed 'good types'. It was an exciting time, and we were on decent bonus money as well. The higher up the table we were, the bigger the bonuses.'

The City players doubtless deserved every penny for surviving Saunders's punishing and notorious training excursions on Mousehold Heath.

'The throwing-up in the bushes depended on what you'd been doing the night before,' reflects Cross. 'We knew what was coming and worked really hard. We would run up the hill, carry weights up the hill, hop up on one leg, bunny hop – it was very unusual, but we got on with it. You laughed at the ones that struggled, and laughed when you fell flat on your face yourself.'

The outcome, of course, was that most other sides could not live with City's standards of fitness.

'We knew we were just so fit that we could run people into the ground. It was a wonderful feeling going out knowing we would be fitter than the opposition, and we did grind teams down.'

City responded to their disappointing defeat at Millwall by beating Cardiff City 2-1 at Carrow Road on 30 October; the game was notable for Cross registering his first Norwich goal and for a costly hamstring injury suffered by Forbes, who would miss the next 15 league games.

Cross's first goal in Canary yellow arrived in what was his fifth appearance for his new club, and the striker was delighted to get off the mark after becoming a little concerned about the wait to find the back of the net:

'It was a feeling of relief really,' says Cross. 'I'd come down as the record signing at the time, at £40,000, and also Rochdale's record sale. However, it wasn't until I got there and read in the local paper that Norwich hadn't paid any more than that for a player before. I'm 20 years of age, with only 50 games in the Third Division with Rochdale under my belt, so I'm thinking, "wow, I've got some responsibility here. Ron Saunders has stuck his neck out and bought me, looking for a striker who's going to score enough goals to get the club up."

'So as games went by I was thinking, "when am I going to get a goal?" I always knew I'd get chances but when chances come you had to put them away. I was really relieved and also pleased that it came at Carrow Road in front of the home fans.

'I was always contributing and working hard, and I knew that was one of the reasons Ron Saunders signed me, he knew I worked hard. I also knew that the rest of the lads appreciated the work I was putting in but I've always felt that a number nine – his job is to score goals so I was conscious of that.'

Back to winning ways against the Bluebirds, Norwich were also progressing well in the League Cup. After despatching Brighton, Carlisle and Grimsby, they faced Chelsea at Carrow Road in the fifth round on 3 November. The attendance of 35,927 was the biggest since 1967, but City were beaten 1-0.

In the league a 1-1 draw at home to bottom-of-the-table Watford on 11 December was a further disappointment, and Forbes was badly missed as City then crashed 3-0 at Carlisle on 18 December – Stan Bowles firing a hat-trick.

'Stan took us to the cleaners. It was an awful pitch. The wind was incredible and it blew across the pitch and spoilt the game, but Stan was so clever on the ball he just dribbled past us and took us to the cleaners. It was a wake-up call,' admits Cross.

City responded by signing midfielder Phil Hubbard from Lincoln City for £20,000 on Christmas Eve. He made his debut in a welcome 3-0 home win over Charlton on 27 December; that was followed by a 2-0 win at Oxford before Hubbard scored his only goal for the Canaries in a 2-1 home win over Fulham on 8 January.

But City suffered a 3-0 hammering at home to Hull in the third round of the FA Cup on 15 January, and a week later were dealt a cruel blow when Silvester – who had scored 12 goals in 26 league games – suffered a serious knee injury in a 1-1 draw at home to Preston on 22 January. The injury would sideline him for 18 months.

Alan Black had by now taken over from Butler at left-back, but City were starting to struggle badly without Forbes and Silvester. Saunders's men shared a thrilling 2-2 draw with Millwall at Carrow Road on 12 February, but the jitters were evident in a 4-0 mauling away to rivals Birmingham on 4 March.

That game marked an inauspicious start to the City career of Scottish striker Jim Bone, who had been signed for £30,000 from Partick Thistle. But Bone scored his first Canary goal in a 1-1 draw at home to high-flying Sunderland the following week – and City also welcomed back the much-missed Forbes.

'We had a bad spell after losing Duncan; Bobby Bell came in on loan from Palace and we signed Boney at the end of February. I hadn't had a good spell, and strikers tend to be a mirror image of the team – if the strikers are playing well and scoring the team probably won't be having a bad spell,' reflects Cross.

With City suffering a tricky spell and Cross himself in the midst of a five-match goalless run, the young striker was grateful for the continued support of his manager:

'Ron was very good; he was a kind of father figure to the younger lads like me. He would cajole us a little bit. It would be "Crossy come in the office; you're not scoring – have you got a girlfriend?" So you're then thinking, "If he thinks I've got a girlfriend he'll think I'm shagging every night." So it's, "no, I haven't got a girlfriend, boss," and he'd reply with, "well, you need to bloody get one – that's what's wrong with you!" You could never win with him in that respect!

'He knew the script; he was a hard man but he was fair. He was always supportive and he'd be aware that if you were doing the right things, then things would come for you in the end.'

A 2-0 win over Hull was followed by a wretched 2-1 defeat at Portsmouth on 18 March, and after one win in eight games there were fears that City could blow it. But Saunders and his troops remained resolute, and City blew away the nerves in style by thrashing Blackpool 5-1 at Carrow Road on 25 March.

On a sun-drenched afternoon at Carrow Road, City got off to the best possible start as Cross won a second-minute penalty which Paddon converted at the Barclay End, and Kenny Foggo headed the second from Cross's pinpoint delivery.

A mix-up between Keelan and Stringer presented Mickey Burns with a gift to make it 2-1, but City responded with a marvellous move as Paddon sent Foggo away down the right, and his cross was met by Cross with a classic centre-forward's header for 3-1. Bone headed a fourth before the break, and in the second-half Paddon hammered home a swerving long-range effort to complete the rout.

'It was a vital game for us,' recalls Cross. 'It was our best performance of the season and just gave us that little kick-start. It was a very hot day – unseasonably hot – but we just knew we had to beat them because we hadn't been playing well.

'I think the fans were thinking that if we didn't win that would be it, and if we hadn't gone up that season it would have been really, really hard to get us going again. I think we were all aware of that, but we won it easily playing excellent football.'

A busy Easter brought four points from key games against Charlton, QPR and Bristol City. Forbes's 81st-minute goal earned a 1-0 home win over Sheffield Wednesday; City then lost 1-0 at Middlesbrough, but the inspirational Forbes struck again to seal a 1-0 home win over Swindon and take his side to the brink of promotion.

The Canaries needed two points from their last two games, and around 3,000 supporters travelled to see goals by Foggo – his 13th league strike of the season – and Paddon spark jubilant celebrations with a famous 2-1 win at Orient on Monday, 24 April.

'Orient was nerve-racking,' says Cross. 'That was the one where you got off the coach and thought, "Christ, if we win today we're up".'

Despite the magnitude of the match, with First Division football now within touching distance, there was certainly no special message or rallying cry from Saunders as the Canaries left the visitors' dressing room at Brisbane Road.

'Nothing was any different really,' remembers Cross. 'We knew how he wanted us to play. We had patterns of play that we set up and we worked on every day in training. We knew we still had the game at Watford if things went wrong, but we were pretty hyped up as we were all conscious of how near we were. Ron was just normal, he made sure we knew what we were doing on our corners, set pieces and throw-ins, and he just wanted us to work hard and support one another.'

Promotion was secure, but with Birmingham in hot pursuit City needed a point from their final game at relegated Watford on 29 April to be crowned champions.

'We celebrated long and hard and I've an idea he may have let us off training for a couple of days, but we realised it would be a shame not to go up as champions so we got ourselves together.'

Norwich wore unfamiliar red shirts to avoid a clash with Watford's yellow, black and red, and it was fitting that newly crowned player-of-the-season Stringer should head his side 1-0 up in the rain at Vicarage Road. The Hornets levelled after the break, and only a miraculous save from Keelan kept City's point safe as he twisted in mid-air to turn Ron Wigg's header over the bar after 88 minutes. At the final whistle City's heroes threw their red shirts into the crowd, and the partying began.

'One thing I remember about Watford is that the game might not have been played because it was so wet. The pitch was awful, absolutely terrible, and we thought we might come a cropper, but Dave Stringer scored with his head from a corner. I don't think we'd have been allowed to throw our shirts in the crowd if they'd been the yellow ones!

'The celebrations afterwards seemed to go on for months. It seemed as if we were out every night, and no one would let us buy a drink. We were like Gods in Norwich for about six months

– people were plying us with drinks and taking us out. It was a marvellous time.'

So the season concluded with City having won 21, drawn 15 and lost just six of their 42 league games, finishing on 57 points – one ahead of Birmingham in the other promotion place. The Canaries had also remained unbeaten at Carrow Road in the league as they entered the top flight of English football for the first time.

When reflecting on the success of 1971/72, Cross looks back proudly on his own contribution, but feels the real hero among City's forward men from that historic campaign is often the forgotten man:

'I only got eight goals that season from signing in October. Jimmy Bone got four but Peter Silvester had got 12 by the end of December before he got his injury. Some people thought that Bone and Cross got the goals that got us up, but I'll tell you who got that goals that got us up – that was Peter Silvester.'

Cross retired in 2016 from his role as opposition analyst at Blackburn Rovers. He remains an occasional guest at West Ham United games and kept a close eye on the Canaries' latest promotion campaign, under Daniel Farke, from his home in the north west:

'I saw the Leeds game at Elland Road and I thought, "wow what a team he's got there" – I was really impressed. Elland Road is a hard place to go, but what a team ethic. It reminded me very much of the way we played – it was almost like a replay of what we used to do. I can't judge the whole season on one game on TV, but I did think, "that's Ron Saunders's Norwich City" – and in that respect what a good job the manager has done.'

1974/75 THIRD IN DIVISION TWO

Relegated after two seasons of top-flight football, Norwich City had developed a taste for the big-time and made a swift return to the First Division in 1974/75. Dave Stringer recalls City's season-long tussle with Manchester United and Aston Villa in both the league and cup.

Norwich City regained top-flight status at the first attempt and reached the League Cup Final at Wembley for the second time in three seasons during manager John Bond's memorable first full campaign in charge.

The Canaries ended the 1974/75 season by winning promotion in the third automatic promotion spot – which had only been introduced a year earlier – behind two of the great names in English football. The Division Two title was won by Manchester United, who were spending a rare season outside the top flight after being relegated with Norwich and Southampton the previous year. Aston Villa, meanwhile, were completing their journey back to the top after suffering the ignominy of dropping into the old Third Division for the first time in the club's history in 1970.

After two seasons competing in the First Division, City's relegation back to the second tier did not come as the greatest of surprises. They had survived their maiden top-flight campaign in 1972/73 thanks to a memorable late goal from defender Dave Stringer that secured a 2-1 win over Crystal Palace at Carrow Road in the penultimate game of the season. In what was a true 'winner-takes-all affair', Stringer's header ensured the Canaries survived and the Eagles suffered the drop to Division Two.

The 1973/74 campaign was dominated by two key departures as the winds of change blew through Carrow Road. In the boardroom, chairman Geoffrey Watling stood down after 17 years at the helm and was replaced by Arthur South in August 1973. Manager Ron Saunders failed to strike up the same kind of positive working relationship with South that he had enjoyed with Watling, and after just two league wins in 16 games he resigned following a 3-1 defeat at home to Everton. His resignation followed an alleged blazing boardroom showdown.

After almost a month without a manager, City named Bournemouth boss John Bond as the new man in the Carrow Road hot seat. For long-serving defender Stringer, who had enjoyed great success under Saunders, and had done as much as anyone to help the Canaries achieve their aim of bringing First Division Football to Norfolk, these were changing times:

'The previous season was our first in Division One and that was a big learning curve for us,' says Stringer. 'Facing the quality of teams in the top division was tough, just as it is now for any promoted team. But we did manage just to stay up in that first season.

'Of course in the second season we found things a little more difficult, plus obviously Ron Saunders left and John Bond came in. John brought lots of new players with him from Bournemouth and there was an awful lot of change happening. At one stage it looked as though we were transferring half our players to Bournemouth and half their players were coming here!'

Despite the new man at the helm looking to implement his own ideas, ways and style of play at Carrow Road, one thing remained the same – the central-defensive pairing of Norfolk-born Stringer and captain Duncan Forbes.

'John kept both Duncan and I in the side. I think that was to try and help keep things organised defensively at the back,' recalled Stringer. 'It took a long time for things to settle, and for John to get us playing how he wanted, and that is usually the case when a new manager comes in.'

A switch of manager at any football club will always bring an element of change, but the exchange of Saunders for Bond really was a journey from one far end of the spectrum to the other.

To compare Saunders and Bond would be on a par with 1988 Wimbledon meets Pep Guardiola ...

'It was chalk and cheese!' chuckled Stringer. 'Ron Saunders was very strict and knew how he wanted us to play. That suited us as well and we did well under him. He was a man for the big occasion and we were successful for that period of time in getting to where we wanted to be.

'John came in and his style of managing and playing was totally different. And that was something we had to get used to as the players who remained at Norwich. Obviously, the new ones coming in from Bournemouth were already well versed in knowing what he required.

'We did a lot more work during the week with the ball, lots of small-sided games, skill work and free-kicks. We were perhaps quite stuck in our ways as a team and John was looking to change that.'

This monumental change in the club's playing culture came against the backdrop of a First Division relegation battle. The fact that City ended 1973/74 propping up the table was therefore of little surprise:

'The relegation had an air of inevitability about it with all the changeover,' acknowledged Stringer. 'I don't think John was under great pressure to keep us up – the objective was to get a team together ready for the start of the following season, one that could get results and get us back up.'

When the 1974/75 fixtures were released, the games with United and Villa always looked key and were never going to lack spice. Canary striker Ted MacDougall certainly had a point to make to United following his unsuccessful spell at Old Trafford; Villa, meanwhile, were now managed by former City boss Saunders.

These rivalries would also extend from the Division Two promotion race to the latter stages of the League Cup, in which all three clubs made it to the last four. Norwich would eventually overcome United over two legs in an epic semi-final – only to be beaten 1-0 by Saunders's Villa at Wembley.

Having already reunited his old Bournemouth strike-force of MacDougall – whom he re-signed from West Ham – and

Phil Boyer at Carrow Road, Bond continued to tweak his squad ahead of the new season. Arrivals in the summer of 1974 included midfielder Peter Morris from Ipswich, defender Tony Powell from Bournemouth and full-back Colin Sullivan from Plymouth.

Ipswich winger Johnny Miller arrived in the autumn, and midfielder Mick McGuire joined the Canaries from Coventry in January 1975. Then, in March 1975, Bond pulled off a master-stroke with the signing of 31-year-old World Cup winner Martin Peters from Spurs for a bargain £50,000. But it was the prolific front pairing who would score the bulk of the goals in 1974/75, with MacDougall netting 23 times in all competitions, and Boyer contributing 21 goals.

Norwich opened the new Division Two season with a 2-1 home win over Blackpool – Powell scoring on his debut – and Colin Suggett's equaliser earned a 1-1 draw at Villa Park in the third match. City won eight and drew six of their first 15 league games, with only a 4-0 thrashing at Fulham blotting the copybook.

The tenth league game of the season comprised the first in the season's series of titanic clashes against Manchester United – and it was first blood to MacDougall as he silenced the boo-boys with a double strike against his old club as the Canaries won 2-0 at Carrow Road in September.

'There was certainly some added motivation there for Ted,' says Stringer. 'He perhaps didn't have the time at Old Trafford that he would have wished to have had. When he was at Bournemouth he was scoring goals for fun, and he got the move to Manchester United which I would have thought was the dream move for him.

'John Bond had him at Bournemouth and liked him as a player; that made Ted feel at home here, I think, and more determined to score goals.

'Ted and Phil Boyer had a great partnership up front. Phil used to do a lot of the donkey work and Ted used to get into the scoring positions for Phil to feed him or work around him.'

Two weeks after the United victory Mel Machin broke his goalscoring duck for the Canaries in style with an unlikely second-half hat-trick to secure a 3-1 win at Nottingham Forest in October.

'Mel used to get forward well from right-back and get into scoring positions; he was given the freedom to do that. That was

John Bond's influence there, he would encourage the full-backs to get forward and get into scoring positions. That way teams had to worry about us rather than we worry about them. As defenders we used to come up with a few decent goals and that all added to the variation that the team had.'

Next up was a Carrow Road visit from Portsmouth on 19 October as Stringer found himself up against legendary former Norwich striker Ron Davies. It was an afternoon when Stringer certainly got one over on his former Canary team-mate:

'I scored at the far post with a header – it was at the River End – I'll always remember it as Ron Davies was marking me. I don't think Ron was ever known for his defensive headers, his strength was heading as a striker at the other end. Let's just say Ron's picking-up at set pieces might not have been as sharp as a defender might have been!'

December began with Miller scoring in the first 30 seconds of an otherwise drab 1-1 draw against Cardiff City at Carrow Road, and in the next home game Boyer scored twice in a minute as City came from behind to beat Bristol City 3-2 in a pre-Christmas thriller.

With City still firing on all cylinders in the League Cup, a worrying sequence of three straight league defeats in January 1975 placed a question mark over the Canaries' promotion prospects. These included a bizarre 3-2 home defeat by York after the visitors went 2-0 up in the first 90 seconds.

But with the League Cup Final still to look forward to, City stopped the Division Two rot with a 2-0 win at Bristol Rovers at the start of February, and then a bumper crowd of 34,509 saw the Canaries twice come from behind to beat promotion rivals West Brom 3-2 at Carrow Road, with goals from MacDougall (2) and McGuire.

Norwich's marathon League Cup run saw them play ten games just to reach the final at Wembley, with the first four ties all going to replays. City beat Bolton 3-1 in a third-round replay at Carrow Road after drawing 0-0 at Burnden Park. In the fourth round City drew 1-1 at West Brom before winning 2-0 after extra-time in an exhilarating replay – MacDougall breaking the deadlock as he rounded the keeper and raised his arms in jubilation even before sliding the ball home.

In the fifth round City were again drawn away, and they drew 2-2 at Sheffield United before winning 2-1 in the replay to set up a mouth-watering home tie with First Division derby rivals Ipswich in the quarter-finals. This time the Canaries reversed the pattern by drawing 1-1 at home before Miller's double-strike against his old club secured a shock 2-1 victory at Portman Road.

Norwich travelled to Old Trafford for the first leg of the semi-final in January 1975, and MacDougall's 88th-minute goal gave City a 2-2 draw to bring back to Carrow Road. They finished the job as Suggett's winner gave Bond's men a thrilling 1-0 second-leg success, and a 3-2 aggregate victory over Tommy Docherty's team.

City had lost 1-0 to Spurs in the 1973 League Cup Final and had been beaten by Wolves in the semi-finals in 1974. And there was more heartbreak as the Canaries never performed against Villa in the final at Wembley on 1 March 1975. Goalkeeper Kevin Keelan kept Villa at bay almost single-handedly, until Machin conceded a penalty ten minutes from time with a spectacular one-handed save on the line from Chris Nicholl's powerful header.

Even then, Keelan turned Ray Graydon's spot-kick brilliantly on to the post, but the Villa man blasted home the rebound to seal a 1-0 victory. It was third time lucky for Saunders, who had lost with Norwich and Manchester City in the previous two finals.

However, Stringer never entertained any notion that the cup run might derail City's promotion push. After all, this was a team that had become almost accustomed to balancing the demands of a cup run with league football over recent seasons:

'In the League Cup we went final, semi-final, final in three years. So, having been used to being in that situation, we were able to handle it. I think perhaps the previous season, when we reached the semi-final with Wolves, that may have taken a little edge off what we were trying to do in the league, but experience teaches you a lot of things and we'd learned not to concentrate on just one thing but to spread our efforts across both.'

Norwich still had everything to go for in the league, and were given a huge lift by the arrival of Peters with ten games remaining. He made his debut in the return league game away to United – and City maintained their unbeaten record against the Red Devils as MacDougall scored yet again to earn a 1-1 draw at Old Trafford.

The introduction of Peters was certainly a timely boost for City, and Stringer acknowledges that the signing of the former England World Cup winner gave a huge injection of belief to the Canary changing room ahead of the promotion run-in:

'His reputation and experience was a big help to the team; he was a leader in that respect. His experience gave him the opportunity to speak to players on the pitch, calm a few down and get them playing football. He could help us keep possession and cause problems for the opposition. He could always find himself in a position where you could pass to him, he always seemed to be in acres of space, and from there he could start an attack or just relieve the defence from being under pressure.

'Everyone understood and respected what he had done and what a great player he was. And he continued to be so with his enthusiasm; he loved the game and you could see that from the way he played and how he conducted himself.'

The closing stages of the season found City locked in a tense battle for the final promotion place behind United and Villa. The Canaries finally secured promotion in their penultimate fixture with a 3-0 win at Portsmouth, with Boyer, Peters and McGuire scoring the goals. That result, coupled with Villa's 2-0 win over Sunderland, meant City were up after losing just once in 14 league games.

Frustratingly for Stringer, who had been ever-present, suspension ruled him out of the final three league games of the season:

'It was the totting up procedure, and as a defender you're in that position where you may pick up the points, which unfortunately I did. So to miss out on the final three games of the season when promotion was won, that was disappointing.'

Although he was ineligible for the fixture, Stringer travelled to Fratton Park with his team-mates, but when the action got under way he was forced to watch from the stands.

So what type of supporter was Stringer down on the south coast that day? 'Nervous! You've always got belief in the team to go out and win a game but it's not the same when you have no influence over things.'

But the afternoon ended with the outcome all of a yellow-and-green persuasion craved, and it was time for the celebrations to begin.

'It was a good journey home; I can't remember too much about the trip home on the coach – so it must have been a good one!'

Having been unable to maintain City's top-flight status following his mid-season arrival from Bournemouth the previous campaign, Bond certainly saw the fruits of his labours rewarded in his first full season in charge. A Wembley final and promotion were viewed as an excellent season's work:

'John was happy that we'd got promoted, that was what he'd aimed to get us to do. It was a great achievement and he was keen to enjoy that as much as the players.'

Four days after securing promotion at Fratton Park, an excited crowd of 35,999 packed into Carrow Road to celebrate promotion – and in the hope of seeing City exact a little revenge over Villa in the final match of an incredible season. With both teams already up, there was only pride at stake – but it was Saunders who enjoyed one last laugh as Villa ran out convincing 4-1 winners.

That final game of the season saw Suggett presented with the Barry Butler Memorial Trophy as City's player of the season. It was fitting reward for his contribution in helping City make an instant return to Division One.

Suggett played in 41 of City's 42 league games plus all 11 matches in the Canaries' marathon run to the League Cup Final at Wembley.

'Colin came in from West Brom originally and was a good player, a solid player,' recalled Stringer. 'He scored some very good goals; not a player who really wanted to work back defensively, but he would always want to put himself in a position to receive the ball in the final third and score goals. He was certainly someone that the opposition always needed to keep an eye on. I always got on well with Colin; he was a very down-to-earth guy and gave 100 per cent in every game.'

Curiously, the final Division Two table of 1974/75 foreshadowed events to follow at a higher level some 18 years later. The very first Premier League season, in 1992/93, culminated in United finally winning their first English title in 26 years, with Villa in second place and Norwich again third.

For Canary legend Stringer, who regularly acts as a match-day host for sponsors and corporate guests at Carrow Road, seeing City win promotion to the top flight once again in 2018/19 reiterates his belief that Norwich City are back where they belong:

'I think when we first broke the ice in 1972, and got to the First Division for the first time, that showed the level that the club could get to and where we want to be. Down the years we have also had teams that have shown they can certainly compete there, finishing well up in the First Division or Premier League table – the challenge is to do that consistently and that is getting harder and harder.'

1981/82 THIRD IN
DIVISION TWO

*Popular right-winger Mark Barham recalls the
Canaries' impressive late surge for promotion
in 1981/82 and the impact of midfield maestro
Martin O'Neill.*

Mark Barham progressed through the youth and reserve ranks at
Carrow Road, and despite being born in Folkestone, he was, in
modern terminology, very much 'one of our own'. He captained
the City youth team to the South East Counties League title in
1979/80. Then, after breaking through to the first team, he went
on to enjoy two promotions, Wembley glory in the 1985 League
Cup Final and two full international caps for England.

When Barham joined the Canaries as an apprentice, he was
joining a First Division club. Therefore, as he made his journey
from youth team to first team, he did so with First Division players
around him passing on valuable snippets of advice and guidance
along the way. His first-team debut came in a First Division match
away to Manchester United.

In short, Barham was brought up on First Division football.
And after six consecutive seasons in the top flight, Norwich
City had slowly gained the reputation of being a recognised and
established First Division team.

Sadly, the 1980/81 season saw many seasons of progress come
to a shuddering halt, as manager John Bond's acrimonious autumn
departure to Manchester City ended in the Canaries' relegation.

For a young player making his way in the game, and proving
more than capable at First Division level, a drop down to Division
Two was far from ideal:

'Obviously I was just coming into the team at the time, and playing in the old First Division, today's Premier League, was my ultimate goal,' recalled Barham. 'So to just get into the team and then get relegated was terribly disappointing. We were transitioning with players that season and it just didn't work for us. It was devastating to think that I'd been playing my football in the First Division and then ended up in the Second Division.'

Since returning to the top flight at the first time of asking under Bond in 1974/75, the Carrow Road faithful had been treated to some exceptional performances on the pitch. City were renowned for an excellent brand of exciting, passing football and a style of play that Carrow Road had not witnessed before. Away from the field of play, Bond's flamboyant personality had certainly raised the club's profile in the media. Such was the Canaries' progress that it was little surprise when Manchester City came calling for Bond.

Much as when Ron Saunders was replaced by Bond back in 1973, the change of manager at Carrow Road in 1980 was met with a downward spiral in terms of immediate results.

'We went from having a seasoned manager in John Bond, who knew how to do everything,' says Barham. 'He knew how to keep players together, when to bring in youngsters and how to work the young ones in alongside the senior pros. John was so good at making all that work – it was an amazing place when I first joined. All of a sudden Ken [Brown] got chucked in to do that, and it took him just a little while to get used to what was going on.'

Barham had enjoyed working with Brown, who had assisted Bond, and felt he was exactly the right man to captain the ship at Carrow Road following Bond's decision to head north. Relegation in 1980/81 was in no way solely down to Ken Brown.

'We were responsible – we were the players on the pitch,' says Barham. 'I don't think it gets said enough these days, but responsibility is not just the manager's problem – it is the players' as well. Ken and Mel [Machin] did their work Monday to Friday on the training ground. But come Saturday that was then our job, and we just didn't perform well enough to keep us where we wanted to be.'

So, with the backing of his players, Brown was keen to lead his troops back to Division One at the first time of asking in what was his first full season at the helm. Relegation had resulted in the departures of midfielder Martin O'Neill to Manchester City and star-striker Justin Fashanu to Nottingham Forest. Many Canaries fans were less than impressed when Brown bought ex-Ipswich striker Keith Bertschin from Birmingham as Fashanu's replacement, and their mood did not improve when an injury-hit City side was thumped 4-1 by Rotherham at Millmoor on the opening day of the season – with winger Barham pressed into temporary service at right-back.

'We started the season with a lot of injuries, and we didn't really have the right people to come into those positions,' recalls Barham. 'I played right-back at Rotherham – Mel Machin and I agreed I wouldn't play there again after the ball came past me at the far post and I let someone head in the fourth!'

City quickly perked up to win four of their first six league games. That run included a first away win of the season at Wrexham on 12 September when Barham struck the winner in a 3-2 triumph – a much-needed response after the Rotherham debacle.

'Traditionally we weren't great away from home and the season before we'd had a torrid time in trying to get points on our travels,' recalled Barham. 'If you can pick up points away from home, it makes you feel so much better. It relieves the pressure on home games and gives you more confidence to play at home.'

Sadly, City's campaign then began a steady decline into mid-table mediocrity. Indeed, the main highlight of the early part of the season was a remarkable sequence in which Scottish striker Ross Jack netted in seven successive league and cup games.

The season reached its lowest point on 28 December when an unhappy Carrow Road crowd saw their side go 3-0 down in 14 minutes to table-topping Luton Town. The final score was 3-1 as new striker John 'Dixie' Deehan – signed on loan from West Bromwich Albion – scored the first of his 70 goals in Canary colours.

Deehan signed permanently for £175,000 in mid-January, and the second coming of midfield inspiration O'Neill after six months at Manchester City sparked an extraordinary revival.

'Ken, as usual, went into the market and pulled out a couple of absolute crackers to get us going,' says Barham. 'You only have to look at Dixie's career to see that he was a proper goalscorer. He had the ability and class to play at centre-forward, and he didn't just score goals – he created things and brought other people into play, and that turned the season around for us with O'Neill coming into the midfield.'

Unsurprisingly, O'Neill's swift return to Norfolk did bring more than a little bit of ribbing the Irishman's way when he returned to the Canaries' Trowse training ground, as Barham fondly recalls:

'He got the usual stick – the boys gave him some banter and put him up the corner out of the way for the first two or three weeks – just mucking about. I think a few of the boys put a sign up saying "Man City dressing room" on our changing room door when we were out training ready to greet him when he got back in!

'At the end of the day, Martin O'Neill was a top player and anyone would want him in their team. He had a genuine ability – he was very hyper, and when you see him on the touchline now you know he hasn't changed. His will to win was second to none.

'Martin was full of experience and had plenty of good stories. He could always draw on those experiences he'd had at Nottingham Forest and tell you what is was like to be a top player.'

O'Neill's presence clearly inspired those around him, particularly the younger players, and his ability to orchestrate play and help team-mates reminded Barham of the effect that World Cup winner Martin Peters had had during his Carrow Road career.

'When you were out on the pitch he could put you in the right positions. This was the thing Norwich were great at, bringing in older players like Martin O'Neill who could actually teach the younger players how to play, at the same time as playing themselves. Those experienced players were one of the reasons behind Norwich's success. Martin Peters was one who would tell me if I was in the wrong place, and explain to me where I needed to be if the ball was in a certain position. That instantly made you look so much better as a player. Having players such as Martin Peters and Martin O'Neill at the club, and them passing their experiences on to the youngsters, was very important.'

O'Neill was certainly the man who launched City's late promotion dash as his deflected 85th-minute shot earned a fortuitous 1-0 victory at Bolton Wanderers on 20 March. The Canaries then beat Cardiff City 2-1 at home and Cambridge United 2-1 away, and made it four successive wins with a 5-0 Easter thumping of Charlton Athletic at Carrow Road – Deehan netting a hat-trick.

A 2-0 defeat at Luton just two days later seemed to end the dream – but the Canaries responded to that setback with successive 2-0 victories against Derby County, Shrewsbury Town and Blackburn Rovers. Norwich had suddenly won seven games out of eight – and they had four matches left in which to gatecrash the top three.

The situation was still delicate. Luton and Watford were streets ahead of the rest, with Sheffield Wednesday occupying the third promotion place on 65 points. Leicester City and Norwich both had 62 points, but the Foxes had a better goal difference and, crucially, had two games in hand.

The stakes could therefore not have been higher when City travelled to face Leicester at Filbert Street in their next fixture on Saturday, 1 May 1982 – a year on from the 3-2 defeat at Carrow Road at the hands of the Foxes which had confirmed City's relegation.

Leicester went into the match in a rich vein of form, having won 11, drawn three and lost just two of their previous 16 league games. But now they were destroyed by a rampant Norwich side who were clearly in no mood to let their belated promotion challenge slip.

Deehan opened the scoring after 22 minutes, and then Barham struck home a half-volley to make it 2-0 just two minutes after half-time. The away supporters in a crowd of 19,630 were celebrating again as Bertschin volleyed home the third after 53 minutes, and then Leicester defender Norman Leet lobbed home a spectacular 61st-minute own goal as the Canaries stormed into an unbelievable 4-0 lead. Larry May's consolation goal two minutes from time could not prevent City storming into fourth place as handsome 4-1 winners.

'There are certain times in a season when things happen and you know things have changed. That game certainly made the players stand up and think to themselves, "Look, we are good enough." To go away to Leicester, who were at that time a decent side, you're thinking they might give us a few problems, so to get a result like that gives you so much confidence. We absolutely stuffed them, and it could have been more than 4-1,' said Barham.

'Travelling home on the bus that day we had a few drinks and thought, "Wow, what a result". We knew we just had to keep that sort of momentum going. And I can still remember the half-volley from that game!'

With three games remaining, the Canaries were now just a point behind third-placed Wednesday, who had hit a sticky patch. Brown's troops maintained their momentum as two nail-biting home wins – 2-1 against Grimsby Town and 2-0 against Orient – made it six wins in a row, and ten in 11 games. Leicester, meanwhile, were starting to struggle after successive defeats against Watford and Grimsby.

By the time Norwich travelled to Sheffield Wednesday for their final match on 15 May, the requirement was clear enough. Third-placed City, on 71 points, would be guaranteed promotion if they picked up a point against the Owls, who were now out of contention. But if Norwich lost they could still be pipped on goal difference if eighth-placed Leicester, on 65 points, beat Shrewsbury and already relegated Orient in their last two games.

Extra spice was added to the occasion by the fact Norwich's fine run had knocked Wednesday out of the promotion race. Jack Charlton's side could not claw back their four-point deficit on the Canaries – but they were in no mood to do their last-day visitors any favours. The Norwich team coach was given a motorcycle escort, and the atmosphere inside Hillsborough was electric.

City fell behind on the hour mark when Andy McCulloch headed home, but Bertschin sparked wild celebrations among Norwich supporters when he met Dave Bennett's cross to equalise with a memorable header just four minutes from time. The goal put a remarkable promotion within touching distance, but with just seconds left a flowing Wednesday move culminated in Mel Sterland crossing for Gary Bannister to head the Owls 2-1 ahead.

The Canaries were distraught, and the restart was delayed for almost five minutes as hundreds of Wednesday fans launched a pitch invasion. Meanwhile television footage proved that a Wednesday fan had been on the pitch when Bannister scored. Dressed in black, the 'Milk Tray' man even dived for Sterland's cross – and would possibly have scored had Bannister failed to connect – yet the goal was allowed to stand.

The final whistle triggered another pitch invasion, but after an excruciating wait it was Norwich who had the last laugh when news finally filtered through that Leicester had only drawn 0-0 at home to Shrewsbury – the Canaries were back in the big time!

Barham played at Hillsborough after having pain-killing injections on a knee injury, but had been forced off by the time Bertschin scored City's 86th-minute equaliser.

'I remember it so well; I'd done my medial ligament the game before against Orient and wasn't sure I was going to be available for Sheffield,' recalled Barham. 'I had a couple of cortisones to make sure I was just able to get on the pitch, but unfortunately we were 1-0 down when I came off and it wasn't looking good.

'Then Bertsch just twisted his neck muscles and headed it in the top corner, and I don't remember much after that because I hit my head on a concrete post above me in the dug-out and knocked myself out!'

Barham had just about regained consciousness by the time Bannister's header ensured a 2-1 Wednesday victory.

'We were all distraught and devastated in the dressing room, and then about ten minutes after we'd got back in, the result came through from the other game to say that they hadn't made it. That sparked amazing celebrations – we just couldn't believe that it had happened for us.

'We went back out jumping round with drink flowing to celebrate with the supporters, then eventually got on the bus back home. On the trip back we got to the pub at Sutton Bridge and there were thousands of Norwich fans standing outside having a pint. Browny pulled the coach over to stop and say hello! We certainly had the drinks bought for us that night and for a few weeks after that too!'

The 1981/82 campaign will forever be remembered for the sensational end-of-season run which saw City rise from mid-table obscurity to claim the third promotion place – but Brown's men had good reason to be thankful for the introduction of the new 'three-points-for-a-win' system. The Canaries finished with 71 points to fourth-placed Wednesday's 70 – but just 12 months earlier the Owls would have pipped Norwich by 50 points to 49.

1985/86 DIVISION TWO CHAMPIONS

Kevin Drinkell recalls his debut season at Carrow Road in 1985/86 when the former Grimsby Town man topped the Canaries scoring charts as Norwich City secured a hat-trick of instant returns to the top flight.

When Kevin Drinkell opted to sever ties with his hometown club, Grimsby Town, in May 1985, he knew the time was right to move on. After all, the opportunity of linking up with Ken Brown's League Cup-winning Canaries offered him a crack at the First Division and the added bonus of European football too.

However, in between Drinkell's discussions with the Canaries about a move to Carrow Road and the actual transfer becoming reality in June 1985, the goalposts shifted rather a long way:

'I decided to sign in May, and when I got the call it was to play for a team that was in the top league, and would be playing in Europe. Then Coventry won a few extra games, and the Heysel Disaster took us out of Europe,' recalled Drinkell.

So rather than stepping up to test himself against the country's finest, Drinkell found himself at a new club but still stuck in the Second Division, albeit he could take heart from knowing that scoring goals in the second tier was already very much his forte.

'In one sense it was a major disappointment for me to be playing in that league where I had played for Grimsby for the previous five seasons. On the other hand I knew that league, and I was now playing with Chris Woods, Steve Bruce and Dave Watson, among others.'

May 1985 proved to be a month when Norwich City's fate was ultimately decided by the actions of others. Firstly, the exceptional end-of-season form of Coventry City's players. Secondly, the behaviour of Liverpool's supporters at the 1985 European Cup Final against Juventus in Belgium.

City had ended their League Cup-winning season with a 2-1 First Division victory at Chelsea on 14 May 1984. The three points won at Stamford Bridge saw the Canaries sign off their 1984/85 campaign with a 49-point tally. It left Ken Brown's men knowing that unless Coventry City, who faced a fixture backlog, won their final three games then Norwich were safe in the top flight once again.

Amazingly, Coventry proceeded to win all three games and amass a further nine points after the regulation season had been completed. The Sky Blues' astonishing form subsequently relegated Norwich, who went down with Sunderland and Stoke City.

Then, just three days after newly crowned First Division champions Everton had surrendered 4-1 at Highfield Road to sentence City to the drop, Liverpool supporters clashed with Juventus fans ahead of their European Cup Final meeting in Brussels on 29 May. Tragically, 39 people (mostly Italians) lost their lives, with hundreds also injured.

The Heysel Stadium disaster subsequently saw all English clubs banned from European competition for five years. The Canaries' long-awaited first foray into Europe was cruelly whipped away from them in an instant.

For many, the icing on the cake of the League Cup victory over Sunderland had been the reward of European football. So for Norwich to suffer relegation, and then lose the opportunity of playing in Europe for the first time, ensured there was a dark cloud lingering over Carrow Road when City reported back for pre-season training in the summer of 1985.

Drinkell was one of a number of new faces, the majority of whom had also been lured to Norfolk by the prospect of European football. They met up with a City squad perhaps still coming to terms with the events of the previous months.

'Three or four of us had joined that summer and were looking to tag on to that, but people like Micky Phelan, Dave Williams and myself, we were used to the Second Division anyway so it didn't frighten us,' said Drinkell. 'As for the existing players, I wouldn't say there was a state of shock, but the circumstances with them being relegated, more or less after the season had finished really, with Coventry playing all those late games – I think they found that a bit hard to take – it's something that would never be allowed to happen today.

'They'd certainly got over the shock of it and were no longer feeling sorry for themselves once the pre-season matches started.'

Despite suffering relegation from the top flight for the third time in the club's history, City took heart from the knowledge that on each of the two previous occasions they had bounced straight back to Division One at the first time of asking.

In addition, manager Ken Brown already had a Norwich City promotion on his CV, having masterminded the Canaries' amazing late surge to promotion in 1981/82.

Furthermore, there was no mass exodus of players. Despite both Woods and Watson having been capped by England during their Canary careers, neither of City's internationals were seeking pastures new. So it was not all doom and gloom as City prepared for an opening-day Carrow Road date with Oldham Athletic.

'Of course, as we look back on this now, almost 35 years on, the biggest difference is the mentality of the players,' reflects Drinkell. 'Players with the quality of Brucey, Watson and Woodsy – in today's world they'd just want away from a club that had come out of the Premier League; they would not be looking to play in a league lower. But back then there was no sign of those guys looking to abandon ship. They just rolled their sleeves up and got on with it. They were all determined to do their bit to help get the club back to where it belonged.'

With such quality among their ranks in 1985/86, it is perhaps hardly surprising that Norwich went on to score 84 league goals in 42 games, conceded only 37, and at one stage remained unbeaten in 18 successive games, of which 14 were won and four drawn. This included setting a new club record sequence of ten successive league wins.

Yet despite such impressive statistics, City started the season poorly – a 1-0 opening-day triumph at home to Oldham was their only win in the first five games. The Canaries lost 2-1 at Blackburn and 4-2 at Millwall – and confidence hit rock bottom following a 2-0 defeat at Portsmouth on 31 August.

Their discomfort was increased by the fact that it was Portsmouth's veteran ex-City striker Mick Channon – so recently a hero of the 1985 League Cup Final victory over Sunderland – who did much to undo his former club.

According to Drinkell, it was then that Ken Brown played a managerial master-stroke – hauling his deflated troops off the team bus and into the pub on the long haul back from Fratton Park:

'The game hadn't gone well, I hadn't scored all season, and the team was a bit low,' recalls Drinkell. 'Ken decided on the way home to stop the bus for a few beers and a heart-to-heart, and to try to get everyone working together.

'It certainly helped me because I wasn't feeling great. I'd been bought to score goals, and I hadn't scored. But Ken's man management was fantastic, and he really took the pressure off. He took the burden on himself, and said, "I'm sure it will turn."

'On the back of that the next week's training was bright and lively and it was no surprise that eventually it all clicked.'

Brown was right. Drinkell broke his duck with a double strike as City walloped Sheffield United 4-0 in their next match – so launching a sequence which would produce just one defeat in 24 league games as the Canaries accelerated up the league. Bizarrely, the only team to beat them in 25 games were Wimbledon, who twice came from behind to run out 2-1 winners and double the Canaries.

Clearly delighted to have got himself off the mark goals-wise after a five game wait, 25-year-old Drinkell was glad things were finally starting to come good following his summer switch from Blundell Park.

'When you look back on your career, and particularly as a striker you get the adulation and jubilation every time you score a goal, but actually it's just a feeling of relief!

'As a new player it was just a matter of trying to prove yourself and it took a couple of months for us all to gel with new players coming in, but that really was a First Division team playing in the Second Division.'

As the season progressed, Drinkell eventually formed an impressive strike partnership with Wayne Biggins, who had joined City in October 1985 from Burnley. Prior to hitting things off successfully with Biggins, Drinkell partnered both John Deehan and Robert Rosario:

'Dixie was someone I'd known all about and I was really looking forward to playing alongside him,' recalled Drinkell. 'But unfortunately John couldn't get over a bunch of little niggly injuries around that time. And I don't think in terms of his Norwich career he ever recovered from that.

'I did enjoy partnering with him, he knew the way the team wanted to play and he certainly helped me integrate into the squad. So although it wasn't a long partnership, those first few months playing with John were a real big help to me.'

City's scintillating form deflected attention from a boardroom shake-up that saw Robert Chase become chairman, with Sir Arthur South and Geoffrey Watling among those to step down following disagreements about the building of the club's new main stand.

Boardroom business mattered little to the players – their focus was purely on winning football matches – something this City side were now achieving on a regular basis. And in Drinkell's eyes a large slice of the credit for this upsurge in form was down to the management of Brown and his trusted coach Mel Machin.

'It was a good partnership between Ken and Mel – it really worked. Training was always designed to get something extra out of you and to stretch you. They had a set style of play they wanted to go with, and I know it seems very out of trend now, but it was a basic 4-4-2. But such was the quality of players we had that if you were, say, a striker or a right-sided midfield player, for example, and found yourself in another part of the pitch, perhaps on the left wing, then you could adapt and play that position for a couple of minutes.

'So it was a build-up of things like that, plus the training and the practising. We got to the stage where the players almost knew what each other were going to do, there was a really good understanding.'

Norwich's run of ten straight league wins in 1985/86 began with a 3-2 win at home to Grimsby on 23 November. The fifth game of the sequence was a 6-1 hammering of Millwall on 21 December – the Lions' late consolation coming via a spectacular long-range effort from a youthful Teddy Sheringham. And City's march to the title was never in doubt after they gained revenge against rivals Portsmouth with a 2-0 success for their ninth straight win.

Pompey's visit to Carrow Road on Saturday, 18 January was a key match and attracted City's biggest home crowd of the season. Second-half goals from Mark Barham and Drinkell gave City a 2-0 win to the delight of home fans among the 18,956 packed into a three-sided Carrow Road.

'It was obviously a big game and marked the transition we'd been on since losing down there early in the season. It was not a case of revenge, or anything like that, but we went into the game thinking, "You caught us on the hop early on, but wait and see how we've improved."'

The run eventually ended on 1 February at Barnsley, where City led 2-1 until Gwyn Thomas's 86th-minute shot was controversially judged to have crossed the line after hitting the underside of the bar.

'Our bonus system was set up so that every time you won, the next week you got a bit more. It was like a roll-on, so we were devastated to draw at Barnsley and get about £20,' laughs Drinkell.

After their winning run ended at Oakwell in February, City enjoyed one of their finest away performances of the campaign when they returned to South Yorkshire a month later. Brown's side turned on the style to destroy Sheffield United 5-2 on Saturday, 22 March.

City had, of course, kick-started their season with a 4-0 home victory over Sheffield United back in September – and they revelled in completing a high-scoring double over the Blades with an exciting victory at Bramall Lane.

Norwich took a sixth-minute lead when Deehan's teasing cross was headed into his own net by United's Paul Smith. Keith Edwards levelled for the Blades after 34 minutes, but Drinkell headed the Canaries 2-1 ahead four minutes before half-time.

Peter Mendham extended City's lead to 3-1 after 65 minutes, but Edwards's second goal of the game narrowed the gap to 3-2 after 80 minutes. But the scoreline was given a little added gloss when Barham's calm 89th-minute finish was followed by a looping Biggins effort in the 90th minute to leave the Canaries comprehensive 5-2 winners.

Promotion was finally secured with four games to spare on 12 April, when City won 2-0 away to Bradford, who were temporarily playing home games at the Odsal Stadium following the 1985 Valley Parade fire tragedy. The Odsal was certainly a strange venue for football, and Norwich City's achievement of securing promotion to football's First Division while playing at a rugby league ground is an item of trivia few other clubs are likely to rival.

'It was like an amphitheatre – I think originally it was a speedway track,' says Drinkell, who got the promotion party up and running with the game's opening goal in the first half. 'From memory there was just a bank of earth at one end, one stand on the side and several standing sections. I remember thinking that there was room for two pitches in the space that had just one, so it was all a little bit vacant, empty and echoey. But we got the result, which was the main thing. In terms of celebrations, there were no great stands full of fans to celebrate in front of – it was a surreal place for football.'

The Canaries sealed the title a week later with a 1-1 draw at home to Stoke and eventually finished a mere seven points clear of second-placed Charlton after taking their foot off the pedal to lose 1-0 at Grimsby and Hull. But the Canaries finished the season on a high with a 4-0 home thrashing of Leeds United after being presented with the championship trophy.

That penultimate away game at Grimsby had seen Drinkell make his first return to Blundell Park since his move to Norwich. Despite returning to his roots as a Second Division champion, it was not a happy homecoming:

'The game at Grimsby was a little bit sad for me – not only did we lose but the reception I got from a couple of oddballs in the crowd was disappointing. It's always a minority, I know that, but when you think I'd been there for ten years, all through my youth, played all my career there and scored over 100 goals for them; to then get abuse from a small section was disappointing.

'I really felt for my parents and my siblings who were at the game – in fact my mum even left at half-time.'

On a happier note, prior to the final home game of the season, Drinkell was presented with the Barry Butler Memorial Trophy after City's fans voted him the club's player of the season.

'As a player that is what you want; you want to integrate yourself into the team first and foremost. In those days it was also about getting on the right side of the supporters too, so at the end of the season to get their seal of approval – that meant as much to me as actually winning the championship.'

Drinkell's season concluded with him netting his 22nd league goal of the season in the final-day victory over Leeds United.

Among his 22 league goals were three braces but no hat-tricks. Curiously, over his three seasons leading the City strike-force, Drinkell scored an impressive 57 goals from 150 appearances but never managed a hat-trick. The ace marksman puts the lack of trebles down to the fact he never fancied taking penalties – a feeling shared by a number of City players from the recent 2018/19 success, no doubt!

Just as today's fans found it hard to comprehend why 2018/19 leading scorer Teemu Pukki did not take the spot-kicks, the story was the same in 1985/86 as Drinkell shied away from penalty duty:

'I never took penalties throughout my career,' says Drinkell. 'In games when a side gets three or four goals up and you get a player with a brace there's often a penalty in those games and the chance to wrap up the hat-trick, but I never had that.

'When I started off at Grimsby we had a couple of senior players who were good at penalties, so all the time when I was coming though at 17, 18, 19, 20 I never got near a penalty. So by the time I was in my early 20s and was asked "Did I want to take a penalty?" it was a case of "Well, I've never taken one before."'

Pukki hammered home 29 league goals in 2018/19, but he too was unable to convert any of his double strikes into a hat-trick. The Finn tried his luck from the spot once but passed the responsibility to others after failing at home to Millwall.

Never the designated penalty taker at Norwich, Drinkell did take one spot-kick – and just like Pukki he failed from 12 yards.

'I took a penalty in a Full Members' Cup game at Charlton and missed it. That was a semi-final too,' recalled Drinkell. 'The final was at Wembley, so that was a big regret as I look back now as it was the nearest I ever came to getting to play at Wembley. It was only a minor cup competition, I know, but it would have been another tick in the box as I look back now.'

2003/04 FIRST DIVISION CHAMPIONS

*Legendary Norwich striker Iwan Roberts recalls
the Canaries' 2003/04 campaign – a season
when City added that little bit of magic to the
mix to create a promotion-winning formula.*

If Norwich City's historic FA Cup adventure of 1958/59 was the
driving force behind the team's promotion-winning success that
followed in 1959/60, then similarities can certainly be drawn
from the events of 2001/02 and the promotion that followed in
2003/04.

Iwan Roberts was part of the City side that came agonisingly
close to winning promotion back to the Premier League in
2001/02. City suffered a heartbreaking penalty shoot-out defeat
to Birmingham in the First Division play-off final that season
but, just like the club's famous '59ers, the players and manager
picked themselves up and channelled their disappointment into a
motivational tool for future glories.

Just as Archie Macaulay kept the majority of his 1958/59 FA
Cup heroes together, Nigel Worthington did likewise with the
bulk of his play-off finalists from 2001/02. The fact that the spine
of the side which suffered play-off heartbreak went on to win
promotion two seasons later was surely no coincidence. Robert
Green, Adam Drury, Malky Mackay, Craig Fleming, Gary Holt,
Paul McVeigh and Iwan Roberts – they all felt the pain of defeat in
Cardiff's Millennium Stadium but they all featured in 40-games
plus as City celebrated success two seasons later.

'We came so close didn't we'" said former Wales international
Iwan Roberts when reflecting on that promotion near-miss back

in his homeland in 2002. 'We had a really good dressing room and we all got on. Don't get me wrong, there were falling outs at times but it was a good group and we all socialised together. Having got to the Millennium that season and having just missed out, it certainly gave us a little taste of what could have been.'

Patience was certainly the key for that group of Canaries who finally made it up and ended the club's nine-season absence from English football's top table. The team did not suffer any kind of play-off hangover once the 2002/03 campaign kicked off. In fact, boss Worthington saw his troops make an impressive start before dropping off the pace and ending the season in eighth position.

If the 2002/03 season taught the Canaries one thing it was their clear need for more goals. The responsibility for finding the net was more often than not placed solely on Roberts's shoulders, and if the big Welshman was not available then the side ultimately struggled to convert good approach play into goals. The fact the City finished in eighth place, and each of the three sides immediately above them all scored 20 goals or more than City, told its own story.

Increasing the team's firepower was boss Worthington's main summer priority, but knowing the problem is one thing, finding the solution is a different beast altogether. The City boss boosted his midfield options with the recruitment of Damien Francis from Wimbledon and secured the services of experienced free agent Marc Edworthy for the vacant right-back berth. He also increased competition for places on the left with the signing of Canadian international Jim Brennan from Nottingham Forest, but, try as he might, Worthington was unable to enhance his striking options prior to the start of the new season.

'We signed some good players ahead of the 2003/04 season but just could not get that striker that Nigel was after,' recalled Roberts.

So City's 2003/04 season kicked off on a blisteringly hot afternoon at Bradford City with David Nielsen and McVeigh leading the line, Zema Abbey on the bench with Roberts out injured. Goals from Mark Rivers and Clint Easton put City two up before the hosts hit back with two goals in the final six minutes to earn a share of the points.

That afternoon at Valley Parade set the tone for what was to be something of a topsy-turvy month at Carrow Road. In the space of just three weeks, City had surrendered a two-goal lead on the opening day, bowed out of the League Cup 1-0 to Northampton Town, signed Elvis Hammond, lost Zema Abbey with a cruciate ligament and seen fellow striker David Nielsen make a sudden departure back to Denmark for 'family reasons'. On the pitch the mixed fortunes continued with two home wins, backed by two away defeats.

Hammond made just four appearances for City and was not the answer to the Canaries' goalscoring problems. However, with a two-week break before their next league fixture at home to Burnley, Worthington pulled off a sensational triple loan signing of Aston Villa striker Peter Crouch, Manchester City forward Darren Huckerby and Portsmouth wide man Kevin Harper.

The trio of new faces certainly gave supporters a much-needed boost and the arrival of such high-calibre players had a major impact among the City players too. Roberts had been around the game long enough to know what was needed to make a promotion-winning team and knew from the off these were the quality of players who could really make the difference at Carrow Road.

'I remember watching a game that Darren was playing in for Nottingham Forest, I think it was, away to Gillingham. It was a game that was live on TV; he scored two, got man of the match and I thought, "I'd love to play with him."

'They were the difference, I knew then we had a real good chance. We had a good squad of players but they gave us that little bit extra and something that every club needs if you are going to get promotion.

'Crouch and Huckerby, they lifted everybody, particularly Darren; we knew what he could do, we knew his pedigree and he'd played for some top clubs. Crouchy was only young at the time and had come from Villa but had already shown at QPR and Portsmouth that he could score goals.'

The three new faces all debuted on Saturday, 13 September 2003 as City beat Burnley 2-0 at Carrow Road. Crouch opened the scoring before being replaced by Roberts, who added the second after being set up by Huckerby. Norwich were suddenly a side with serious fire power, up to tenth in the table and a team moving in the right direction.

Goals and wins followed on a consistent basis and when Huckerby netted his first Carrow Road goal, to set City on their way to a 2-1 victory over Crystal Palace in late September, the result left Norwich fourth in the table.

For Roberts, the new faces limited his number of starts, but the experienced striker was always one to put team before self and could see first-hand the positive influence that his new team-mates were having both on the pitch and in the changing room:

'I knew with Nigel bringing them in, especially Crouchy, that I wouldn't start as many games that season. It didn't really bother me because I knew what they would be bringing to the table. The thing is that whenever you sign a player there is always a risk – are they going to settle into the dressing room? What are they like as characters? But those two, they settled quicker than snow. Plus Kevin Harper – they were cracking lads.'

Come match days and City's fans were soon lapping up the winning performances and enjoying the exciting style of football that was being produced, with Huckerby's pace in particular causing havoc for opposing defenders. For Roberts, the good results all came on the back of the work that was taking place on the training pitches. It was at the club's Colney Training Centre during the week that Huckerby's incredible level of professionalism and attitude to training really set the tone for others to follow.

'I played with Craig Bellamy at Norwich and obviously with Hucks. They are very similar – very driven, focussed and hard working. They put demands on others and you have to work as hard and put the same amount of effort in as they do. I wouldn't say Hucks would dig you out but Craig would. If he saw someone not working as hard as he was he'd have no problem in letting them know! Darren wasn't like that but certainly other players saw him working his socks off and knew they had to do likewise.'

Following a 3-1 win away to Walsall on 1 November 2003, Kevin Harper returned to Portsmouth and City also faced a brief spell without Crouch after he scored but later saw red at the

Bescot Stadium, ruling him out of a Carrow Road date with Watford.

December began with Norwich gaining a point from a gritty performance in a goalless match away to Millwall. The fixture signalled the end of Crouch's loan spell. Although City expressed their desire to extend the player's stay in Norfolk, Villa boss David O'Leary indicated that he was looking to give Crouch a crack at showing what he do could at Villa Park in the Premier League. When Crouch returned to his parent club he left with the Canaries sitting third in the First Division table.

There was no doubting the clear influence that the loan signings had made on City's fortunes and on Saturday, 13 December 2003, Norwich City found themselves at a major crossroads. The Carrow Road clash with Cardiff City marked the final game of Huckerby's loan spell and he signed off with an outstanding display on what was billed as his 'farewell' performance.

Huckerby had already scored four goals before facing Lennie Lawrence's Cardiff in what looked almost certain to be his 16th and final game in Canary colours.

The match erupted in the 34th minute when Huckerby collected the ball on the half-way line in front of the emerging new South Stand structure. He accelerated smoothly into a thrilling 50-yard diagonal run which left a succession of Cardiff defenders trailing before he skipped past the keeper and finally slid the ball back into the unguarded River End goal.

The Canaries doubled their lead in the 54th minute when Huckerby set up Roberts to make it 2-0. Future City striker Peter Thorne reduced the deficit with a 59th-minute header, but the Canaries were not pegged back for long.

Central-defender Fleming made it 3-1 after 71 minutes when Ian Henderson's shot fell at his feet, and in the 79th minute Huckerby tormented Cardiff again with a twisting, turning run followed by a close-range shot which was deflected in off Tony Vidmar.

Such was the impact of Huckerby's performance, the Norwich board found themselves under great pressure to bring him back to the club on a permanent basis. It was evident to all that Huckerby was the key to City's success and that he possessed the ability to almost single-handily lead Norwich to promotion.

Not only were the Carrow Road crowd demanding that Huckerby should stay, but the dressing room also acknowledged that he really was the difference, as Roberts explains:

'His last game on loan was Cardiff at home and he scored that ridiculous first goal which was typical Darren. At the final whistle you're just thinking, "We're going to miss that". He was instrumental in my goal too, but it was a sad feeling in the dressing room, and a sad place as Hucks was going back to Manchester.

'We all knew that financially Darren was earning a lot more than anybody else but it didn't bother the dressing room whatsoever because we knew how important he was and what he would add in value on the pitch.'

Despite the clear love for Huckerby both in the stands and in the dressing room, as well as his phenomenal contribution on the pitch, signing him on a permanent basis was a big financial ask for Norwich City. At the time the club were also in the process of constructing a new South Stand and, as is so often the case at Carrow Road, cash was in short supply.

Norwich lacked no desire to sign Huckerby, but how to finance the deal was the conundrum that faced the Carrow Road hierarchy. However, a major plus-point was that the player himself also wanted the move. With both men having young families, Roberts and Huckerby swiftly struck up a good friendship, and Roberts felt Huckerby had the appetite for a permanent move almost from day one of his initial loan.

'As soon as he walked through the door we got on,' confirmed Roberts. 'He loved Norwich – hence he's still here now, as many of us are. He didn't need convincing. If the club feels right, and the city feels right for you as a person, you can soon see the picture. Once he pulled on the Norwich shirt and saw the love he was getting from the fans, and the respect from his team-mates, he didn't need any convincing.'

With Christmas approaching and no sign of Huckerby returning on a permanent basis, City appeared to have switched their attentions elsewhere and completed the permanent signings of Peterborough United's in-form striker Leon McKenzie and Charlton Athletic frontman Mathias Svensson, who had slipped down the pecking order at The Valley.

News of the two signings was met positively by the Norwich fans, although there was an underlying frustration that it wasn't the permanent acquisition of Huckerby – after all, that was the news they were all really craving. It was a sentiment that was matched in the dressing room by Roberts:

'Look, everyone wanted Hucks to stay. I can understand people thinking that the club had gone for the cheaper option. I'd seen Matty [Svensson] play many times for Charlton; he was another grafter, a hard worker and he'd put himself about. He had a nasty streak in him which you always want, but did he have the blistering pace and creativity that Darren had? No.

'And the same with Leon – they were both out-and-out centre-forwards so I knew I was going to be in direct competition with both for a starting place. I wouldn't say it left me disappointed – that would be wrong and disrespectful. Whoever comes through the door you welcome them with open arms and make them as welcome as possible; you want them to settle in very quickly, as the quicker they settle the more beneficial it is for the team.'

For McKenzie, settling in quickly was not exactly a problem. He instantly won the Norwich fans over as he marked his debut with a brace to secure City both three points and local bragging rights with a 2-0 victory over arch-rivals Ipswich Town at Portman Road. The win also sent City top of the league for Christmas.

Three points from a trip to Portman Road and the Canaries top of the table – it seemed things could not really get much better for Norwich fans. But on Boxing Day 2003 they certainly did when, prior to City's match with Nottingham Forest, the club's majority shareholders, Delia Smith and her husband Michael Wynn Jones, emerged from the Carrow Road tunnel with Huckerby and his permanent signing was confirmed to an ecstatic home crowd. The announcement was pure theatre and in hindsight it was arguably the moment Norwich City were effectively promoted.

'I think we knew a couple of days before. We had to keep things quiet and could not broadcast it to anybody but we were all chuffed to bits,' recalled Roberts. 'It was the best Christmas present the club could have given the fans – that's for sure.'

Boosted by the Huckerby signing, City won their two festive fixtures – a 1-0 victory over Forest at Carrow Road and a 4-0 romp away to Derby County. After bowing out of the FA Cup at Everton, it was now a case of full speed ahead for promotion.

A surprise 1-0 defeat at home to struggling Bradford City resulted in Worthington fielding a three-pronged attack of Roberts, Huckerby and McKenzie for the Canaries' trip to lowly Rotherham United on 17 January 2004. An incident-packed affair unfolded as the two sides shared eight goals on an afternoon when tempers flared at Millmoor as a half-time tunnel fracas saw the Millers' Guy Branston sent off and his manager, Ronnie Moore, later sent to the stands.

'There have not been too many games in my career that have ended 4-4! It was certainly a lively one,' acknowledged Roberts, who was delighted to be back in the starting line-up, particularly with the number of forward options Worthington now had at his disposal. 'I hadn't started for a couple of games but got the first goal. I scored eight goals that season but only started 13 games – but I was involved in about 40-odd. I knew what was going to happen because of the strength and choices we had in those forward positions.

'It was a real one-off sort of game, you don't get many like that. They were struggling as well; we probably felt all we had to do was turn up, which is always fatal really.'

Crucial games came thick and fast and City showed their promotion mettle to see off Sheffield United at a rain-soaked Carrow Road on 31 January 2004, and it was the Huckerby/ Roberts partnership that once again came good for the Canaries. Roberts netted the only goal of the game to send Neil Warnock's Blades back up north empty handed.

'Yes, second half at the River End,' remembers Roberts. 'Hucks got away from Phil Jagielka, who was playing at right-back for them that day, and there was just no way he was ever going to catch him.

'I was trying to catch him up and he then pulled the ball back and, despite a slight deflection, it came to me perfectly. I struck it first time and hit it into the ground and I think the pace and bounce of the ball beat Paddy Kenny.

'It was one of the most important goals I scored for the club because it was two teams who were both really neck-and-neck at the time. At that stage it was a six-pointer and to win the game 1-0 and score the winning goal was a really satisfying moment.

'After Bradford and Rotherham we needed to bounce back and that was a big statement against a good Sheffield United side.'

A Huckerby special then secured a 1-0 win at Wimbledon, before City won 2-0 at Coventry and then engineered useful points from tough Carrow Road assignments with West Ham United (1-1) and second-place West Bromwich Albion (0-0).

Next up was the second East Anglian derby of the season. With the new Jarrold Stand now fully open and operational, City were determined to secure a league double over Town and add another three points to their promotion push. A few less than complimentary remarks from Ipswich's Fabian Wilnis made victory all the more sweet as goals by Malky Mackay (2) and Huckerby condemned the Tractor Boys to a 3-1 defeat.

'He [Wilnis] was always one to say something stupid and give you more incentive and more fire in your belly to go out and ram his words down his throat. It was just a really silly thing to say that we lacked the real quality that was needed to get promoted. You certainly get so much pleasure in proving people like him wrong.'

After comfortably defeating Town, City remained top of the pile with a dozen games to play and went on to secure promotion with four fixtures to spare. They landed the title in their penultimate match away to Sunderland when a 1-0 defeat mattered little as results elsewhere saw them up as champions.

For Roberts, the title triumph in 2003/04 signalled the end of his Norwich City career and the Carrow Road favourite looks back on his time with the Canaries as being a case of mission accomplished:

'It was a magnificent feeling, I couldn't have asked for a better ending,' he acknowledges. 'From day one when I first signed for the club, in my first interview I said I wanted to help get the club back into the Premier League and in my last season we did it.

'For myself, Malky [Mackay] and Flem [Craig Fleming], we'd seen some dark days and had some bad seasons, finishing in the bottom half and seeing Carrow Road half empty. Having had those tough seasons you appreciate the good days that little bit more.'

So having been so close in Cardiff, Norwich City and Iwan Roberts finally won promotion in 2003/04 – but, despite a great team effort, Roberts knows that one man really made all the difference:

'I've told Darren many times, I didn't win a lot in my career – a couple of play-off finals with Leicester, but my main medal that I cherish is my championship one, and I wouldn't have got that if it wasn't for him.

'We might have finished in the top six and made the play-offs – we had a good side and a good spine and players with plenty of experience. But when Hucks walked through the door we knew we had a proper good chance.'

2009/10 LEAGUE ONE CHAMPIONS

*Top appearance maker in the Canaries' 2009/10
League One title-winning season, midfielder
Simon Lappin reflects on an eventful campaign at
Carrow Road.*

Norwich City began the 2009/10 season with a humiliating 7-1 home defeat at the hands of Paul Lambert's Colchester United – but ended it as runaway League One champions after moving quickly to bring the young Scottish manager to Carrow Road.

That first-day battering for Bryan Gunn's team comprised the rudest of wake-up calls as the Canaries began their first season in English football's third tier in 49 years.

For Scottish midfielder Simon Lappin, who would go on to feature in 44 of City's 46 League One fixtures, missing out on the opening-day massacre was perhaps a blessing in disguise:

'I was disappointed not to start the game, I'd had a good pre-season under my belt and I'd signed a new contract,' recalled Lappin. 'I'll be forever grateful to Gunny for giving me that contract and I was looking to get back in the side. I'd been out until Gunny took over and I wanted to get back playing consistently. So to be sat on the bench on the first game of the season was disappointing.

'You need to make sure you are always ready to go on and I got a shout at 5-0 when Gunny said, "Are you ready?" and I'm thinking, "We're 5-0 down, I don't know what I can do to salvage this here!"'

Gunn's call to Lappin proved to be just a question rather than an instruction and the former St Mirren man continued to look on from the bench. Despite not being involved on the pitch, Lappin's role as an unused substitute presented him with a front-row seat to reflect on the magnitude of the defeat and the mood in the dressing room post-match.

'Obviously it was a really disappointing start to the season; to lose your first home match is far from ideal but in the manner we did, 7-1 … the dressing room was numb, just in shock really. This wasn't what was meant to happen.

'We'd had an okay pre-season and won the majority of our games but the biggest thing that he kept saying to the players was that pre-season doesn't count for anything – it all comes down to this first game of the season. And, of course, it couldn't have turned out any worse to be honest.'

The 7-1 hammering was Norwich's worst-ever defeat at Carrow Road and a personal nightmare for new Australian goalkeeper Michael Theoklitos, signed from Melbourne Victory. He would never play for the club again. It was also a dreadful day for central-defender Michael Nelson – but the former Hartlepool skipper fought back to play a big role in City's success.

In the immediate aftermath of the opening-day disaster, Lappin remembers the general mood in the camp being one of looking to the future. Therefore, attention switched instantly to a League Cup tie at Yeovil just three days later, which offered City an almost immediate chance to right the wrongs of the Colchester catastrophe.

'It was a tough day for Michael and of course whenever we talk about goalkeepers it gets highlighted as it is more costly when they make an error. But we were a great group and it was almost a feeling of, "Let's just start again here and scrub that first game of the season." It was only one game, three points and there were still 45 games to go.

'We got a good result in the cup at Yeovil which again I was disappointed not to start. After a 7-1 game you're thinking, "Well, there's going to be plenty of changes here," but you just have to bide your time until the chance comes along.'

Summer signing Grant Holt smashed a hat-trick as City recorded a 4-0 League Cup victory at Yeovil and Lappin got his first taste of competitive action for 2009/10 when he replaced Adam Drury at left-back in the later stages.

The much-improved result at Huish Park on Tuesday, 11 August 2009, was still not enough to save Gunn's job. The City boss was dismissed ahead of the second league game of the campaign at Exeter City.

The decision to relieve Gunn of his duties so early into the season, particularly after backing his summer overhaul of the squad, left the entire club stunned. After responding to the Colchester defeat in such a positive way, the players were left wondering just what would happen next – particularly those summer recruits who had been brought to the club by Gunn ahead of the new season.

'I'm sure the new signings were all thinking, "What's going on here?"' acknowledged Lappin. 'With us playing Yeovil and then Exeter we stayed down there. We got a call to say there was a meeting going on downstairs and that was when the news was broken to us. Everybody was really disappointed for Gunny, particularly with his standing in the club and that it was so early in the season. But with football that is sometimes the way it goes.

'For me, Gunny was great, getting me back in the side and giving me another contract. I really felt for him because I knew what the club meant to him. It was a strange time. We'd had a good pre-season, were looking to bounce back and then this all happens within a week. It was all hard to take in at the time. You're thinking, "We got a result in the cup and it's only been one game," but that's the way football goes sometimes. The change happens and a couple of days later there's a new man in charge.'

A 1-1 draw at Exeter, with Ian Butterworth taking over as caretaker manager, was followed by the confirmation on Tuesday, 18 August 2009 that Norwich City's new manager would be Paul Lambert. Having overseen the 7-1 victory for Colchester United just ten days earlier, Lambert was now City manager and would be assisted by former Carrow Road favourite Ian Culverhouse and head of football operations Gary Karsa.

The trio watched from the stands as City lost 2-1 at Brentford later that evening. However, it was not long before Lambert was making his mark at Colney.

'We lost the game at Brentford and then had a day off, I believe. We then all met him for the first time the following day. He came in as the manager with Ian and Gary and I can remember the very first meeting we had. It was basically just a general chat and he really put it to us and said what did we think had gone wrong? A few of the senior player spoke and then he said, "I'll give you my take on things." And from there on in he'd laid down the law as to what he expects and what he demanded of us. You knew there and then that if you didn't meet his demands you wouldn't be there. There were lads who'd only come in that summer but they found themselves gone very quickly.'

Lambert's tenure as City boss began against one of his former clubs, Wycombe Wanderers, and he certainly kept the squad on their toes with reference to team selection for his Carrow Road bow.

'I remember in training we played three 20-minute games and he rotated around with different players in different positions. I actually thought I did okay in those games and it's just how human nature works when a new manager comes in – you're eager to impress. Everyone was in the same boat, there was a clean slate and you were trying to get yourself in the side.

'Nobody had a clue about the starting line-up until the Saturday. I remember the gaffer then just read out 18 names; nobody had a clue where they were actually playing. Ian Culverhouse then came in and smiled as if to say, "This is the way Paul Lambert works." He then told us the positions. Then, before we went out to warm-up, the gaffer said a few bits and then he told us what he demanded and that we just need to go out and play. We went out and played with hunger and real desire to do well.

'At half-time we were 3-1 up and the goal we had conceded was really poor from our point of view. Instead of saying how well we'd played he laid down the marker of that goal we conceded – it doesn't happen. He was absolutely irate about the goal we lost, and right then he was setting the boundaries and laying down a marker of what won't be acceptable.'

A much-changed City side, captained by Grant Holt, ran out 5-2 winners and Lappin and his team-mates had been made aware of the standards that were needed if they wanted to remain in Lambert's side.

With a first league win of the season under their belts it was, in Lambert's eyes, now a case of making up for lost time. He felt the squad he had inherited were not fit enough for the task in hand and soon began to increase the workload and tempo of City's training sessions.

'The first Tuesday session we had with them, it was one of the toughest training days I've ever done,' recalled Lappin with a look of dread. 'Everybody that was there that day would tell you the same; it just seemed to go on for hours. It probably only lasted 90 minutes but it was constant and we were all thinking we can't train like this all the time. But slowly, over time, the tempo of training got to that level and it just became second nature to us and that transpired on to the pitch. We had to be fit for the way we wanted to play and they certainly got us fit and ready to play that way.'

Lambert's flying start against Wycombe was followed by a 4-1 Carling Cup exit at home to Premier League Sunderland, but a 2-0 win at Hartlepool provided further encouragement. The Hartlepool game also marked the debut of on-loan Newcastle goalkeeper Fraser Forster, who took over from Spurs loanee Ben Alnwick. Forster was to play a starring role, with 18 clean sheets in 38 league appearances, and became one of the most important players in the City squad, according to Lappin.

'I remember his first game; nobody knew he was coming in and we met him at the hotel and everyone was just thinking, "Who is this monster?" He was an absolute giant, lovely big guy and some of the saves he made in training – well, you saw it in games, but in training you were thinking, "How the hell's he saved that?" He was a massive signing for us and he saved us on many occasions.'

The 2-0 victory over Hartlepool heralded a barren run of four league games without victory in September, culminating in a 1-1 draw at Gillingham on September 26 – Declan Rudd making his senior debut and becoming City's fourth keeper of the season after Forster was sent off for bringing down Curtis Weston.

That left City 14th in League One, with just ten points from nine games – a colossal 15 points behind leaders Leeds United, and 13 behind second-place Charlton. Incredibly, however, the Canaries would win 17, draw two and lose just one of their next 20 league games.

Rudd made his full debut as City thrashed Leyton Orient 4-0 on 29 September. That was followed by a 5-1 demolition of Bristol Rovers four days later. Among the scorers in both games was Jamie Cureton – his last goals for the club.

But City's main scorers for this season were now well in their stride, with Wes Hoolahan causing havoc behind an exciting front pairing of Holt and Chris Martin. The trio ended the season with 67 goals between them in all competitions, with Holt bagging 30, Martin 23 and Hoolahan 14.

City suffered a cruel setback when a rare error by Forster saw him kick the ball straight to Jermaine Beckford to gift the striker an injury-time winner in a televised 2-1 defeat at Leeds on 19 October. Lambert's team were sixth but still trailed Leeds by 11 points.

The league trip to Southampton on 21 November ended in a 2-2 draw – a scoreline which was repeated when City returned to St Mary's in the Johnstone's Paint Trophy area semi-finals. Alan Pardew's men progressed on penalties, and later beat Carlisle 4-1 in the Wembley final.

The Canaries began their FA Cup campaign with a 7-0 romp away to non-league Paulton Rovers – Martin plundering four goals, with Holt (2) and Hoolahan also on target. But City exited the competition as they slid to a 3-1 defeat at Carlisle in the second round.

But there was no stopping Lambert's men in the league, and a 3-0 home win over Huddersfield on 19 December began a sequence of eight successive league victories for a City side who had by this time signed defender Russell Martin from Peterborough.

'I can always remember the Huddersfield game because we were due to have our Christmas night out afterwards. Huddersfield battered us in the first half – they were camped in our half. And I remember at half-time – and this wasn't our motivation to win the game, but the gaffer said, "If you don't win this game you can forget about your night out!" Second half we steamrollered them with goals from Gary Doherty, Wes and Chrissy Martin.'

Norwich's great form coincided with the important festive period and produced a 2-0 victory over Millwall at Carrow Road on Boxing Day, before City began 2010 by moving into the automatic promotion places with a hard-fought 1-0 victory away to Wycombe on 2 January. The Adams Park success came thanks to a crucial second-half goal from midfielder Korey Smith.

'It wasn't a great footballing performance but it was dogged and determined and on a difficult pitch, from what I remember, but a massive three points,' was Lappin's recollection of the match that first elevated City into the top two.

After Lambert's decision to up sticks and swap Colchester for Carrow Road, there was no love lost between the two clubs, and a legal battle over suitable compensation remained on-going when City headed to the Weston Homes Community Stadium on 16 January. Despite the local media and the Essex club trying to up the ante pre-match, Lambert and his players made sure they did their talking on the pitch. On a rain-soaked afternoon in Essex, City certainly gained a large slice of revenge for their 7-1 mauling on the opening day as Lappin and his team-mates recorded an emphatic 5-0 victory.

'It was just another game. Never once did Paul or the staff say, "Look we're going back here and this is our old club" – that never came into it. It was just another game on our calendar and we had to go and win it.

'We won convincingly. It was nice afterwards, not just to put that first game of the season to bed – but nice to get one over them.'

Not only did the match at Colchester provide an element of revenge for the first game of the season and another vital three points in the race for promotion, it was also notable for the first rendition of the now famous 'Simon Lappin, King of Spain' chant from the stands.

'My wife went to that game and sat in with the supporters,' recalled Lappin. 'I'd heard my name being mentioned in this song to the tune of "London Bridge is falling down" but I never knew what the exact words were. When I heard from my wife what they were singing I found it really funny!

'Not that you're looking for any kind of limelight, as that's not the kind of person I am, but you know you're doing something right when the fans have a song for you. It's still talked about to this day – my daughter talks to her wee friends at school about it and it's great that I had that and I loved it.'

A week later City finally moved to the top of League One on goal difference from faltering Leeds after digging out a gritty 1-0 home win over Brentford on 23 January. City were reduced to ten men when Holt was sent off in the first half – but clinched the points thanks to Martin's late strike.

City's eighth straight win comprised a 2-1 victory over Hartlepool on 30 January. The Canaries trailed for 63 seconds before Cody McDonald headed an equaliser; then former Stockport left-back Michael Rose scored the winner on his debut. It was a record 11th straight home league win for City in a single season.

Norwich suffered their first league defeat in three and a half months when they lost 2-1 at Millwall on 6 February. They bounced back to win 2-1 at Brighton, but then that proud home run was finally ended as Lee Barnard scored twice to give Southampton a 2-0 win at Carrow Road on 20 February.

With 14 games left, City were three points clear of Leeds at the top, but a reassuring eight points clear of third spot. The Canaries then put their foot down to win four in a row against Southend, Oldham, Yeovil and Huddersfield – where on-loan Preston striker Stephen Elliott scored twice in a 3-1 win.

The Canaries were held to a 1-1 draw at Swindon, but promotion was all but guaranteed when Leeds visited Carrow Road for League One's 'Match of the Day' on Saturday, 27 March.

Chris Martin headed a dramatic 89th-minute winner as Norwich City sealed a colossal victory over second-place Leeds to go 11 points clear at the top of the table, having achieved an amazing 26-point swing since September.

Leeds were searching desperately for a late winner of their own when they were caught on the break by Lambert's men. Midfielder Stephen Hughes delivered a perfect, curling cross from the right flank for Martin – a 62nd-minute substitute for Stephen Elliott – to race to the near-post and glance an unstoppable diving header past Shane Higgs in the River End goal.

Carrow Road exploded with excitement and relief as the Canaries – who were now also 11 points clear of third-placed Millwall – took a giant step towards both automatic promotion and the title. There was still time for exasperated Leeds substitute

Trésor Kandol to be shown a red card for grabbing Darel Russell around the neck just 58 seconds after coming on.

It had been a tough, tense battle against a Leeds side desperate to cling on to the Canaries' coat-tails after letting slip their own commanding early-season lead at the top of the table. And, remarkably, Simon Grayson's match-day squad included four players who would go on to join the Canaries – midfielders Jonny Howson, Bradley Johnson and Robert Snodgrass, plus striker Luciano Becchio.

'To win that Leeds game in the fashion we did was fabulous,' said Lappin. 'It was a great ball from Stephen Hughes from the right-hand side and Chrissy doing what he did best.'

With eight games left to play, City won only one of their next four and a 2-1 defeat at Orient on 13 April left them a reduced six points clear of Leeds and seven clear of third-place Millwall with four fixtures remaining. But there were no slips, and in the next game Nelson's header earned a 1-0 victory at Charlton to guarantee promotion on the same ground where relegation had been confirmed the season before.

City secured the title with a 2-0 home win over Gillingham – Darel Russell opening the scoring before Nelson made it two goals in two games. City celebrated with a 3-0 win at Bristol Rovers, and the surprise 2-0 home defeat by Carlisle on the final day mattered little. City were runaway League One winners, having amassed 95 points to Leeds's 86 points at the end of an exhilarating campaign.

'Obviously the moments you remember are the big ones – winning promotion at Charlton, securing the title against Gillingham and then getting presented with the trophy, plus the parties that followed. But really it was the whole meteoric rise from the day when Paul, Gary and Ian came in. It was just amazing to be a part of it. An incredible season and I was very fortunate to have been part of that dressing room.

'Everybody in that squad played their part. It's no coincidence that teams I've been involved with that have been successful have had that togetherness, which in that team was unbelievable. It was a great dressing room to be involved in.'

Prior to holding aloft the League One trophy following City's final game of the season at home to Carlisle United, skipper Grant

Holt was presented with the Barry Butler Memorial Trophy as City's player of the season. Holt's 24 League One goals played a key role in City's success and made him a more-than-worthy recipient of the award.

'He was almost like a Roy of the Rovers figure – captain and scoring all those goals,' laughed Lappin. 'Some of the goals he scored were incredible. But he'd be the first to say it, he wouldn't have been able to have done any of that without the boys around him. It was a real collective effort from everybody. Strikers always get the limelight but Holty, Wes and Chrissy were unstoppable that season. It was our job to get the ball to them and they make things happen.'

However, the ultimate driving force behind this title-winning season was City's motivational leader – Paul Lambert.

'Ian would put on the training session and the manager would step in and say his bit, but it was a match day when Paul would really come alive,' recalled Lappin. 'He just had this knack of making you feel like you were the best player in your position in the world. You would walk out the dressing room door feeling as though you were filling the doorway.'

2010/11 CHAMPIONSHIP RUNNERS-UP

A summer signing from Brighton & Hove Albion, all-action midfielder Andrew Crofts instantly knew he was joining a team on the up. From early on in the Canaries' 2010/11 campaign, Crofts felt the close-knit City squad and their motivational manager Paul Lambert were on the road to the Premier League.

After guiding Norwich City to the 2009/10 League One title in his first season at the helm, manager Paul Lambert wasted little time in building on the feel-good factor that surrounded the club in the summer of 2010.

When quizzed as to the club's aspirations for 2010/11, his stock answer tended to be, 'We'll aim to be competitive' – while new summer signings were simply described as 'here to give the existing lads a hand'. It was a smart move from an astute manager who was keen not to burden his squad with any unnecessary levels of expectation from the outside world.

As City geared up for life in back in the Championship, Lambert introduced a number of new faces to the group. Remarkably, almost every one of them would be a roaring success over the coming season. Lambert and his trusty assistants, Ian Culverhouse and Gary Karsa, clearly appeared to have the Midas touch when it came to recruitment.

Ahead of the new season, in came goalkeeper John Ruddy, defenders Steven Smith and Elliott Ward, midfielders Andrew Crofts, David Fox and Andrew Surman plus striker Simeon

Jackson. With the exception of Smith, who struggled to adjust to life south of the border following his move from Glasgow Rangers, all of the summer recruits played vital roles in a memorable campaign.

Box-to-box midfielder Crofts was signed from Brighton & Hove Albion in May 2010 as one of the first acquisitions following promotion. He had faced City twice the previous season in League One fixtures, and his tenacious ball-winning skills and desire to succeed had clearly left an impression on the City boss.

The midfielder remembers his initial talks with Lambert, but at that juncture there was no big promotion spiel from the City manager. However, once the squad was fully assembled, the group were left in no doubt about their aims for the season.

'The first meeting I had with the gaffer was really all about how he was looking for the team to play and how he saw me fitting into things,' says Crofts, who went on to feature in all bar two of City's 2010/11 Championship fixtures. "But I remember as clear as day the first team meeting we had in pre-season; it was before the first day's training and it was, "We're looking to get promoted".

'It was clear from the start that we should be looking to get promoted and we should fear no-one. The way the gaffer presented it, everyone bought into it and there was a feeling of "Let's give this a right good go." So the belief was there from pre-season.

'As a new signing, joining a club that had just got promotion from League One to the Championship, I was thinking that perhaps consolidation, or top ten, might be the aim, but no, the gaffer was clear from day one he wanted promotion and I was buzzing to hear that.'

Not only was Crofts delighted to learn of his new manager's high aspirations for the season ahead, but he was also thrilled with what awaited him in the changing room at Colney:

'As a new player you're always excited to meet the dressing room, meet the personalities and characters and see what the environment is like,' added Crofts. 'I think most people know I'm an outgoing person, I'm bubbly and enthusiastic, and I always tend to fit into changing rooms easily anyway. But at Norwich it was so easy. I knew a couple of the players and I think everybody knows I'm big pals with Russell Martin. He'd been there from the previous season and that helped me a lot. But that changing room we had was on another level; we were all such good mates and we loved going to battle together.'

As far as transfers go, it was apparent from the off that Andrew Crofts and Norwich City were very much the perfect match.

'Pre-season went really well, we played Everton and Newcastle at Carrow Road and I just loved it. To say I loved playing at Carrow Road would be an understatement – every time I walked out on to the pitch I so looked forward to playing.'

City's first match of the campaign, at home to Watford, was chosen to kick off the new Championship season, and as a result was pulled forward to Friday, 6 August 2010, and broadcast live on Sky television. A 3-2 defeat proved to be something of a mixed bag for Wales international Crofts.

'First half against Watford was disappointing, we went behind and could have done better,' recalled Crofts. 'Second half we had a good go, and to be fair we were a lot better. It was great to get a goal, and my first goal for a big club like Norwich was a big thing for me personally. But I'm a team player, and I was more disappointed that we didn't get anything from that game,' says Crofts.

Following a straightforward midweek win over Gillingham in the League Cup, City were keen to get their first Championship victory of the season under their belts when they travelled to Scunthorpe United on 14 August.

'There was no dwelling on that Watford result; we were disappointed that we lost the first game, but at the same time we knew we could soon put that one behind us.'

A first league goal of the season from skipper Grant Holt gave City all three points from their trip to Glanford Park and from that moment on the Canaries' 2010/11 Championship campaign had lift-off.

'From day one you looked around and thought, "We've got a proper team here." The Watford game was disappointing but we quickly got that one out of our system. We beat Scunny and after that we were always picking up points and always in games – we'd gelled and hit it off.'

A Carrow Road meeting with Swansea City proved a watershed moment for goalkeeper John Ruddy. The former Everton stopper had not enjoyed the most comfortable of starts to his Canary career, and he was struggling to convince fans that he was the man to fill Fraser Forster's gloves after the on-loan keeper returned to Newcastle United following a highly impressive loan spell during the previous season.

An entertaining match appeared set for a goalless finish but a highly eventful ending unfolded in the final six minutes. After 84 minutes Swansea were awarded a penalty after Ruddy's rocky start continued when he upended Scott Sinclair, but the City man instantly redeemed himself with a stunning spot-kick save. From the moment that he repelled David Cotterill's penalty in front of a delighted Barclay, Ruddy's confidence appeared to grow and grow. The save was made all the more sweet as Norwich forced two late goals to win the match 2-0. Swans defender Ashley Williams turned the ball into his own net after 87 minutes before substitute Jackson opened his Canary account in injury time to make it 2-0.

A much-changed City line-up then exited the League Cup at Blackburn Rovers before a full-strength side ended August with a useful point from their trip to Nottingham Forest. Crofts netted City's goal at the City Ground as Lambert handed a Canary debut to central-defender Leon Barnett, who had joined on loan from West Bromwich Albion.

An impressive run of four wins from six games ahead of an international break in early October saw City defeat Barnsley and Leicester City at Carrow Road while recording away successes at Preston North End and Bristol City. The 4-3 victory over Leicester City under the Carrow Road floodlights was perhaps the pick of the lot – certainly in the entertainment stakes.

So as Crofts prepared for international action with Wales, he was able to reflect on an impressive start to his Canary career. It also offered him and his team-mates the chance to see the benefits of their gruelling pre-season schedule.

'As a new player you always want to try and make a good impression, and as a box-to-box midfielder you want to chip in with a few goals, so I was pleased with those opening few months. I'd settled in with the group, shown the players what I was about and shown the fans what I could do.

'Pre-season was proper, it was tough and we did lots of work on how we were going to play. We played the diamond and everybody knew their roles and responsibilities.'

The next phase of fixtures began with a gritty 0-0 draw away to league leaders Queens Park Rangers and that point signalled a run of five draws in eight games. It also saw City defeat Middlesbrough 1-0 at Carrow Road, while suffering reverses at the hands of Crystal Palace and Cardiff City.

Remarkably, the team had not suffered back-to-back league defeats all season, a wonderful trait that they would maintain throughout the entire campaign. Incredibly, that impressive record made it two seasons on the spin under Lambert that Norwich had managed to not suffer simultaneous league defeats – they set the ball rolling on that statistic during their League One campaign.

'We never lost two league games in a row and that was something we were really proud of,' says Crofts. 'If we lost a game we just had to get something from the next game – that was something that was just installed in us. Again, it was almost demanded from the gaffer and the boys all bought into it.'

November ended with the first East Anglian derby of the season as Roy Keane's Ipswich Town arrived at Carrow Road on Sunday, 28 November 2010. After a one-season hiatus in hostilities, following City's League One campaign, the East Anglian derby was back and Norwich City were bang up for it.

City's 3-2 defeat at Portman Road back in April 2009 had placed a major dent in the club's faint hopes of Championship survival in 2008/09. City fans were ridiculed by followers of their bitter rivals as they left the ground in sombre mood that day – but revenge is a dish best served cold, and the Canaries handed out the first sizeable portion in style in November 2010. Little did anyone know at the time, but City were about to embark on a decade of derby dominance.

Grant Holt stole the headlines and wrote his name into Norwich City folklore as he hammered home a hat-trick in a comprehensive 4-1 Canary victory. Despite Simon Lappin and Chris Martin being the only two players in City's starting line-up with previous experience of an East Anglian derby, this new-look side soon grasped the importance of the occasion.

'Local derby games are always special,' acknowledges Crofts. 'You don't realise how big it [Norwich City v Ipswich Town] is until you are part of it. The gaffer was great in the build-up to it – he made sure we all knew how big it was, but also made sure we prepared as we would for any other game. Knowing what it means to the fans, it certainly helped you to do that little bit extra, or run that little bit harder, and we had an excellent result.

'Holty grabbing the hat-trick was amazing. Often derby games are close but we made it comfortable and enjoyed two special wins that season, which was amazing.'

The derby triumph also saw Arsenal midfielder Henri Lansbury make his City debut after joining on loan from the Gunners. Lansbury teed up Holt's second goal and made a terrific immediate impression. Such was his influence that the loan was extended for the remainder of the season, and the youngster chipped in with four league goals. Just like fellow loanee Leon Barnett, Lansbury had little problem in settling into a vibrant Canary changing room.

'H [Henri Lansbury] was wicked; the recruitment that Norwich made that year, it was evident that we were all the same type of characters. He was quick, grafted like everybody else and had real talent and an ability which matched his desire and work-rate. He settled in really quickly, scored some important goals, he was great in the changing room and great on the pitch.'

Victory over Ipswich was the first of six wins from an impressive run of ten league games that saw Lambert's men lose just once. That run of results saw Norwich well-placed to mount a serious promotion push come the end of January 2011.

The first month of the new year had seen City convert Barnett's loan from West Bromwich Albion to a permanent deal. They also completed the signings of Colchester United left-back Marc Tierney and MK Dons striker Aaron Wilbraham.

February began with a midweek visit from Millwall, and once again City showed all of their battling qualities to come from behind to win 2-1. Victory was sealed thanks to a last-gasp goal from Lansbury four minutes into stoppage time.

'That's a great habit to have, scoring late goals,' says Crofts. 'I think if you look at any successful team in any division over the years, it's always the ones who get the late goals and have that belief and go to the end who end up succeeding, and we had that in abundance.'

A narrow 2-1 defeat at Burnley followed the win over the Lions, but once again City bounced back from a defeat at the first attempt as another late goal, this time from Grant Holt, saw City beat Reading 2-1 at Carrow Road.

'Most of the time I thought we had the better of teams, and when you feel like that you know you've got a chance. It was always a good thing knowing that the other teams amongst it will have come in and seen that Norwich have scored late; that will have been really deflating for them.'

City ended February on a winning note as they overcame Barnsley 2-0 at Oakwell to record a league double over the Tykes. Always a team game, yes, but this was very much the 'Andrew Crofts show'. The midfielder netted his seventh and eighth goals of the season in the first half to set City on the way to all three points and to cement their place in the play-off pack. Having headed his side in front, the midfielder then proceeded to score City's second goal of the game as he sent a volley on the turn past Luke Steele in the Barnsley goal for what was viewed by most as City's goal of the season.

'I've scored some good goals, but that was one I was very, very proud of. I know it gets played a lot since then and with the comparisons to the [Justin] Fashanu one. People always talk about it and it's one that's always in my memory – it is one of those moments I'll never forget.

'The fact that we won 2-0 was the main thing, but it was nice to get a brace – the first one was a header from a ball in by Marc Tierney. Second one came from a really clever ball from Wes, who found me nicely. I managed to turn and swivel and it went in – I probably should have had a hat-trick, to be fair – I had a couple of chances second half, but you can't complain at two goals, a clean sheet and three points – great memories.'

Crofts was keen to place on record the role that Wes Hoolahan played in his stunning strike at Oakwell. As well as being idolised by the Norwich fans, ultra-talented playmaker Hoolahan was also held in the highest of regard by his team-mates:

'Wes was a real talent, but it was his work-rate coupled with his ability that really made him stand out. A clever, intelligent player, full of energy, full of life and he just loves playing football – and that was infectious.'

Despite Hoolahan's excellence more often than not being a vital factor in Canary victories, a week later the Irishman was very much the villain of the piece when City faced basement side Preston North End at Carrow Road on Saturday, 5 March 2011.

Former Canary Chris Brown had given the visitors a surprise lead on the hour-mark, but City responded almost immediately as Holt rattled home his 14th league goal of the season. Norwich were then presented with a glorious opportunity to win the game when they were awarded a 72nd-minute penalty following a handball by North End midfielder Darren Carter.

Hoolahan took the responsibility for converting from 12 yards but a nonchalant chipped effort was gratefully clutched by visiting keeper Iain Turner. The match ended 1-1. Suffice to say that when Hoolahan's head hit the pillow that night he could probably still hear the voice of a furious Lambert ringing in his ears.

'The gaffer was not happy. And yes, he obviously gave Wes a fair bit in the dressing room afterwards!' recalled Crofts. 'I remember sitting next to Wes and he was so gutted and so disappointed.'

However, if a team or a player is to be judged by their response to a disappointment, then what followed away to Leicester City three days later was the perfect example of why this Norwich team was in it for the long haul. City had defeated the Foxes 4-3 at Carrow Road back in September, and the two sides served up another goal-glut at the Walkers Stadium as Norwich came out on top in a five-goal thriller. A memorable 3-2 victory moved City up to third in the table and level on points with second-place Swansea.

'That night at Leicester, that just summed up Wes and summed up everything at Norwich that season,' says Crofts. 'He was down after the penalty miss, but next match and he opens the scoring with a header! That was what we were all about, and that showed Wes's character – he was brilliant in that game.'

Success at the Walkers Stadium was followed by a hat-trick of home wins, interspersed with useful draws away at Hull

City and Watford. Despite taking an early lead against Bristol City, it took late goals from Lansbury and Surman to see off a resilient Robins side on Monday, 14 March. A 6-0 thrashing of relegation-threatened Scunthorpe United saw hat-tricks for both Holt and Jackson as City got April off to the best start possible. Loan signings Dani Pacheco from Liverpool and Sam Vokes from Wolves added further striking options for the promotion run-in, and both debuted against the Iron.

City then defeated Nottingham Forest 2-1 at Carrow Road in front of the live Sky television cameras on Friday, April 15. That win over Forest subsequently set things up for a never-to-be-forgotten Easter period.

The second East Anglian derby of the season was brought forward 24 hours from Good Friday and played at Portman Road on the evening of Thursday, 21 April. With Ipswich still smarting from their 4-1 mauling at Carrow Road earlier in the season, Town were now under the management of Paul Jewell and looking to give their fans one final hurrah as their season petered towards an uneventful mid-table finish.

Any season when the Canaries record a league double over their arch rivals is a special one in the supporters' eyes, but what happened in 2010/11 was simply fairytale stuff from a Canary perspective. On an unforgettable evening for the City fans inside Portman Road, and for the many thousands watching a beam-back at Carrow Road, Norwich produced a ruthless display of finishing and went one better than in the Carrow Road clash – this time winning 5-1.

The euphoria that surrounded the win was immense, and the three points elevated the Canaries into the second automatic promotion place behind leaders Queens Park Rangers and ahead of Cardiff City.

Jackson was then the hero of the hour as he grabbed his second Carrow Road hat-trick in three games when City beat Derby County 3-2 in an astonishing game on Easter Monday. In a season of many last-gasp winners, Jackson's hat-trick goal won the game with almost the last kick of the match. The goal meant City kept the destiny of the second automatic promotion place in their own hands at Cardiff's expense, and sparked absolute pandemonium at Carrow Road. Even keeper Ruddy ran the length of the pitch to celebrate with his team-mates in front of an ecstatic Snake Pit.

Jackson's late heroics meant Norwich held on to second spot in the table – at 2-2 they had briefly dropped to third after Cardiff won 1-0 at Preston.

With two games to play, Norwich City's fate was in their own hands as a remarkable second successive promotion hovered into view. Portsmouth away and Coventry City at home were now all that stood between City and a place in the Premier League.

In the two-way battle with Cardiff for the second promotion spot, both clubs were in action on Monday, 2 May, with the Bluebirds hosting Middlesbrough ahead of City's evening meeting with Portsmouth at Fratton Park. Dave Jones's Cardiff side were fully expected to win at home to Boro and ramp the pressure up on City ahead of their game with Pompey. However, Jones's men buckled dramatically under the weight of expectation at the Cardiff City Stadium and handed the initiative to the Canaries.

'I remember it so well – we were in the hotel and managed to grab the first ten to 15 minutes of the Cardiff game on the TV,' recalls Crofts. 'Middlesbrough went 1-0 up early on and we're thinking, "Get in there!"

'Then literally a couple of minutes later they go two-up and all the boys are in the hotel hallway thinking this could be our day. Then it's 3-0 and it's, "Oh My God!" – we're walking out to get on the bus just looking at one another and I remember Simon Lappin squeezing his head as if to say, "This is it, this is it."

'So we get there knowing Cardiff have just lost 3-0 and if we win, we're up. It really ratcheted things up and we're all thinking, "Let's get this done."'

Norwich were in no mood to let this opportunity pass them by and duly sealed promotion thanks to a second-half header from in-form striker Jackson.

'Jacko was proper hot over the last few months. He went into every game thinking he was going to score, and the team thinking he was always going to score. That's such a massive boost for any team, and especially at that time of the season.

'First half, we battered Portsmouth and should have been three or four up. You're thinking, "Is this going to be one of those days when we just don't manage to score?"

'I remember the goal well. The ball's been cleared up-field, I brought it down and popped it inside to Foxy and he's played an unbelievable ball into Jacko, who tucked it away with his head. Great jubilation – but there was still a fair bit of the game to go and we had to make sure we saw it through. The scenes after that one were off the scale!'

At the end of the game the travelling masses spilt on to the pitch to celebrate with their heroes as City headed back to the top flight just 24 months after relegation to the third tier. This was a remarkable achievement and one that Crofts felt was just reward for the phenomenal spirit that ran through the club – forged by Lambert and embraced by everyone.

'Every game we were in, we gave it everything and the fans knew that. The connection that the players had together, I think it rubbed off on the fans. The relationship between the fans and the players was so united and the gaffer had a massive hold on that. He created it and we all bought into it – everything was just so tight and united.

'The set-up was surreal really; it was a pleasure to play and a pleasure to go into training every day. We worked so hard as a team and staff, the whole club was united and everyone was singing off the same page.'

2014/15 CHAMPIONSHIP PLAY-OFF WINNERS

*Skipper Russell Martin recalls the pain of
relegation and the feeling of relief as the Canaries'
2014/15 season finally concluded with Wembley
glory and promotion to the Premier League.*

With two seasons of Premier League experience behind them,
Norwich City were beginning to feel part of the top-flight
furniture as they embarked on a third straight campaign among
English football's elite in 2013/14.

Despite a host of big-money signings arriving in the summer
of 2013 to strengthen the squad, things did not go to plan and the
Canaries' three-season spell in the Premier League came crashing
to an abrupt end.

The relegation was a massive blow to the club's progress and
the feeling of disappointment and failure certainly hit the playing
staff, particularly those who had been with the club on its meteoric
rise from League One to the Premier League under Paul Lambert.
One player to really feel the pain was defender Russell Martin:

'After two years in the Premier League you feel that you've
proved yourself and you've earned the right to be there really, so
to then get relegated – it was tough,' confirmed Martin.

The 2013/14 relegation was almost something City sleepwalked
into. They were never cast adrift at the foot of the table but, when
push came to shove in the vital closing weeks of the season, this
was a team that just could not amass the points needed for survival.

'It was quite tight for a while and at one stage I thought we
were going to be comfortable,' added Martin. 'You get a good few

points on the board and you think that should be enough but then other teams go on good runs and it puts you under pressure.'

Only three points from a home match with Arsenal, coupled with favourable results elsewhere and a miraculous swing in goal difference could have saved City as they went into their final fixture. Realistically they were down before a ball was even kicked that day as a season of frustration came to a close.

'It was a horrible feeling, the worst I've had. It was terrible. For the lads who'd worked so hard to get us there it obviously hurt us that bit more than perhaps the ones who'd just come in.

'That was probably one of the reasons we went down. There were players that knew the full background story of us being a League One club and then others who just saw us as a Premier League club and came along to earn some good money and put themselves in the shop window. For those that had been there in League One and the Championship it certainly meant a bit more.'

Relegated, and with uncertainly over the manager's role after Neil Adams stepped in to the breach following the sacking of Chris Hughton with five games to play, confusion reigned at Carrow Road in the immediate aftermath of the drop.

After the club scoured Europe in search of the best possible management team to guide the team back to the Premier League, the ship was finally steadied when Adams was appointed manager on a permanent basis.

'There were a few grumblings and a few people wanted away,' recalled Martin. 'It was inevitable we were going to lose a few people like Snoddy [Robert Snodgrass], who had been one of our best players, but when we came back for pre-season, and the summer had gone, everyone's head was fixed on making sure we got back up as quick as possible really.'

As the Canaries bade farewell to Johan Elmander, Jonas Gutierrez and Joseph Yobo, whose lucrative Carrow Road contracts had fortunately expired, misfiring striker Ricky van Wolfswinkel was loaned to Saint Etienne and Leroy Fer sold to QPR. Adams was certainly shuffling his pack and looking to address the Canaries' goalscoring problems post-Grant Holt.

'The club had had Premier League money for three years so we had a squad that was strong for the Championship. Neil had come in as manager and the lads were all quite pleased with that, then the new signings started to come in.

'You looked at our front line and it was really refreshed. Grabbs [Lewis Grabban] and Cammy [Cameron Jerome] – they both gave us something different and we looked really strong for the Championship. Kyle [Lafferty] didn't perhaps play the number of games he would have liked but he had a good impact in the dressing room, he was always positive – we had a good group of players who really cared and wanted to get the team back up.'

Despite an opening-day 1-0 defeat away to Wolverhampton Wanderers, a new-look City side soon hit its straps and back-to-back home wins over Watford and Blackburn Rovers were followed by a Grabban goal to secure victory in the East Anglian derby away to Ipswich Town on 23 August 2014. When City followed up a 4-2 win at Cardiff City with a 3-0 victory away to Brentford the chant of 'We've got our Norwich back' was booming out from the away fans and echoing around Griffin Park.

As September ended with a 3-1 win at Blackpool it looked as though Adams's side was embarking on a straightforward procession back to the Premier League.

'We started the season fairly well, but we all knew it was never going to be that easy. Although we started well and were playing some really good football we were a little bit open. We were free-flowing as a team but open, and Neil was happy with that as he wanted to entertain and score goals, but other people wanted to make sure the other side of it was set up right as well.'

That level of openness and vulnerability at the back began to rear its ugly head as a tricky October loomed. Norwich picked up just six points from a potential 15 following a home defeat to Charlton Athletic (0-1) plus 1-1 Carrow Road draws with Rotherham United and Leeds United. On the road City suffered their customary defeat at Fulham and drew 0-0 at Sheffield Wednesday before finally ending the month with a less than inspiring 2-1 win over Bolton Wanderers at Carrow Road.

'We had started well but the disappointing thing was that as soon as we hit a little rough patch, which you're always going to at some point in a season, everything was brought into question about Neil's background and experience.'

An awful start to November saw City thumped 4-0 away to Middlesbrough and suffer a 2-1 defeat at Nottingham Forest. Adams was now a manager under serious pressure.

The City boss made the decision to part company with coach Mark Robson, who was then replaced by the vastly experienced and highly respected Mike Phelan. A former Canary himself, Phelan's arrival began with a 2-1 defeat at home to Reading. However, results then did begin to get back on track as City won 1-0 at Wigan, thrashed Huddersfield Town 5-0 and drew 2-2 at Derby County.

The festive period saw a hapless Millwall side dismantled 6-1 at Carrow Road on Boxing Day but, such was the lack of consistency in results and performances, City followed their mauling of the Lions with a 2-1 defeat at Reading 48 hours later. The patience of the club's board was being run thin and, following an FA Cup third-round defeat away to League One Preston North End, Adams was shown the exit door.

'I felt sorry for Neil, it was a tough time. The club had given him the job but didn't support him through it,' reflected Martin. 'But as a player you have to acknowledge what the club want and you have to get on with it.'

With City in touch with the play-off pack, there was certainly a feeling that the popular Adams had been more than a little harshly treated. And after being handed the captaincy by Adams, Martin had great sympathy for his manager:

'I was disappointed for Neil as he was such a good guy. He was in a different job to what he had been in before, and having been a player here before it obviously meant so much to him as well.

'I think he started to feel it a little bit and there were a few lads who – I wouldn't say didn't work hard enough for him, but there were always a few who felt that he'd come from the under-18s as a coach, and they didn't need coaching – yet Neil wanted to coach. It was hard to put your finger on where it all went wrong. We were very close to being a really good team but for some reason it wasn't quite clicking.

'Ultimately the club made a decision and it proved to be a good decision in the end with Alex Neil coming in.'

Following Adams's departure, the club acted swiftly in appointing his successor as the little-known Alex Neil arrived from Scottish club Hamilton Academical. It was a surprise appointment that in truth left both the fan base and dressing room a little underwhelmed.

'Mike Phelan was there and I think he made it evidently clear he wanted the job. The lads were not sure who was going to get it and as soon as we heard it was Alex Neil – I'll be honest, not many of us knew too much about him! A few of the lads that had played in Scotland, like Whitts [Steven Whittaker], knew a little bit but at that time no-one knew much of what to expect.'

Suffice to say the Scot wasted little time in making his mark at Colney. Such was Neil's appetite to hit the ground running at Norwich that he abandoned a watching brief in the stands at Bournemouth, on 10 January, after Jonny Howson had been shown the red card. He made his way down to the dugout and helped the City bench mastermind a memorable 2-1 win with ten men.

'He came in and stamped his authority on the place really quickly and that was probably really what the group needed. Some managers come in and say, "Right, this is how we're doing it," but with Alex it was very straightforward, it was black or white, no grey areas; you do it his way or you don't do it, basically.

'He instilled some belief and we became much more aggressive and reflected what he wanted on the pitch. He had a clear way of doing things and didn't hang about in getting his message across.

'Although a lot of managers come in and assess the situation I think he thought he had a good knowledge of it and just made it clear that we were going to be really fit, pressing high and on the front foot – that's how he went about it.'

The City players instantly responded to Neil's approach and after a disappointing 2-1 defeat at home to Brentford was followed by a goalless draw at Birmingham, the Canaries then embarked on a sequence of six straight Championship victories.

City's excellent form propelled them not only right back into the play-off picture but also with a real chance of hunting down the top two of Bournemouth and Watford.

'There were a couple of games when you started to think this could be us and could be our year. One was Blackburn away, when

I really felt the togetherness was really strong and we had a huddle on the pitch at the end of the game. It wasn't planned or anything but there was then a real connection growing back between the fans and the players again; that was something we'd probably lost from the previous season.'

The feel-good factor inspired by Bradley Johnson's stunning late winner at Ewood Park saw confidence flowing through the City squad ahead of the second East Anglian derby of the season. With Ipswich also in the play-off frame, the stakes could not have been much higher when the two old foes locked horns at Carrow Road on Sunday, 1 March 2015. Unfortunately for Town, Johnson picked up where from where he had left off at Ewood Park and let fly with a rocket-like effort to give Norwich an early lead. Grabban then netted a second goal after the break to seal another routine City victory over their Suffolk rivals.

Norwich continued to impress under Neil, and when two tough away assignments at Bolton and Leeds yielded six points Norwich appeared serious contenders for a top-two finish.

'Bolton away, when Hoops [Gary Hooper] nicked a late winner, you certainly felt the momentum building and belief is such an important part of it. We'd done unbelievably well to put ourselves in a position where three or four weeks from the end of the season we could actually get automatic promotion, because at one point that looked well beyond us.'

After a crucial home match with Middlesbrough ended in a frustrating 1-0 defeat, City's penultimate game of the season was drawn at Rotherham, and that proved to be the end of their pursuit of a top-two finish.

With a final home game against Fulham next on the agenda, City knew a win would secure third place and guarantee that the second leg of the play-off semi-final would be played at Carrow Road. However, for skipper Martin there was still more than a tinge of disappointment that they had not been able to bag one of the top-two automatic promotion berths that he felt he and his team-mates deserved:

'The frustrating thing for us was that we'd battered Watford twice, 3-0 in both games, but they were going to finish above us. That certainly showed what we were capable of though.

'The Boro game was make or break, we felt if we had won that then we would have kicked on and got into the top two.

'In the end I'd probably say that was the best thing that happened to us, that home game against Middlesbrough, when they caught us a bit cold and beat us 1-0. That match prepared us so well for the play-off final when we met them again.'

A 4-2 final-day victory over Fulham at Carrow Road saw Norwich end the campaign with 86 points and third place. Results elsewhere meant Ipswich finished the season in sixth spot and it would be an East Anglian derby in the play-off semi-finals.

The last time the two sides had met in a semi-final had been 30 years previously when Norwich defeated Town in the 1985 League Cup semi-final en route to beating Sunderland in the Wembley final. The pre-match hype and excitement reached fever pitch but City captain Martin confirms this was the match the Norwich players really wanted.

'We had played against them twice that season and beaten then twice, so we were really comfortable with playing them again. I know it meant a lot to the fans but for us it was just really clear-cut, they were the team we wanted to play. We kept it quiet but we had all agreed that Ipswich was our preferred team and once it panned out that way there was a feeling that this was how it was meant to be.

'It was perfect, a great atmosphere against our local rivals, who we'd already got the better of, and Alex had a plan of how he wanted to play against them. We knew once we got something at their place, and then got them back to ours, it was game on.'

Having ended the regular season eight points and three places better off than their bitter rivals, City showed their extra quality to see off Town and book a first trip to Wembley in 30 years. The first leg ended 1-1 at Portman Road in a game that City controlled for large periods. Despite Town producing a brave showing in the first half of the second leg, Norwich upped the gears after the break. A Wes Hoolahan penalty, plus goals from Nathan Redmond and Jerome, secured a 3-1 win and an aggregate 4-2 triumph over Mick McCarthy's men, who stood little chance after the dismissal of Christophe Berra for handball in conceding the spot-kick just after the interval.

Monday, 25 May 2015 will go down in history as one of the greatest days in Norwich City Football Club's history. It was the day that Alex Neil's team produced an excellent display to defeat Middlesbrough 2-0 in the play-off final and secure promotion back to the Premier League.

The yellow army flocked to Wembley in their thousands and created a sea of yellow and green in their half of the stadium. First-half goals from Jerome and Redmond – whose crisp finish rounded off a scintillating team move – put Norwich firmly in the driving seat and gave Boro a problem they simply had no answer to.

It was a day no Norwich City fan fortunate enough to be there will ever forget. It was also the stand-out day of Martin's career.

'That was the ultimate for me – leading the team up the steps at Wembley, and to do it in front of all those fans and your family was brilliant. It was magical and something you can only dream of really. That was the highlight of my career.'

A key factor in City's performance on the day was perfect preparation, as Martin explains:

'Alex was brilliant throughout the whole week in the build-up to the final with his preparation and the way he conducted himself. It wasn't just down to Alex though. Nick Davies, the head of sports science, he got the training load right, the days we trained right and the days off right.

'We went down to London for a couple of days and went to the Grove for a nice meal to take our mind off things. We trained really well on a good pitch, went to see Wembley and knew where our families were going to be sitting, so we got all that sort of thing out the way. We made sure we stayed at the Hilton at Wembley so we could just be ready to get up and go on the day.

'It was such a relaxed week or ten days leading up to the final. You just had that feeling it was going to go for us. On the day Middlesbrough turned up late and a bit flustered and it just felt like it all fell into place.

'I remember being with Steven Whittaker right at the start of the day and seeing fans outside in yellow and green at about 9am going to get their breakfast in restaurants, and both of us felt that we ought to be feeling anxious or nervous but we were just so relaxed. That was the feeling that Alex and the staff gave us that week and it was perfect.'

Once that final whistle blew at Wembley, and before Martin led his troops up the steps to collect the play-off winner's trophy, there was a brief time for reflection:

'It was hard to take it all in at the time but the overwhelming and overriding feeling was one of relief that we'd done it. It was almost like a feeling of redemption for us as a group of players who'd been though the relegation. We knew we had paid the fans back and given them what they deserved. They didn't deserve relegation the year before but they certainly deserved Wembley. We all did.'

On the up – *City players celebrate their point at QPR in April 1960. The result left the Canaries on the verge of promotion to the Second Division*

Into the big time – *action from City's 2-1 win at Orient in April 1972. The result secured Norwich City a place in Division One for the first time in the club's history*

Celebration time – City fans invade the pitch at Vicarage Road after landing the Second Division title in 1972

Bond's boys – manager John Bond (far left) and his promotion-winning squad face the camera ahead of their 1975/76 campaign back in the top flight

King Ken – *boss Ken Brown celebrates City's 1981/82 promotion at Sheffield Wednesday, Brown would oversee another immediate return to the top flight in 1985/86*

Shrewd signing – *striker Kevin Drinkell ended his first campaign at Carrow Road as City's leading scorer, the club's player-of-the-season and a Second Division champion*

Star turn – *Darren Huckerby was the inspiration behind City's 2003/04 success. Iwan Roberts was first on the scene to congratulate the flying winger on his wonder-strike against Wimbledon in February 2004*

*Farewell Iwan –
Canary legend Iwan
Roberts together
with children Ben,
Chase and Eva waves
goodbye following his
final game at Carrow
Road in 2004 as City
celebrate promotion to
the Premier League*

Champions! A proud Simon Lappin shows the League One trophy to the Carrow Road faithful in May 2010

Debut action – Andrew Crofts made his Canary bow against Watford in August 2010. The midfielder proved to be a key member of City's promotion-winning side

Blue Murder – Canary cult hero Grant Holt wheels away after completing his unforgettable hat-trick in the 2010 East Anglian derby as Norwich thrashed Ipswich 4-1

Wembley winners! Russell Martin raises the Championship play-off trophy in 2015

Significant strike – Moritz Leitner fires home City's equaliser at Portman Road in September 2018. The goal relieved growing pressure on head coach Daniel Farke and sparked Norwich's surge up the table

Youth and experience *– young right-back Max Aarons and ever-present goalkeeper Tim Krul both played crucial roles in the Canaries' 2018/19 title triumph*

Victory parade – club captain Grant Hanley scaled the roof of the open topped bus to hoist the Championship trophy during the 2019 celebrations

2018/19 CHAMPIONSHIP CHAMPIONS

Experienced goalkeeper Tim Krul was ever-present in his debut season at Carrow Road as the Canaries pulled off the most unexpected of promotions in 2018/19.

The whole essence of this publication is to acknowledge that promotion seasons are invariably the best seasons, and the beauty of the Canaries' tenth and most recent post-war promotion was that their title triumph came from absolutely nowhere!

City's previous campaign had ended with an uninspiring 14th-place Championship finish, in what was head coach Daniel Farke's first season at the helm. From day one the Carrow Road faithful got fully behind their new German leader, but as the season progressed the patience of even the most optimistic of supporters was put to the test. After the summer optimism that tends to go hand-in-hand with a new voice and fresh ideas coming from the touchline, plus the introduction of several new faces to the squad, the 2017/18 season was not one that will live too long in the memory.

In truth, City were almost single-handedly carried through the campaign by midfield star James Maddison. Angus Gunn performed well in goal during a season-long loan from Manchester City, there was the odd flash of brilliance from Josh Murphy, while Grant Hanley added some stability at the back and Jamal Lewis appeared a more-than-useful find at left-back. However, but for midfielder Maddison's 14 league goals, then City would almost certainly have been relegated. Other than Maddison's classy displays, and Timm Klose's late equaliser against Ipswich Town, watching football at Carrow Road in 2017/18 at times bordered on the mundane.

After the aforementioned Klose goal against Ipswich, home fans endured back-to-back goalless Carrow Road clashes with Bolton Wanderers and Nottingham Forest, neither of which did a great deal to fuel the enthusiasm for signing up to a 2018/19 season ticket. So when City ended the campaign with a 5-1 mauling at Sheffield Wednesday and a final league position below bitter rivals Ipswich Town, suffice to say there was not a huge level of optimism as to what might lie ahead in the following season.

The summer break saw the anticipated big-money departure of Maddison, who joined Leicester City, as the Canaries looked to balance the books now that Premier League parachute payments had come to an end following the club's relegation in 2016. Murphy also departed Carrow Road when he linked up with Premier League new boys Cardiff City and the impressive Gunn returned to his parent club.

If the Maddison monies were used to balance the books, then the fee received for Murphy did perhaps allow Farke and sporting director Stuart Webber some room for manoeuvre in their attempts to improve a squad which had seen three key men depart.

Ahead of the new season Norwich secured the signing of 21-year-old Argentine midfielder Emi Buendia from Getafe in Spain. They also captured Mortiz Leitner from FC Augsburg; the midfielder had been on loan at Carrow Road during the second half of the previous season and agreed to return on a permanent basis. City then fended off strong interest from Championship rivals Millwall to land the services of Wolverhampton Wanderers' versatile midfielder Ben Marshall. Season-long loan moves were secured for Sheffield Wednesday striker Jordan Rhodes and Germany under-21 international right-back Felix Passlack from Borussia Dortmund.

Meanwhile, two free agents also agreed to join the Canaries. The first was Finnish international striker Teemu Pukki, who had spent the previous four seasons in Denmark with Brondby. The second was former Newcastle United goalkeeper Tim Krul, the one-time Holland number one, having been back-up keeper at Brighton in 2017/18.

A vastly-experienced stopper, Krul was delighted to agree a two-year deal at Carrow Road as he looked to get his career back on track after a long-term injury had hampered his progress while at St James' Park.

'It was really nice to sign on the dotted line. I spoke with the manager and people at the club and it moved very quickly,' said Krul, upon his arrival at Colney. 'The manager rang and explained everything – what his plans were, what he expected of me – and I really liked what I was hearing.

'The manager said he knew what my qualities were and that he was keen to get me back to the level I was at before my injury.'

City's seven new recruits were also joined by an eighth new face as Kenny McLean linked up with his new team-mates. The Scottish international midfielder had signed for City from Aberdeen in January 2019, but the deal saw him initially loaned back to the Dons for the remainder of the 2018/19 campaign.

Krul made his first appearance in a Norwich shirt in a 3-1 pre-season friendly win over League One Luton Town at Kenilworth Road. Despite the challenge of Michael McGovern and Remi Matthews for the goalkeeper's role, it was unsurprisingly Krul who was handed the number-one shirt and a place in the starting line-up for City's first game of the new 2018/19 Championship season away to Birmingham City.

Flying winger Onel Hernandez was the Canaries' opening-day hero, netting a brace as City twice came from behind to secure a useful point. Little did anyone know at the time, but Hernandez's injury-time equaliser would set the tone for a season of dramatic Norwich City late shows.

For the record, of those who had started Farke's first game as City boss at Fulham 12 months previously, only left-back James Husband was named in the City side to face Blues a season later.

An entertaining, if ultimately unrewarding first home fixture saw West Bromwich Albion edge a crazy seven-goal game 4-3. The match saw Pukki and Rhodes each mark their Carrow Road debuts with a goal – the latter also missing a crucial penalty with the match delicately poised at 1-1.

A League Cup victory over Stevenage was marred by an injury to McLean and was followed by a last-gasp 2-1 defeat at Sheffield

United. Having taken just one point from the first nine available, City registered their first league win of the season when goals from Pukki and Alex Tettey gave Farke's men a 2-0 victory at home to Preston North End.

After being brushed aside 3-0 by a highly impressive Leeds United at Carrow Road, City found themselves with one win, one draw and three defeats on the board prior to the first East Anglian derby of the season.

A much-changed Norwich team won a League Cup tie 3-1 away to Cardiff City ahead of derby day, but that did little to ease the growing pressure that Farke was beginning to find himself under. Norwich's league results were a concern, and among sections of the fan-base questions were beginning to be asked as to whether City had the right man at the helm. If the German ever needed a win, it was now. With a two-week international break to follow the Portman Road clash, a defeat might well have made his position precarious.

Farke made a brave call to hand teenage right-back Max Aarons a league debut, but when Gwion Edwards gave Town a 57th-minute lead it appeared Ipswich's nine-year wait for a derby win could be coming to an end. With temperatures beginning to rise among the travelling fans, Farke was saved by fellow countryman Leitner, who levelled with a sweetly struck shot from just outside the area 19 minutes from time.

With the match ending 1-1, most of the 25,690 crowd, regardless of allegiance, departed Portman Road with the view that both East Anglian clubs could well be in for a long season.

Following the international break, next on the agenda was a Carrow Road date with Middlesbrough on Saturday, 15 September. Quite what happened on the training pitches at Colney over that 13-day spell between the draw at Ipswich and this visit from high-flying Boro, only those involved will know – but suddenly something clicked, and, more importantly, it clicked in the cut and thrust of a Championship fixture.

Against an unbeaten Boro side, who had not even conceded a goal since the opening day of the season, Norwich turned on the style as Pukki netted the game's only goal just prior to the hour mark. This proved to be City's fourth straight win over Boro and all without conceding a goal. More important, though, was the manner and style of the victory. The passing was purposeful and the defending resolute – despite City being without injured captain Grant Hanley.

The morale-boosting victory over Tony Pulis's Boro triggered an instant upsurge in form as City won back-to-back away games at Reading and Queens Park Rangers, before a Mario Vrancic penalty sealed a 1-0 home win over Wigan Athletic. So after September had begun with a 1-1 derby-day draw at Ipswich, and concerns growing among fans about Farke's credentials to manage the team, the month remarkably ended with four straight Championship wins plus a League Cup victory at Wycombe Wanderers.

Norwich now appeared full of confidence and a team blessed with a serious goal threat – demonstrated by Pukki having notched three goals in the last four league games. October commenced with a 1-1 draw at Derby County, and City's next fixture certainly proved to be a key landmark in the season. Norwich arguably played as well as at any stage of Farke's reign when they faced Stoke City at Carrow Road on Saturday, 6 October. Frustratingly, though, it proved to be an afternoon when they just could not convert their impressive approach play into the goals their performance warranted. However, at full-time the Carrow Road faithful gave the team a huge ovation in recognition of their efforts. The reaction of the crowd that day, despite the disappointment of a 1-0 home defeat, seemed to trigger a bond of trust between fans and players – the effort and endeavour of the team was there for all to see, and the crowd gave their seal of approval.

Seven days later City came from behind to win 2-1 at Nottingham Forest. With Pukki out injured, defender Klose stepped up to the mark as a surprise two-goal hero. Victory at the City Ground on 20 October began a three-game week for the Canaries, with home matches against Aston Villa and Brentford to follow.

Once again City came from behind, this time thanks to a clinically executed second-half brace from Rhodes as they defeated Aston Villa 2-1 in front of the live Sky television cameras.

City completed an excellent week's work with a 1-0 victory over Brentford, as they made it seven wins from nine Championship fixtures to continue their charge up the table. Buendia netted his first goal in English football and Norwich had a great chance to double their lead on the stroke of half-time, but for the second time this season Rhodes fluffed his lines from the penalty spot.

The spot-kick miss mattered little as City held on for three points, but their margin of victory could well have been greater as goalkeeper Krul acknowledged:

'It was another great three points,' said the City keeper. 'We made things a bit too difficult for ourselves. I think we could have killed off the game much earlier. We should have been 2- or 3-0 up and that would have helped us relax at the back a bit more as a team.'

Victory over the Bees resulted in a perfect nine-point week for the Canaries and Krul felt Norwich were now at a stage of the season when things were really starting to move in the right direction.

'We are building something special here. We've got a lovely set-up and we've got some real talent,' he explained. 'People are believing in the manager's philosophy, everybody is fully giving everything and everyone is committed. It's a real team effort.'

Although City bowed out of the League Cup at Bournemouth, they swiftly returned to winning ways and built further league momentum with an emphatic 4-0 victory over Sheffield Wednesday on Saturday, 3 November. Pukki marked his return to the side with a double strike in a fixture that also saw the in-form Buendia score again, while substitute Dennis Srbeny netted his first league goal of the season. With a performance about as far removed as possible from the end-of-season no-show that City produced at Hillsborough just five months earlier, this win briefly elevated Norwich to top spot in the Championship table.

If entertainment, goals and excitement had been in short supply in Farke's first season at the helm, the head coach was certainly making up for lost time now. A week on from hitting four at Hillsborough, the Canaries did it again at home to Millwall in a truly exhilarating match that will never be forgotten by those inside Carrow Road.

Trailing 1-0 at the break, City levelled through Pukki after 49 minutes. The Finn then failed to fire City in front from the penalty spot, as Ben Amos repelled his effort, before Leitner fired Norwich in front with 11 minutes remaining. The lead proved a brief one though, as the Lions grabbed an unlikely equaliser just two minutes after Leitner's strike. The visitors then stunned Carrow Road when Jed Wallace put them 3-2 ahead after 83 minutes.

Behind for the second time in the game, and having missed yet another penalty, many teams might have filed this one in the 'not our day' drawer. Not Norwich City though; Farke's men piled forward and grabbed a remarkable equaliser two minutes into injury-time from substitute Rhodes, who had had only been on the pitch for four minutes.

Remarkably, the drama did not stop there, and Carrow Road erupted when Pukki netted his second and City's fourth in the seventh minute of additional time. In front of an ecstatic Barclay, Pukki was mobbed by team-mates as City celebrated the most extraordinary of victories.

Such was the never-say-die attitude of Farke's players, who just kept going and going, that their relentless approach against the Lions saw comparisons drawn with City's 2010/11 promotion winners, who also made netting late goals part of their trademark. As the Canary faithful filtered away from Carrow Road, still trying to comprehend what they had just witnessed, it was at this juncture that a few began to wonder ... maybe, just maybe, this could be City's season.

Norwich hit four goals for a third consecutive game as they returned from the long haul to Swansea with another three points following an impressive 4-1 victory. The flow of goals then came to a brief end as November concluded with a 0-0 draw away to Hull City.

Having the belief to come from behind, plus the desire and fitness to grab late goals, were qualities that City demonstrated perfectly to record December wins at home to Rotherham United and Bolton Wanderers. An excellent four points from trips to Bristol City and Blackburn Rovers then teed City up for the hectic festive period, with Farke's men sitting second in the table ahead of their Boxing Day clash with Nottingham Forest.

If Canary fans thought the late finishes against Millwall and Bolton had been dramatic then Boxing Day 2018 took things to a new level. Trailing 3-0 with 13 minutes to play, City reduced the arrears through Vrancic, but as the clock ticked down, and the match went into additional time, it looked like the Bosnian's goal was little more than a consolation strike. However, with the match in its 94th minute, substitute Hernandez netted a second Norwich goal. Then, with almost the last kick of the match, Carrow Road almost exploded as Hernandez rifled home a mind-blowing 98th-minute equaliser.

Just three days after the stunning comeback against Forest, the Carrow Road faithful were treated to another goal-fest when Derby County provided the opposition for the Canaries' final game of 2018. Swift out of the blocks, City engineered a two-goal lead only to be pegged back to 2-2 before the break. When Pukki netted his second goal of the game nine minutes from time to restore Norwich's lead, Farke's side looked set for three points.

Amidst the celebrations that marked Pukki's goal, one of the floodlights at the River End failed and the referee took both sides off until the issue was rectified.

The teams re-emerged from the tunnel after a 20-minute delay, and the break had certainly had a derogatory effect on the Canaries. Not only did they let their lead slip, they even managed to end the game empty handed after Jack Marriott netted a 92nd-minute winner to give the Rams an incredible 4-3 victory.

The calendar year of 2019 began with 1-1 draws at Brentford and West Bromwich Albion, with an FA Cup defeat at the hands of League One Portsmouth sandwiched in between.

Norwich therefore went into their televised Friday-night match with Birmingham City on 18 January on the back of five games without a win. With a trio of crucial fixtures coming up against promotion rivals Sheffield United and Leeds United, plus the second East Anglian derby of the season, it was vital City returned to winning ways.

With the Birmingham clash offering not only three points, but also the chance to put the pressure on the other promotion hopefuls, who were playing the next day, City grabbed their opportunity with both hands as goals from Pukki, Vrancic and Tom Trybull secured a morale-boosting 3-1 victory.

That win over Birmingham teed things up perfectly for the next three pivotal fixtures. Despite leading twice, City could not beat Sheffield United at Carrow Road on 26 January, as an entertaining clash between two well-matched sides deservedly ended 2-2.

Next up was the eagerly anticipated trip to Leeds United on Saturday, 2 February, and the meeting of the division's top two was unsurprisingly selected for live television and a 5.30pm kick-off. Norwich picked the perfect opportunity to produce their performance of the season, recording a 3-1 win and overtaking Leeds at the summit of the Championship table.

Demoralised by the defeat, Leeds's frustrations boiled over at full-time when former Canary loanee Patrick Bamford became embroiled in a spat with City's Ben Godfrey. Not for the first time, Krul's experience came to the fore as the keeper removed his team-mate from the altercation, before providing the Leeds striker with a few words of advice.

'He was giving Ben Godfrey all sorts, grabbing him. So I said "Come on" and I pushed him away, told him the game was over. I said, "Come on, I'm old and wise enough for that."'

Having recorded a monumental win at Elland Road, City were in pole position with 16 games to go, but the magnitude of fixtures continued to grow as Norwich prepared for the visit of local rivals Ipswich Town.

Despite Town propping up the Championship table, and very much the division's whipping boys, Norwich fans remained mindful that form can often go out the window come derby day. The fact that Ipswich were heading up the A140 with former Canary boss Paul Lambert at the helm also added additional spice to the occasion. For City keeper Krul, the pre-match wish was for him and his team-mates to just carry on producing the outstanding levels of performance that had served them so well thus far. The exceptional Elland Road performance had set the standard they aimed to emulate.

'We've been on top form for the last 20 games – even more,' said Krul, ahead of derby day. 'I really, really feel like that. You don't always win but if you keep plugging away like we have been, then I think the results will keep coming, for sure.

'It's a massive game. We had a great draw away to them at the start of the season, and if we put a performance on like the one at Leeds then we will be really confident. But derby days are different again. We will be in a similar atmosphere to Leeds and the Norwich fans will be up at a height after our win. So we will have to give Ipswich what we gave Leeds, for sure.'

An early Hernandez goal settled the nerves before a second-half brace from Pukki wrapped up a straightforward 3-0 win against relegation-bound Town. On an afternoon when City didn't really need to get out of second gear to confirm a decade of dominance over their rivals, the match will be fondly remembered by City fans for Town boss Lambert's red card. Following an awful tackle by Jon Nolan on Aarons, just before half-time, Lambert became embroiled in an altercation with City goalkeeper coach Ed Wootten, and the one-time Carrow Road hero was subsequently banished to the stands.

After the euphoria of victories against Leeds and Ipswich, City's midweek match away to Preston just proved to be a bridge too far as they went down 3-1 at Deepdale. The defeat at Preston saw the Canaries surrender top spot and keeper Krul was keen for a reaction when City faced lowly Bolton three days later, in the second part of a north-west double header.

'We have been under pressure all season about having to win certain games and we have produced – so Saturday we need to put ourselves under a bit of pressure and say, "Yes, that's a game we need to win now,"' said Krul prior to City's match at the University of Bolton Stadium.

'It's 32 games in and we are up there. To be fair, we went to Leeds and everybody thought the pressure was on – and the boys stepped up to it. Same with the derby, the boys stepped up to it.

'The last few weeks it has felt different because of the hype. We need to take it game by game but it's easier said than done because you're so excited about what could be. We all know what we are playing for and if there is ever a chance to do it, it is this season.

'It's no coincidence that we are up there after 32 games and we just have to stand up and be counted. If you really want to go to the Premier League, these are the months you have to show it.'

City certainly responded to Krul's pre-match rallying cry, and demonstrated that the defeat at Deepdale was nothing more than a minor blip, as they dominated throughout to win 4-0 at Bolton. Their victory over Wanderers triggered the start of an eight-match winning run that would take the Canaries to the brink of promotion.

Among that series of fixtures was a Buendia-inspired 1-0 victory over Swansea City on Friday, 8 March as the three-way battle for automatic promotion between City, Leeds and Sheffield United gained further momentum.

'It would be a big shame if we can't now finish in the top two because we've proven on a lot of occasions that we are one of the best teams in the league, if not the best,' said Krul following victory over the Swans.

'We've shown some amazing football this season, we've dug it out and come back so many times from being behind. I just hope we can keep going.'

The winning run came to an end when the Canaries were held 2-2 at home by Reading on Wednesday, 10 April. Against the Royals, City certainly missed the suspended Buendia following his red card in the 4-0 win over Queens Park Rangers. They would also have to manage without their little magician in the next two games at Wigan and at home to Sheffield Wednesday.

With the finishing line in sight, City's winning run was followed by a series of draws as the long trip to Wigan ended 1-1, before an outstanding last-gasp free-kick from Vrancic salvaged a point from the Good Friday meeting with the Owls.

Buendia returned for the Easter Monday match at Stoke City, which finished 2-2, and later that day Leeds suffered a 2-0 defeat at Brentford – leaving City six points ahead with two games remaining. Against all the early-season odds, Norwich were now on the verge of promotion back to the Premier League – just a point from their final home game against Blackburn Rovers would see them promoted.

An expectant Carrow Road crowd gave their heroes a tremendous welcome ahead of a Saturday evening match with Rovers as Norwich looked to seize the opportunity to win promotion at Carrow Road for the first time since 1960.

First-half goals from Marco Stiepermann and an absolute rocket from the in-form Vrancic set City on their way to a memorable 2-1 triumph, and a place back among English football's elite.

Amid the promotion celebrations, goalkeeper Krul reflected on a remarkable personal journey back to the Premier League, admitting City's promotion success had made for the most memorable season of his career so far:

'The most exciting one has been this one, for sure,' said Krul, when asked where the achievement ranked in his career. 'I finished fifth with Newcastle and that was an incredible journey, three points off the Champions League, and I had some great moments with Holland. But this, to play every moment of this journey, I can't describe how I feel.

'We were hoping for a top-ten finish, so to be in the top two from November has been some journey. We've had some amazing nights at this stadium, some crazy nights, some massive ups and downs; it's amazing – what a journey.'

The City stopper was also keen to pay tribute to Farke, who he felt had prepared the side perfectly game-in, game-out across a gruelling campaign.

'The preparation, he's so professional,' said Krul. 'If you knew the amount of hours we've put in on the training pitch, it's the most I've trained in my career. We've had some sessions where we've trained for two and a half or three hours – and then another session in the gym in the afternoon.

'He's worked us hard and look at the amount of times we've turned games around in the last ten minutes – that's not a coincidence, the boys are fit.

'It's the German mentality; they work hard and he's a true believer that if you work hard then the results will come.'

With promotion assured, City soon switched their attentions to securing the Championship title. They went into the final game of the season away to Aston Villa with a three-point lead over second-place Sheffield United – the Blades also having achieved automatic promotion.

In identical fashion to the Blackburn match eight days earlier, City knew a point was all they needed. Once again Farke's men over-delivered and signed off with a 2-1 win against a Villa side that would feature in the end-of-season play-offs.

An amazing campaign, that witnessed City producing some exceptional football, ended with City lifting the Championship trophy at Villa Park, and 29-goal striker Pukki being presented with the golden boot as the division's top scorer.

The Championship trophy was certainly the icing on the cake, and a fitting reward for a wonderful achievement. Bizarrely, City's season began and ended just three-and-a-half miles apart, kicking off at St Andrew's and ending at Villa Park – but what a journey in between. The one player who was there every single step of the way was ever-present goalkeeper Krul.

'To play every second, to lift the trophy, to have the promotion at home, there are so many meant-to-be moments – my parents in the crowd [at Villa Park]; I think it's the best season for me,' said the popular Dutchman.

'I know we were playing it down when we went up, but it meant so much to us to finish off this season top. We've been so good all season. So many challenges have been thrown at us, I think we deserve it.'

A to Z Player Profiles

THE PLAYERS

AARONS, Max
Date of birth: 4 January 2000
Place of birth: Hammersmith
Position: Defender
Promotion campaign: 2018/19 Championship champions
2018/19 League statistics: 41(-)2

The introduction of Max Aarons for a league debut in the white-hot atmosphere of an East Anglian derby demonstrated the belief that head coach Daniel Farke had in this teenage full-back. Aarons's arrival on the first-team scene coincided with the team's instant upturn in fortunes and surge up the league table.

The London-born defender formed an excellent full-back partnership with Jamal Lewis and the pair's desire to get forward and support the attack formed a vital component of Norwich's play. Rarely beaten in one-on-one situations, Aarons emerged as a brave, committed defender who timed his tackles to perfection. His level of consistency throughout the season, for a player of such limited experience, was arguably his greatest asset.

Not only was Aarons instrumental in keeping the opposition at bay and helping to support forward moves – he also chipped in with goals himself. The young right-back netted in the home win over Rotherham United on 1 December 2018 and then headed a second-half equaliser away to Bristol City a fortnight later. A memorable breakthrough season was capped when Aarons was named the EFL's young player of the season at the Football League awards.

ABBEY, Zema
Date of birth: 17 April 1977
Place of birth: Luton
Position: Striker

Promotion campaign: 2003/04 First Division champions
2003/04 League statistics: 1(2)-

Signed from Cambridge United in December 2000, Zema Abbey played a small part in the Canaries' 2003/04 First Division success. However, it was his early-season injury, sustained in the Canaries' 1-0 defeat at Sheffield United on 23 August 2003, that really proved to be a major turning point in the season.

With the severity of Abbey's injury confirmed, coupled with David Nielsen's desire to leave the club, City boss Nigel Worthington was left with only Iwan Roberts and youngsters Ian Henderson and Ryan Jarvis at his disposal in the striking department. That was until Norwich secured the ambitious triple loan signings of Kevin Harper, Peter Crouch and Darren Huckerby.

Although Abbey featured in just three league fixtures, the club ensured their injured striker received a Championship winners' medal and took part in the end-of-season celebrations. The club followed up Abbey's winners' medal gesture with the offer of a three-month contract in the summer of 2004 to prove his fitness. However, he was eventually released in September 2004 after a loan spell at Boston United.

ADEYEMI, Tom
Date of birth: 24 October 1991
Place of birth: Milton Keynes
Position: Midfielder
Promotion campaign: 2009/10 League One champions
2009/10 League statistics: 2(9)-

A product of the club's academy, Tom Adeyemi made his senior debut in difficult circumstances after entering the fray as a substitute in City's opening-day 7-1 mauling at home to Colchester United on Saturday, 8 August 2009.

However, Adeyemi went on to enjoy an impressive debut campaign under Paul Lambert and featured in 11 league fixtures. His two league starts came in the 1-1 draw at Exeter City, in the immediate aftermath of Bryan Gunn's departure, and the impressive pre-Christmas 3-0 victory over Huddersfield Town at Carrow Road.

A memorable breakthrough season for the popular youngster was capped when he was voted Apprentice of the Year at the Football League awards in March 2010.

ALLCOCK, Terry

Date of birth: 10 December 1935
Place of birth: Leeds
Position: Striker
Promotion campaign: 1959/60 Division
   Three runners-up
1959/60 League statistics: 44(n/a)16

The name of legendary City striker Terry Allcock sits proudly second in the club's list of all-time goalscorers with 127 goals scored in a Canary career that spanned from 1958 to 1969.

A hero of the memorable 1958/59 FA Cup run side, Allcock played a major role in the team's promotion from Division Three the following season. Featuring in all bar two of City's league fixtures, Allcock ended the 1959/60 campaign as joint top scorer alongside Jimmy Hill, with both players netting 16 goals.

Allcock's importance to the side could never be underestimated and it will be of little surprise to learn that City failed to win either of the two games he missed en route to promotion.

ALNWICK, Ben

Date of birth: 1 January 1987
Place of birth: Northumberland
Position: Goalkeeper
Promotion campaign: 2009/10 League One champions
2009/10 League statistics: 3(-)-

Goalkeeper Ben Alnwick joined the Canaries on loan from Tottenham Hotspur at the start of the 2009/10 season as cover for new City number one Michael Theoklitos.

Alnwick's debut came in the League Cup at Yeovil after Theoklitos's nightmare performance against Colchester United in the 7-1 opening-day defeat. His league bow arrived four days later in a 1-1 draw away to Exeter City. Ironically, he played under three different managers during his first four games for City – Bryan Gunn at Yeovil, Ian Butterworth at Exeter City and Brentford, then Paul Lambert against Wycombe Wanderers.

An injury sustained against former club Sunderland in the League Cup cut short his loan spell, with the keeper returning to White Hart Lane in September 2009 for treatment, and the Canaries completing the loan signing of Fraser Forster from Newcastle United.

ANDERSON, Terry

Date of birth: 11 March 1944
Place of birth: Woking
Date of death: January 1980 (between 24 and 31 January)
Place of death: Great Yarmouth
Position: Midfielder
Promotion campaign: 1971/72 Division Two champions
1971/72 League statistics: 32(2)-

A talented right-winger, Terry Anderson's skills graced Carrow Road for an eight-year period and were rewarded with a Second Division championship medal in 1971/72 as the Canaries reached the top flight for the first time.

An instrumental figure in Ron Saunders's super-fit promotion-winning side, Anderson featured in 34 of City's 42 league games en route to the First Division and laid on chances for strikers David Cross and Peter Silvester on a regular basis.

He missed the promotion clincher at Orient, but he returned to the side in the final game to help seal the title at Watford when he appeared as a substitute, replacing Alan Black at Vicarage Road.

ANDREU, Tony

Date of birth: 22 May 1988
Place of birth: Cagnes-sur-Mer, France
Position: Midfielder
Promotion campaign: 2014/15 Championship play-off winners
2014/15 League statistics: -(6)-

Goalscoring midfielder Tony Andreu followed his former Hamilton Academical boss Alex Neil from New Douglas Park to Carrow Road in February 2015.

Despite playing a starring role for Neil's over-achieving Accies, Andreu struggled to make a major impact south of the border and had to settle for just six brief substitute appearances as the

Canaries won promotion via the play-offs. His City debut came at Carrow Road on Saturday, 7 February 2015, when he replaced Wes Hoolahan during the second half of a comprehensive 4-0 victory over Blackpool. On the six occasions that Andreu featured, City gained impressive results, registering four wins, one draw and just one defeat. The Frenchman subsequently enjoyed successful loan spells with Rotherham United and Dundee United before joining Coventry City.

ASHMAN, Ron
Date of birth: 19 May 1926
Place of birth: Whittlesey
Date of death: 21 June 2004
Place of death: Scunthorpe
Position: Defender
Promotion campaign: 1959/60 Division Three runners-up
1959/60 League statistics: 46(n/a)2

The Canaries' record league appearance maker, Ron Ashman turned out in a colossal 592 league fixtures for the club – a record that is unlikely to ever be surpassed.

Ashman was captain of the 1959/60 promotion-winning team that ended the campaign as runners-up to Southampton under the management of Archie Macaulay.

Ever-present in all 46 league games alongside fellow team-mates Barry Butler, Roy McCrohan and Bryan Thurlow from the 1958/59 FA Cup adventure, Ashman also chipped in with two goals as City secured 1-1 draws at Bradford City and Newport County.

BARHAM, Mark
Date of birth: 12 July 1962
Place of birth: Folkestone
Position: Midfielder
Promotion campaigns: 1981/82 third in Division Two and 1985/86
    Division Two champions
1981/82 League statistics: 25(2)4
1985/86 League statistics: 35(-)9

Former England midfielder Mark Barham enjoyed two separate promotions with the Canaries as City twice won promotion under the astute management of Ken Brown in 1981/82 and again in 1985/86.

Always associated with the club's 1985 League Cup triumph at Wembley, Barham was also a key player in the 1981/82 promotion-winning campaign that saw Brown's side remarkably win ten of their final dozen games to seal the third and final promotion place.

Barham featured in 27 league games, scoring four goals, in the 1981/82 success, and was an even more influential figure in 1985/86, chipping in with nine goals as the Canaries returned to the top flight at the first time of asking as Second Division champions.

BARNETT, Leon

Date of birth: 30 November 1985
Place of birth: Stevenage
Position: Defender
Promotion campaign: 2010/11 Championship runners-up
2010/11 League statistics: 25(-)1

Signed initially on loan from West Bromwich Albion in August 2010, central-defender Leon Barnett made his Norwich City debut in a 1-1 draw away to Nottingham Forest on 28 August 2010.

Drafted into the City squad to cover for injuries to Zak Whitbread and Michael Nelson, Barnett gave an assured display alongside Elliott Ward at the City Ground. His impressive performances won him instant respect from the crowd and he soon became a regular face in Paul Lambert's side. Barnett headed home his first goal for the club to secure a 1-1 draw at home to Leeds United in November 2010.

In December 2010 the club announced that an agreement had been reached to make his move from the Hawthorns to Norfolk a permanent one with effect from 1 January 2011. After suffering a hamstring injury in the 2-1 victory at home to Reading on 12 February, Barnett was ruled out for the remainder of the season, with Whitbread returning to the side for the promotion run-in.

BASSONG, Sebastien
Date of birth: 9 July 1986
Place of birth: Paris
Position: Defender
Promotion campaign: 2014/15 Championship play-off winners
2014/15 League statistics: 18(-)- + play-offs 3(-)-

Cameroonian international defender Sebastien Bassong will surely cite 2014/15 as one of the most successful campaigns in his career – after all he helped get two clubs promoted in one season!

Deemed surplus to requirements by then City boss Neil Adams, Bassong was loaned to Championship rivals Watford in the first half of the season. He made 11 league appearances for the Hornets. However, come January 2015, new City boss Alex Neil recalled Bassong to the fold and he returned to the City side for a goalless draw away to Birmingham City on 31 January 2015.

His performance at St Andrew's, alongside Russell Martin at the heart of the defence, certainly made an impression on Neil, and Bassong missed just one match over the remainder of the campaign.

He was a star performer in the play-off final at Wembley as City secured their place in the Premier League together with Bassong's other 2014/15 club, Watford, who had landed the Championship runners-up spot in April 2015.

BELL, Bobby
Date of birth: 26 October 1950
Place of birth: Cambridge
Position: Defender
Promotion campaign: 1971/72 Division Two champions
1971/72 League statistics: 3(-)-

Famed for being the answer to the quiz question 'Who was Norwich City's first loan player?', Bobby Bell made three appearances in the 1971/72 season while on loan from Crystal Palace.

His Canary debut came in the hugely entertaining 2-2 draw with promotion rivals Millwall at Carrow Road on 12 February 1972. Match number two for Bell saw him and his new colleagues keep a clean sheet in a goalless draw at home to struggling Cardiff City in a game the home side really should have won. Bell's final outing for the Canaries ended disappointingly as City's 23-week stay at the top of the Second Division table came to a temporary end as they crashed to a 4-0 defeat against Birmingham City in front of over 40,000 at St Andrew's.

BENNETT, Dave

Date of birth: 26 April 1960
Place of birth: Oldham
Position: Midfielder
Promotion campaign: 1981/82 third in Division Two
1981/82 League statistics: 21(1)3

Signed by John Bond in 1978 but a star performer for Ken Brown, skilful winger Dave Bennett played a key role in City's 1981/82 promotion as the Canaries bounced back to the top flight at the first time of asking.

Used only sporadically until the 1981/82 promotion campaign, Bennett won himself a place in Brown's starting line-up for the opening-day fixture away to Rotherham United and went on to enjoy a further 20 starts and one appearance from the bench.

Injuries interrupted his season, but he contributed countless opportunities for others and weighed in with three league goals including late strikes to seal victories away to Derby County and at home to Orient as City closed in on promotion.

BENNETT, Elliott

Date of birth: 18 December 1988
Place of birth: Telford
Position: Midfielder
Promotion campaign: 2014/15 Championship play-off winners
2014/15 League statistics: 3(6)- + play-offs –(1)-

Popular right-sided midfielder Elliott Bennett suffered a knee ligament injury on the opening day of the 2013/14 season and only returned to action with a late substitute appearance in the final game of the season. After missing an entire season, Bennett worked overtime during the summer break to gain full fitness ahead of the new 2014/15 season under Neil Adams and took his place in the City side for the opening-day defeat away to his first club, Wolverhampton Wanderers. That proved to be both Bennett's first and last league start under Adams.

As the season progressed, Bennett's flexibility often saw him named among the City substitutes and he started two further Championship fixtures under Alex Neil in the second half of the season as the Canaries drew at Birmingham City in January 2015 and defeated Fulham on the final day of the regulation season. He tasted action as a late substitute in the closing stages of the play-off semi-final victory over Ipswich Town and took his place among the substitutes for the Wembley final.

BENNETT, Ryan

Date of birth: 6 March 1990
Place of birth: Grays
Position: Defender
Promotion campaign: 2014/15 Championship play-off winners
2014/15 League statistics: 3(4)-

Central-defender Ryan Bennett suffered an injury in the 1-0 East Anglian derby victory over Ipswich Town at Portman Road in August 2014 and was subsequently sidelined for the majority of the first half of the 2014/15 campaign.

He returned to the starting line-up for the 2-1 defeat at Reading on 28 December 2014 and also played in the FA Cup third-round exit at League One Preston North End, in what proved to be Neil Adams' final game in charge of the Canaries.

Due to the form of captain Russell Martin, and a return to favour for Seb Bassong following the appointment of Alex Neil as manager, Bennett found himself among the substitutes more often than not as Norwich navigated their way back to the Premier League via the end-of-season play-offs.

BENSON, John

Date of birth: 23 December 1942
Place of birth: Arbroath
Date of death: 30 October 2010
Place of death: Macclesfield
Position: Defender
Promotion campaign: 1974/75 third in Division Two
1974/75 League statistics: 9(1)-

One of the many who followed manager John Bond from AFC Bournemouth to Carrow Road in the 1970s, defender John Benson made ten appearances in the Canaries' 1974/75 promotion-winning campaign. The majority of his outings came at right-back when covering for Mel Machin. However, his ability to slot into a number of defensive positions with little fuss also saw him play in central defence when he replaced skipper Duncan Forbes for the 2-0 win over Millwall at Carrow Road on 5 October 1974.

Under the guidance of Bond, Benson began his coaching career at Norwich when he took charge of the youth team in 1979. He returned to Carrow Road for a third spell when he briefly assisted then-boss John Deehan in April 1994.

BERTHEL ASKOU, Jens

Date of birth: 19 August 1982
Place of birth: Videbaek, Denmark
Position: Defender
Promotion campaigns: 2009/10 League One champions and 2010/11 Championship runners-up
2009/10 League statistics: 21(1)2
2010/11 League statistics: 2(3)-

A Danish central-defender, Jens Berthel Askou initially joined the Canaries on a trial basis during the club's pre-season tour of Scotland in the summer of 2009. After impressing manager Bryan Gunn the Dane then agreed a two-year deal at Carrow Road.

He marked his league debut with a goal as the managerless Canaries took a point from their long trip to Exeter City and he was on target again in Paul Lambert's first game in charge as City defeated Wycombe Wanderers 5-2. After forming a useful partnership with Gary Doherty at the heart of the City defence during the first half of the 2009/10 season, he suffered an injury in December 2009 during the 3-3 draw at Yeovil and lost his place in the team to Michael Nelson.

Berthel Askou made five league appearances at Championship level in 2010/11 but was clearly not in manager Lambert's long-term thinking once the Canaries had returned to the second tier.

BERTSCHIN, Keith

Date of birth: 25 August 1956
Place of birth: Enfield
Position: Striker
Promotion campaign: 1981/82 third in Division Two
1981/82 League statistics: 35(1)12

Striker Keith Bertschin was the Canaries' leading league goalscorer in 1981/82 and his dozen goals clearly played a significant part in the team's instant return to the First Division.

Bertschin netted the only goal of the game to secure a narrow win over Barnsley at Oakwell in February 1982, and he really came to the fore in the final weeks of the season as he scored in all of City's last five league fixtures.

On the final day of the season it looked as though his 86th-minute equaliser had given City the point they needed to secure promotion away to Sheffield Wednesday. However, the home side instantly regained the lead but it mattered not as Leicester City's draw with Shrewsbury Town meant City were going up regardless.

BIGGINS, Wayne
Date of birth: 20 November 1961
Place of birth: Sheffield
Position: Striker
Promotion campaign: 1985/86 Division Two champions
1985/86 League statistics: 28(-)7

Wayne Biggins enjoyed a fairytale first season at Carrow Road following his transfer from Fourth Division Burnley in the summer of 1985.

Biggins established an impressive strike partnership with Kevin Drinkell as the Canaries took the Second Division by storm in 1985/86. He marked only his second league appearance with a goal as City drew 1-1 away to Brighton & Hove Albion in November, and from that moment on he was ace marksman Drinkell's chosen strike partner.

In total Biggins netted seven league goals, including a brace in the 4-1 demolition of Huddersfield Town in March, and ended his debut season at Norwich with a Second Division title winners' medal and the opportunity to play in the First Division the following season.

BLACK, Alan
Date of birth: 4 June 1943
Place of birth: Alexandria, Scotland
Position: Defender
Promotion campaign: 1971/72 Division Two champions
1971/72 League statistics: 19(1)-

Long-serving Canary left-back Alan Black joined Norwich City from Sunderland in 1966 and was the first signing made by then Norwich manager Lol Morgan.

The Scot soon made the Canary left-back berth his own but shared duties with Geoff Butler during the historic 1971/72 campaign. The second half of the season saw Black make 20 appearances in total, which included outings in the memorable end-of-season fixtures at Orient and Watford, where firstly promotion and secondly the title were secured.

A strong, committed and reliable performer, Black was a popular and well-respected character during his Carrow Road career. His involvement in the team that brought First Division football to Norwich for the first time won him a place in the club's Hall of Fame.

BLY, Terry
Date of birth: 22 October 1935
Place of birth: Fincham, Norfolk
Date of death: 24 September 2009
Place of death: Grantham
Position: Striker
Promotion campaign: 1959/60 Division Three runners-up
1959/60 League statistics: 25(n/a)7

The goalscoring hero of the club's historic 1958/59 FA Cup run, Norfolk-born Terry Bly played a key role for City again the following season as Archie Macaulay's side secured promotion to the Second Division.

Bly certainly picked up from where he left off as the 1959/60 campaign got under way, the striker was on target along with Jimmy Hill as City secured an opening-day 2-2 draw with Southampton at the Dell. He also helped City get the calendar year of 1960 off to a positive start when he scored twice in the first half to secure a 2-0 victory at Reading on 2 January 1960. His Elm Park brace proved to be his final goals for Norwich as, after five further Third Division appearances, he joined Peterborough United in June 1960 following the Canaries' promotion.

BONE, Jimmy
Date of birth: 22 September 1949
Place of birth: Bridge of Allan, Scotland
Position: Striker
Promotion campaign: 1971/72 Division Two champions
1971/72 League statistics: 13(-)4

Jimmy Bone may not have amassed hundreds of appearances for Norwich City but he certainly made his mark at Carrow Road in a short and successful Canary career.

He arrived from Partick Thistle in February 1972 for a fee of £30,000 with the brief of filling the goalscoring boots of injured City marksman Peter Silvester. Bone marked his home debut with a goal against Sunderland in a 1-1 draw on 11 March 1972. Along with David Cross, Bone was also on target in the 2-0 Easter Saturday victory at Charlton that inspired the superb Pink 'Un headline 'Hot Cross Bone Day' to accompany the match report.

Bone netted four goals in 13 outings as Ron Saunders's side won the Second Division title and brought First Division football to Norfolk for the first time. He then took the mantle of scoring the club's first goal in the top flight.

BOYER, Phil

Date of birth: 25 January 1949
Place of birth: Nottingham
Position: Striker
Promotion campaign: 1974/75
    third in Division Two
1974/75 League statistics:
    40(-)16

Recruited from AFC Bournemouth for a then club record fee of £145,000 in February 1974, Phil Boyer's goals were not enough to prevent the Canaries sliding to the drop in 1973/74.

The following campaign once again saw Boyer form a formidable striker partnership with Ted MacDougall as City won promotion from the Second Division at the first attempt. The Boyer/MacDougall partnership yielded 32 league goals as City ended the campaign in third place behind Manchester United and Aston Villa.

Boyer's 16 goals in 1974/75 included four braces, his double strikes coming against Orient and Oldham away and in the Carrow Road clashes with Bristol City and Nottingham Forest.

His impressive goalscoring form continued in the First Division the following season and he became the club's first full England international when he debuted against Wales on 24 March 1976.

BRENNAN, Bobby

Date of birth: 14 March 1925
Place of birth: Belfast
Date of death: 1 January 2002
Place of death: Norwich
Position: Midfielder
Promotion campaign: 1959/60 Division Three runners-up
1959/60 League statistics: 20(n/a)4

Another hero of the Canaries' 1958/59 FA Cup run, Bobby Brennan also made his mark on the club's promotion-winning campaign the following season.

Widely regarded as one of Norwich City's most skilful players of all time, Brennan was blessed with tremendous close control and the capability to almost glide past opponents. He also had the ability to chip in with goals and contributed four in the 1959/60 campaign, with his final goal for the club coming in the 3-0 Carrow Road victory over Halifax Town on 18 April 1960 in the penultimate home game of the season.

A goalless draw away to Queens Park Rangers signalled the end of his 250-game Canary career and how fitting that promotion was achieved in Brennan's final season at Carrow Road.

BRENNAN, Jim

Date of birth: 8 May 1977
Place of birth: Ontario, Canada
Position: Defender
Promotion campaign: 2003/04 First Division champions
2003/04 League statistics: 7(8)1

Signed from First Division rivals Nottingham Forest on a Bosman-style free transfer in the summer of 2003, Jim Brennan arrived at Carrow Road with the view of adding competition for places at left-back and on the left side of midfield.

A deep-seated abductor muscle injury delayed his debut until November 2003 and he was never able to really force himself into the first-team picture on a regular basis. He started seven league games as the Canaries won the First Division title under the management of Nigel Worthington in 2004.

The highlight of Brennan's time at Carrow Road was his cracking goal against Coventry City at Highfield Road in City's 2-0 triumph in February 2004 during the 2003/04 campaign.

BRIGGS, Keith

Date of birth: 11 December 1981
Place of birth: Glossop
Position: Defender
Promotion campaign: 2003/04 First Division champions
2003/04 League statistics: 1(2)-

A promising right-back, Keith Briggs joined Norwich City from Stockport County for a fee of £65,000 in January 2003 and debuted the following month in a 2-2 draw with Stoke City at Carrow Road on 1 February 2003. Despite his promise shown at Edgeley Park, he found first-team opportunities scarce at Carrow Road due to the form of first Steen Nedergaard and then Marc Edworthy in the 2003/04 promotion season.

Briggs won a place in the City line-up for the opening-day match away to Bradford City but was replaced at half-time by Edworthy. His other two league outings in 2003/04 were substitute appearances in the Carrow Road clashes with Millwall and Watford.

BRIGGS, Max

Date of birth: 9 September 1948
Place of birth: Bramerton, Norfolk
Position: Midfielder
Promotion campaign: 1971/72 Division Two champions
1971/72 League statistics: 21(6)-

Home-grown hero Max Briggs made 27 appearances in the Canaries' 1971/72 Second Division title-winning season before finally going on to play First Division football the following season, some four years after his Canary debut. Often the Canaries' twelfth man, Briggs had to wait until 20 November 1971 for his first league start of the promotion campaign, but his adaptability served him well as he made a further 20 starts under the watchful eye of Ron Saunders.

Norfolk-born Briggs took great delight in featuring in the run-in to promotion, and particularly the historic matches at Orient and Watford, as promotion and then the title were confirmed.

BROOKE, Garry

Date of birth: 24 November 1960
Place of birth: Bethnal Green
Position: Midfielder
Promotion campaign: 1985/86 Division Two champions
1985/86 League statistics: 8(5)2

Talented midfield playmaker Garry Brooke joined City in May 1985 and became the first of many players that Norwich boss Ken Brown lured from Tottenham Hotspur to Carrow Road in the 1980s.

Often substitute at Spurs, Brooke made the switch from White Hart Lane to Norfolk in pursuit of regular first-team football, and despite starting City's opening four Second Division games in 1985/86 he soon found himself twelfth man at Carrow Road.

Brooke made a goalscoring return to London when he netted in City's 4-2 defeat at Millwall in August and was also on target in the 4-0 rout away to Carlisle United on 12 October 1986. However, as the season progressed he found starts harder to come by due to the ultra-consistent form of midfield trio Dave Williams, Mike Phelan and Peter Mendham.

BRUCE, Steve

Date of birth: 31 December 1960
Place of birth: Corbridge
Position: Defender
Promotion campaign: 1985/86 Division
   Two champions
1985/86 League statistics: 42(-)8

Steve Bruce etched his name into Norwich City folklore when he headed home the Canaries' winning goal in the 1985 League Cup semi-final second-leg victory over arch rivals Ipswich Town.

Famed for that 87th-minute bullet header at the Barclay End, Bruce enjoyed an excellent debut season at Carrow Road despite City suffering relegation on the back of their League Cup Final triumph at Wembley.

A true crowd favourite throughout his stay in Norfolk, Bruce was ever-present alongside fellow central-defensive partner Dave Watson as City ran away with the Second Division title to secure an instant return to the top flight. The 1985/86 campaign saw the big defender as an asset in both penalty areas; not only did Bruce do his bit to keep the opposition at bay but he also scored eight league goals en route to the title.

BUENDIA, Emiliano
Date of birth: 25 December 1996
Place of birth: Mar del Plata, Argentina
Position: Midfielder
Promotion campaign: 2018/19 Championship champions
2018/19 League statistics: 35(3)8

An inspirational signing from Getafe ahead of City's 2018/19 promotion-winning campaign, Argentinian Emi Buendia enjoyed a memorable debut campaign with the Canaries – ending the season third in the player-of-the-season poll.

Buendia is an attacking midfielder, blessed with a wonderful eye for a forward pass, who also boasts exquisite close control. His ability to create in the final third was a key facet of City's attacking play, and as the season progressed he became widely recognised as the team's most creative spark. Not only was Buendia the man to make City tick as an attacking force, but his appetite to win the ball back when out of possession was equally as impressive.

His debut came in City's first league win of the season, when he entered the fray to replace Ben Marshall as Norwich overcame Preston North End 2-0. A full debut came in the East Anglian derby with Ipswich and his first goal arrived in the 1-0 win over Brentford at Carrow Road on 27 October 2018. A cracking strike to seal all three points at home to Swansea followed by a brace against Hull City saw Buendia as City's star performer in the month of March.

BUTLER, Barry
Date of birth: 30 July 1934
Place of birth: Stockton
Date of death: 9 April 1966
Place of death: Norwich
Position: Defender

Promotion campaign: 1959/60 Division Three runners-up
1959/60 League statistics: 46(n/a) 1

Barry Butler was the heartbeat of the Norwich City defence for a nine-season spell, playing a starring role in the historic 1958/59 cup run, promotion to the Second Division in 1959/60 and League Cup glory in 1961/62.

A true leader both on and off the pitch, Butler was highly respected by team-mates and opponents alike, with his professionalism and determination to recover from injures an example to all around him. He was ever-present in the 1959/60 promotion campaign and netted a rare goal in the 5-1 demolition of Mansfield Town at Carrow Road on 28 December 1959.

The popular defender was killed in a tragic road accident in 1966, aged just 31, and the club's player-of-the-season trophy is awarded in his memory.

BUTLER, Geoff

Date of birth: 29 September 1946
Place of birth: Middlesbrough
Position: Defender
Promotion campaigns: 1971/72 Division Two champions and
  1974/75 third in Division Two
1971/72 League statistics: 23(-)-
1974/75 League statistics: 17(1)-

A Second Division champion in 1971/72, a place in City's side for the 1973 League Cup Final at Wembley and a promotion winner again in 1974/75 completed a hat-trick of highlights in Geoff Butler's 196-game Norwich City career.

He shared left-back duties with Alan Black in the 1971/72 success, with that position perhaps being the only role in the side where a clear first choice didn't exist. Butler was ever-present from the opening-day draw away to Luton Town through until Christmas. However, the festive period saw the transfer-listed Black return to the side.

Butler featured in the 5-1 victory over Blackpool at Carrow Road in March 1972 and played 23 games in total as City sealed promotion to the top flight as Second Division champions. He made 18 league appearances in 1974/75, netting a vital equaliser away to Millwall in April 1975 as Norwich returned to the top flight after a single season absence.

CANTWELL, Todd

Date of birth: 27 February 1998
Place of birth: Norwich
Position: Midfielder
Promotion campaign: 2018/19 Championship champions
2018/19 League statistics: 18(6)1

A true product of the Norwich City Academy, Norfolk-born Todd Cantwell joined the Canaries' academy at the age of ten.

Cantwell is a midfield technician with an eye for a pass, an awareness of others and the ability to score goals. He emerged briefly on the first-team scene in 2017/18 when he made his debut in City's FA Cup third-round replay away to Chelsea. He ended the 2017/18 season with a beneficial loan spell in Holland with Fortuna Sittard.

After featuring in League Cup victories over Stevenage and Cardiff City, Cantwell's full league debut came in City's midweek 2-1 triumph away to Reading on 19 September 2018. Daniel Farke remained loyal to his young winning team and Cantwell became a regular starter over the following months. He netted his first goal for the club in the 3-1 Carrow Road victory over Rotherham United on 1 December 2018 and in doing so became the first English player to score a league goal for City in 2018/19.

CLAYTON, Paul

Date of birth: 4 January 1965
Place of birth: Dunstable
Position: Striker
Promotion campaign: 1985/86 Division Two champions
1985/86 League statistics: 1(-)-

A former Sprowston High School pupil, Paul Clayton was an FA Youth Cup winner with City in 1983, his eight goals during the run including two against Everton in the final.

The striker's senior debut arrived as substitute in a 0-0 draw at home to Coventry City in December 1983 and he proceeded to make a total of 15 senior appearances for the Canaries.

Clayton only just made the cut for this publication after appearing in the Canaries' final game of the 1985/86 campaign. Boss Ken Brown was keen to acknowledge the efforts of his squad over a long and gruelling campaign and Clayton played the full 90 minutes of City's final day 4-0 romp over Leeds United at Carrow Road. That match proved to be his final first-team outing in Canary colours with a loan spell in Sweden preceding a £25,000 switch to Darlington in March 1988.

COOPER, Kevin

Date of birth: 8 February 1975
Place of birth: Derby
Position: Midfielder
Promotion campaign: 2003/04 First Division champions
2003/04 League statistics: 6(4)-

Kevin Cooper joined the Canaries on a three-month loan deal from Wolverhampton Wanderers at the tail-end of the 2003/04 championship-winning season, as manager Nigel Worthington strengthened his squad ahead of the final promotion push.

A clever and experienced midfielder, Cooper had the ability to operate wide on either flank and proved a useful member of the Canaries squad during the end of season run-in.

After featuring in ten games for City, he collected a title winners' medal and joined the squad for the civic celebrations that followed promotion. However, despite rumours of a permanent move to Carrow Road, nothing materialised and the player returned to his parent club at the end of the season.

CROFTS, Andrew

Date of birth: 29 May 1984
Place of birth: Chatham
Position: Midfielder
Promotion campaign: 2010/11 Championship runners-up
2010/11 League statistics: 44(-)8

Wales international midfielder Andrew Crofts was signed by Paul Lambert in the summer of 2010 from Brighton & Hove Albion and became a vital player in City's 2010/11 promotion from the Championship.

Playing in all bar two of City's 46 league games, Crofts marked his Canary debut with a goal in the opening game of the season against Watford. He netted a further seven league goals in 2010/11, including a memorable brace in a 2-0 win at Barnsley in February 2011 – the second was a stunning volley on the turn, evoking memories of Justin Fashanu's goal of the season against Liverpool in 1980. Unable to cement a regular place in the City side following promotion to the Premier League, Crofts was granted a return to

Brighton for an undisclosed fee in August 2012 by new City boss Chris Hughton.

CROSS, David
Date of birth: 8 December 1950
Place of birth: Heywood
Position: Striker
Promotion campaign: 1971/72 Division Two champions
1971/72 League statistics: 32(-)8

Following the Canaries' great start to the 1971/72 campaign, manager Ron Saunders splashed out a club record £40,000 to secure the services of striker David Cross from Rochdale in October 1971.

An old-fashioned front man, Cross provided real aggression and aerial prowess to the Canary front line and chipped in with eight league goals to help his new club win promotion to the top flight for the first time.

He made an almost instant impact at Carrow Road with three goals in four games in late October and early November as City recorded vital victories over Cardiff City and Hull City before securing a useful point away to Sheffield Wednesday. Cross also starred for City in the First Division the following season and played in Norwich's 1973 League Cup Final against Tottenham Hotspur at Wembley.

CROSSAN, Errol
Date of birth: 6 October 1930
Place of birth: Montreal, Canada
Date of death: 23 April 2016
Place of death: Langley, Canada
Position: Midfielder
Promotion campaign: 1959/60 Division Three runners-up
1959/60 League statistics: 43(n/a)13

A member of both the Canaries' and the Canadian FA's halls of fame, speedy right-winger Errol Crossan was a true crowd favourite during a Canary career that spanned from September 1958 to December 1960.

A hero of the 1958/59 FA Cup team, Crossan netted four goals in the cup run, including the second goal in the memorable 3-0 third-round victory over Manchester United at Carrow Road plus the quarter-final equaliser away to Sheffield United.

Like so many of the cup heroes, Crossan formed part of the 1959/60 team that won promotion from the Third Division. He scored an impressive 13 goals from midfield, just three less than joint leading scorers Terry Allcock and Jimmy Hill, as Norwich returned to the Second Division along with champions Southampton.

CROUCH, Peter
Date of birth: 30 January 1981
Place of birth: Macclesfield
Position: Striker
Promotion campaign: 2003/04 First
   Division champions
2003/04 League statistics:
   14(1)4

Peter Crouch joined the Canaries from Aston Villa in September 2003 on a three-month loan deal to add some attacking options to Nigel Worthington's squad following a long-term injury to Zema Abbey and the return to Denmark of David Nielsen.

At 6ft 7in he is believed to have become the Canaries' tallest-ever player when he made his debut against Burnley on 13 September 2003, an occasion he marked with a goal in a 2-0 Carrow Road triumph.

Extremely popular with his team-mates and the fans, Crouch had a great first touch and formed a useful partnership with fellow on-loan striker Darren Huckerby as City catapulted up the table during his time at Carrow Road. The Canaries wanted to keep him at the club on a season-long loan, but with Aston Villa struggling for goals he was called back to Villa Park.

CROWE, Matt
Date of birth: 3 July 1932
Place of birth: West Lothian

Date of death: 27 May 2017
Place of death: Port Elizabeth, South Africa
Position: Midfielder
Promotion campaign: 1959/60 Division Three runners-up
1959/60 League statistics: 45(n/a)4

A giant figure in the Canaries' 1958/59 FA Cup team, left-half Matt Crowe was widely regarded as Archie Macaulay's finest signing as Norwich boss, having been recruited for a bargain £500 from Partick Thistle in May 1957.

Crowe was ever-present during the cup run and missed just one league match en route to promotion the following season after sitting out the 1-0 victory over Newport County at Carrow Road in October 1959.

He scored four goals in the 1959/60 promotion-winning campaign, the most vital securing a 1-0 home win over a stubborn York City at Carrow Road on 2 April 1960. The dependable Crowe was ever-present once again in 1960/61 as City impressed in the Second Division.

CUELLAR, Carlos
Date of birth: 23 August 1981
Place of birth: Madrid
Position: Defender
Promotion campaign: 2014/15 Championship play-off winners
2014/15 League statistics: 8(-)-

A vastly experienced Spanish defender, Carlos Cuellar joined City on a short-term contract for the 2014/15 Championship season.

The former Glasgow Rangers, Aston Villa and Sunderland man was signed by Neil Adams to provide know-how and cover for City's defensive ranks. But he marked his debut with an own-goal in the 3-1 League Cup triumph over Crawley and went on to play just ten games in total before leaving the club after promotion was achieved via the play-offs at the end of the season.

Cuellar's league debut away to Nottingham Forest on 8 November 2014 saw City snatch defeat from the jaws of victory as they conceded two late goals at the City Ground in a frustrating 2-1 loss. However, his final outing in green and yellow ended on a happier note as a Jonny Howson-inspired Norwich won 4-1 away to Millwall in March 2014.

CULVERHOUSE, Ian

Date of birth: 22 September 1964
Place of birth: Bishop's Stortford
Position: Defender
Promotion campaign: 1985/86 Division Two champions
1985/86 League statistics: 30(-)-

The 1985/86 Second Division title-winning season saw Ian Culverhouse emerge as the Canaries' first-choice right-back and begin the start of a 369-game ten-year Carrow Road playing career.

Once of Ken Brown's many astute signings from Spurs, Culverhouse made a £50,000 switch from White Hart Lane to Carrow Road in October 1985, making his debut in a comfortable 4-0 win away to Carlisle United later that month. Following his initial bow at Brunton Park, Culverhouse remained ever-present until both promotion and the title were assured. He sat out the final away match of the season at Hull but returned to the side for the end-of-season celebrations as City ended the campaign with a comprehensive 4-0 victory over Leeds United at Carrow Road.

Having enjoyed one Canary promotion as a player, Culverhouse returned to Carrow Road in August 2009 when his coaching talents helped City achieve back-to-back promotions under Paul Lambert.

CURETON, Jamie

Date of birth: 28 August 1975
Place of birth: Bristol
Position: Striker
Promotion campaign: 2009/10 League One champions
2009/10 League statistics: 3(3)2

Jamie Cureton enjoyed two spells with Norwich City, having begun his long and successful goalscoring career at Carrow Road in the early 1990s. His appetite for the game and eye for goal soon saw him progress through the youth and reserve teams before making his first-team debut in 1994.

However, it was during his second stint with the club that he helped the Canaries achieve promotion. He had returned to Carrow Road in the summer of 2007 after an excellent season as the Championship's top scorer with Colchester United in 2006/07 and was City's leading scorer at the same level in 2007/08.

After City suffered relegation to the third tier in 2008/09, Cureton formed part of the squad that won the 2009/10 League

One title. With a trio of goal getters in superb form in the shape of Grant Holt, Chris Martin and Wes Hoolahan, Cureton was often left as a frustrated onlooker. However, the popular striker made a contribution with goals from substitute appearances against Leyton Orient and former club Bristol Rovers in October 2009.

DALEY, Luke
Date of birth: 10 November, 1989
Place of birth: Northampton
Position: Striker
Promotion campaigns: 2009/10 League One champions and 2010/11
   Championship runners-up
2009/10 League statistics: 3(4)-
2010/11 League statistics: -(1)-

A product of the Canaries' academy, jet-heeled frontman Luke Daley was handed his first-team debut by Bryan Gunn when he replaced Jamie Cureton in the second half of City's Championship match at home to Burnley in February 2009.

His pace and eye for goal clearly made an impression on Paul Lambert, who in turn rewarded Daley with a first senior start in City's League Cup tie with Sunderland at Carrow Road in August 2009. A full league debut came away to MK Dons the following month.

A series of niggling injuries and the form of other strikers limited Daley's first-team opportunities while at Carrow Road. His final appearance for the club came in an eventful 3-3 draw at Reading during the club's 2009/10 promotion-winning season from the Championship.

DARLING, Malcolm
Date of birth: 4 July 1947
Place of birth: Arbroath
Position: Striker
Promotion campaign: 1971/72 Division Two champions
1971/72 League statistics: 4(-)1

Versatile frontman Malcolm Darling featured in the early part of City's 1971/72 Second Division title-winning season after arriving from Blackburn Rovers in May 1970.

Darling came to Carrow Road from Ewood Park after City boss Ron Saunders sanctioned a move for Bryan Conlon, who headed in the opposite direction. With the ability to operate anywhere across the front line, Darling offered many options but was never able to establish a regular starting place in Saunders's side.

The promotion season saw him start four of City's first five league games and he was on the scoresheet in the opening home game of the season in a 3-1 victory over Portsmouth. His appearance in the 1-0 Carrow Road triumph over Carlisle United on 4 September 1971 proved to be his final game for City, with the Scot then moving on to Rochdale.

DEEHAN, John
Date of birth: 6 August 1957
Place of birth: Solihull
Position: Striker
Promotion campaigns: 1981/82 third in Division Two and 1985/86
  Second Division champions
1981/82 League statistics: 22(-)10
1985/86 League statistics: 22(4)4

With ten goals from 22 outings, striker John Deehan boasted the Canaries' best goals-to-games ratio among the 1981/82 promotion-winning squad.

Signed from West Bromwich Albion midway through the 1981/82 campaign, Deehan marked his City debut with a goal but could not help prevent a 3-1 defeat at home to Luton Town on 28 December 1981. His arrival, and ultimately his goals, proved vital in City's bid for promotion. He hammered home a further nine goals, including a hat-trick in the 5-0 demolition of Charlton Athletic at Carrow Road on 10 April 1982, as Norwich went on to secure their place back among football's elite.

A League Cup winner in 1985, Deehan also featured in City's 1985/86 Second Division title success. However, that season saw Kevin Drinkell and Wayne Biggins often chosen as the men to lead the line, with Deehan contributing four goals from 26 appearances.

DOHERTY, Gary
Date of birth: 31 January 1980
Place of birth: Carndonagh, Ireland
Position: Defender
Promotion campaign: 2009/10 League One champions
2009/10 League statistics: 38(-)6

With the flexibility to operate with equal effectiveness as a central-defender or as a striker, Gary Doherty was recruited from Tottenham Hotspur in August 2004.

Signed by Nigel Worthington, Doherty experienced a rollercoaster Carrow Road career, playing for City in the Premier League, Championship and League One. An extremely popular and well-respected character in the dressing room, Doherty captained the team on many occasions during his time at Carrow Road and was voted player of the season in 2005/06.

After a difficult start to the 2009/10 League One season, Doherty went on to form a solid partnership in the heart of the City defence, firstly with Jens Berthel Askou and then with Michael Nelson, during the second half of the title-winning campaign. Doherty's final season at the club saw him chip in with six league goals from his 38 appearances, and he ended the campaign third in the supporters' player-of-the-season poll.

Manager Paul Lambert decided against activating the one-year option City had on Doherty's contract and he left the club in the summer of 2010.

DONACHIE, Willie
Date of birth: 5 October 1951
Place of birth: Glasgow
Position: Defender
Promotion campaign: 1981/82 third in Division Two
1981/82 League statistics: 11(-)-

Acknowledged as one of the First Division's best full-backs during the 1970s while with Manchester City, Scottish international Willie Donachie had a brief spell with the Canaries during the club's 1981/82 Second Division campaign.

His time at Carrow Road was sandwiched between two spells in the USA with Portland Timbers. Donachie was unable to displace regular Canary left-back Greg Downs on a permanent basis and was limited to 11 league and three League Cup appearances during his five-month Norwich City career.

Ironically, Donachie debuted on 3 October 1981 in a 2-1 defeat at home to Oldham Athletic, a club he would later serve with great distinction and success as number two to another former Canary, Joe Royle.

DONOWA, Louie

Date of birth: 24 September 1964
Place of birth: Ipswich
Position: Midfielder
Promotion campaign: 1985/86 Division Two champions
1985/86 League statistics: -(2)-

Two brief appearances from the bench in the opening month of the Canaries' 1985/86 Second Division campaign proved to be the final outings in a City shirt for exciting winger Louie Donowa as his 80-game and 15-goal Norwich career came to a close.

An integral member of the City side that enjoyed League Cup success at Wembley in 1985, Donowa had also tasted FA Youth Cup glory with the Canaries in 1983.

His contribution to the 1985/86 success consisted of replacing David Williams in the 4-2 defeat at Millwall on 24 August 1985 and then entering the fray at Fratton Park for Paul Haylock as City went down 2-0 to Portsmouth. He later joined Second Division rivals Stoke City on loan before trying his luck in Spain.

DORRANS, Graham

Date of birth: 5 May 1987
Place of birth: Glasgow
Position: Midfielder
Promotion campaign: 2014/15 Championship play-off winners
2014/15 League statistics: 12(3)3 + play-offs 1(2)-

Talented Scottish midfielder Graham Dorrans joined the Canaries on an initial month's loan in February 2015 from West Bromwich Albion before completing a permanent switch to Carrow Road. He helped City to secure promotion via the play-offs in 2014/15, making his City debut in the comprehensive 3-0 victory over Watford at Vicarage Road on 21 February 2015.

He scored vital goals in back-to-back away victories against Bolton Wanderers and Leeds United in early April as City chased hard for automatic promotion. Always neat and tidy on the ball and with a good eye for a pass, Dorrans featured on 21 occasions during City's ill-fated 2015/16 Premier League campaign.

The Scot remained at the club following relegation in 2016, but as Norwich attempted to balance the books ahead of their final season with parachute payments he joined his boyhood heroes Glasgow Rangers in the summer of 2017.

DOWNS, Greg

Date of birth: 13 December 1958
Place of birth: Carlton
Position: Defender
Promotion campaign: 1981/82 third in Division Two
1981/82 League statistics: 28(-)1

The exceptional performances of attacking left-back Greg Downs won him the Barry Butler Memorial Trophy as City's player of the season during the 1981/82 Second Division promotion-winning campaign.

The early part of the season saw Downs replaced at left-back by the experienced Willie Donachie for an 11-game spell. However, Downs returned to the side during the festive period and then made the number-three shirt his own, missing just one further match as City produced a memorable end-of-season run to land the third and final promotion berth.

His only goal of the campaign looked to have secured a point away to Newcastle United in January 1982, only for Imre Varadi to pop up with a winner for the hosts. Downs's marauding runs forward made him a popular player during his Canary career and he remains a regular visitor to Carrow Road, often summarising for BBC Radio Norfolk.

DRINKELL, Kevin

Date of birth: 18 June 1960
Place of birth: Grimsby
Position: Striker
Promotion campaign: 1985/86 Division Two champions
1985/86 League statistics: 41(-)22

Striker Kevin Drinkell proved to be an instant goalscoring success for the Canaries following his transfer from Grimsby Town in the summer of 1985 and was yet another shrewd acquisition by Ken Brown.

Drinkell arrived at Carrow Road with an impressive goals-to-games ratio from his time at Blundell Park and proceeded to hammer home the goals that inspired Norwich to the Second Division title and an instant return to the top flight.

His 22-league goal haul unsurprisingly saw him voted the club's player of the season at the end of his debut campaign. An old-fashioned centre-forward, Drinkell's style of play won him many admirers and saw comparisons made with David Cross, who in 1971 also stepped up from the lower divisions to score the goals that helped Norwich to promotion.

DRURY, Adam

Date of birth: 29 August 1978
Place of birth: Cottenham
Position: Defender
Promotion campaigns: 2003/04 First Division champions, 2009/10 League One champions and 2010/11 Championship runners-up
2003/04 League statistics: 42(-)-
2009/10 League statistics: 35(-)-
2010/11 League statistics: 19(1)1

Together with Wes Hoolahan and Russell Martin, Adam Drury is one of just three players to savour promotion success with the Canaries on three separate occasions.

Signed by Nigel Worthington from Peterborough United in 2001, Drury went on to enjoy 11 seasons at Carrow Road, playing 361 games. He was voted player of the season in 2002/03 and captained the 2003/04 First Division championship-winning team.

A reliable and ultra-consistent defender, Drury was rarely beaten in one-on-one situations. His experience was used wisely by boss Paul Lambert in the 2009/10 League One triumph. The following season saw Drury on target in City's epic 4-3 Carrow Road victory over Leicester City in September 2010. During the 2010/11 campaign Drury shared left-back duties with Marc Tierney as City completed a remarkable back-to-back promotion success to elevate the club from League One to the Premier League.

EASTON, Clint

Date of birth: 1 October 1977
Place of birth: Barking
Position: Midfielder
Promotion campaign: 2003/04 First Division champions
2003/04 League statistics: 8(2)2

Recruited from Watford in June 2001, Clint Easton enjoyed an impressive debut campaign at Norwich City in 2001/02 as the Canaries reached the First Division play-off final.

A creative player with the ability to operate in a number of roles across the midfield, Easton was predominately used on the left flank and made ten league appearances in the 2003/04 campaign, in what proved to be his final season with the Canaries.

Easton made a flying start to 2003/04 and was on target in City's opening-day fixture at Bradford as Nigel Worthington's men secured a 2-2 draw at Valley Parade. He also netted the first home goal of the season as City cruised to a routine 2-0 victory over Rotherham United, but, following the arrival of Darren Huckerby, Easton found attacking opportunities down the left flank hard to come by. His final appearance for Norwich came against his former employers as the Hornets pulled off a surprise victory at Carrow Road on 15 November 2003.

EDWARDS, Robert

Date of birth: 22 May 1931
Place of birth: Guildford
Position: Striker
Promotion campaign: 1959/60 Division Three runners-up
1959/60 League statistics: 1(-)-

Frontman Robert 'Bob' Edwards boasted a good goalscoring record while plying his trade for Swindon Town and joined the Canaries in December 1959. With City missing the services of key goalscorers Terry Bly and Terry Allcock for their Third Division match away to Chesterfield on 12 December 1959, Edwards did not have to wait long for his Canary debut. Norwich trailed 2-0 at the break at Saltergate, and although Edwards and his new team-mates engineered a route back into the game thanks to a second-half goal from James Moran they were unable to force an equaliser.

With substitutes and squad rotation very much future inventions, the Chesterfield outing proved to be Edwards's only first-team appearance for the Canaries. He maintained his goalscoring form at reserve-team level for City before moving on to Northampton Town in 1961.

EDWARDS, Robert
Date of birth: 25 December 1982
Place of birth: Shropshire
Position: Defender
Promotion campaign: 2010/11 Championship runners-up
2010/11 League statistics: -(3)-

A vastly experienced central-defender, Rob Edwards joined the Canaries on a short-term loan deal from Premier League Blackpool in February 2011.

A former Welsh international, Edwards arrived at Carrow Road to provide defensive cover after injury ruled Leon Barnett out for the remainder of the season. With Barnett sidelined, City were left with just Elliott Ward, Zak Whitbread and the out-of-favour Jens Berthel Askou as their only recognised central-defenders following the departure of Michael Nelson to Scunthorpe in January 2011.

Edwards made just three appearances for Paul Lambert's side, all as a substitute and all in home matches – his final outing being the memorable Simeon Jackson-inspired 3-2 victory over Derby County as City closed in on promotion. He debuted in a 1-1 draw with Preston North End and also featured in the closing stages of the 2-1 win over Nottingham Forest. After Norwich had secured their promotion to the Premier League, Edwards returned to Bloomfield Road.

EDWORTHY, Marc
Date of birth: 24 December 1972
Place of birth: Barnstaple
Position: Defender
Promotion campaign: 2003/04 First Division champions
2003/04 League statistics: 42(1)-

Having been released by Wolves in the summer of 2003, following their promotion to the Premier League, experienced right-back Edworthy found himself without a club. After trial periods with Reading and Stoke City failed to result in a contract, he was technically unemployed on the eve of the 2003/04 season, yet ten months later he was picking up a First Division championship winners' medal with the Canaries.

He arrived at Norwich just two days before the start of the new season with a view that both the club and player would have an opportunity to look at one another. A two-year contact was agreed 24 hours before the Canaries' opening game of the season at Bradford, where he made his City debut as a second-half substitute.

Edworthy instantly made the right-back berth his own and formed part of a solid and reliable back four during the Canaries' 2004/05 championship-winning season.

ELLIOTT, Stephen
Date of birth: 6 January 1984
Place of birth: Dublin
Position: Striker
Promotion campaign: 2009/10 League One champions
2009/10 League statistics: 4(6)2

Republic of Ireland international forward Stephen Elliott joined the Canaries on loan in March 2010 from Preston North End.

He signed for Paul Lambert's promotion-chasing side for the remainder of the 2009/10 League One campaign and is fondly remembered for chipping in with two vital goals in City's 3-1 win away to Huddersfield Town on 13 March 2010.

Signed to keep the goalscoring trio of Grant Holt, Chris Martin and Wes Hoolahan on their toes, Elliott covered for injuries and suspensions but only managed to force his way into the starting line-up on four occasions. In total he made ten appearances in a City shirt after making his initial bow at home to Yeovil Town in a routine 3-0 Carrow Road triumph on 6 March 2010. His aforementioned double strike against the Terriers was undoubtedly the standout performance from his time at Norwich and the Irishman returned to Deepdale at the end of the title-winning campaign.

FASHANU, John
Date of birth: 18 September 1963
Place of birth: Kensington
Position: Striker
Promotion campaign: 1981/82 third in Division Two
1981/82 League statistics: 4(1)1

Famed for his starring role with Wimbledon's 'Crazy Gang' and their 1988 FA Cup triumph, John Fashanu made his Football League debut for Norwich City during the club's 1981/82 promotion-winning campaign. Following the footsteps of older brother Justin, John progressed through the youth and reserve ranks to earn a professional contract at Carrow Road. His first-team breakthrough arrived when he replaced Clive Woods in the 2-1 home win over Shrewsbury Town on 17 October 1981.

Fashanu's lively showing from the bench against the Shrews won him a place in the starting line-up for City's next outing a week later when they travelled to Watford. The powerful striker netted his first goal for the Canaries in a 4-1 romp over Derby County at Carrow Road in November 1981. Unable to cement a regular place in the City side, he joined Lincoln City in 1983.

FER, Leroy
Date of birth: 5 January 1990
Place of birth: Zoetermeer, Netherlands
Position: Midfielder
Promotion campaign: 2014/15 Championship play-off winners
2014/15 League statistics: -(1)-

An athletic midfielder and Dutch international, Leroy Fer made only the briefest of contributions to the Canaries' 2014/15 season.

Having joined the club in July 2013 from FC Twente, Fer was an impressive performer for Norwich in a difficult 2013/14 campaign. Speculation about his Carrow Road future began in the aftermath of City's relegation from the Premier League at the end of 2013/14, with a number of clubs reported to be courting his services.

With a deal to remain in the Premier League with Queens Park Rangers close to completion, Fer was not involved in City's opening-day defeat at Wolves but made a final appearance in yellow and green as a late substitute, replacing Wes Hoolahan in the closing stages of City's 3-0 Championship triumph over Watford at Carrow Road. The Dutchman made the point of applauding all corners of the ground at full-time in a farewell gesture to thank the City fans for their support during his 14 months with the Canaries.

FLEMING, Craig
Date of birth: 6 October 1971
Place of birth: Halifax
Position: Defender
Promotion campaign: 2003/04 Division One champions
2003/04 League statistics: 46(-)3

An outstanding Norwich City servant, defender Craig Fleming chose the 2003/04 season to produce arguably his finest season in a City shirt as the ever-present centre-half landed the Barry Butler Memorial Trophy when he was voted by the fans as City's player of the season.

The accolade capped a tremendous season for Fleming, whose ultra-consistent performances alongside Malky Mackay were a significant factor in the team's journey to the Division One title and the return of top-flight football to Carrow Road.

Never renowned for his goalscoring, Fleming also chipped in with three goals in the charge to the title. The defender netted in the 4-1 demolition of Cardiff City at Carrow Road, the 4-0 post-Christmas victory at Derby and during the final-day celebrations as Nigel Worthington's side wrapped up a classic campaign with a 3-1 win away to Crewe Alexandra.

FOGGO, Kenny

Date of birth: 7 November 1943
Place of birth: Perth
Position: Midfielder
Promotion campaign: 1971/72 Division Two champions
1971/72 League statistics: 38(2)13

Scottish winger Kenny Foggo starred in the Norwich City side that sealed the club's first-ever promotion to the top flight in 1971/72. He weighed in with an impressive 13 league goals to become the club's leading scorer for a third consecutive season as the Canaries landed the Second Division title.

Fittingly, Foggo's final strike of the season came in the crucial 2-1 promotion-sealing win at Orient on 24 April 1972. Not only did the Scot top City's scoring charts in 1971/72, but his tricky wing play also provided countless opportunities for others. Foggo's contribution to the Canary cause made him a particularly popular character in both the dressing room and on the terraces.

Despite playing a key role in the promotion-winning season, Foggo made just two top-flight appearances before joining Portsmouth in January 1973. He departed Carrow Road with an extremely respectable 57 goals from 201 appearances and was the first City player to twice be awarded the Barry Butler Memorial Trophy as the club's player of the season.

FORBES, Duncan

Date of birth: 19 June 1941
Place of birth: Edinburgh
Position: Defender
Promotion campaigns: 1971/72 Division Two champions and 1974/75 third in Division Two
1971/72 League statistics: 27(-)2
1974/75 League statistics: 39(-)1

Captain and leader of the Canaries' 1971/72 promotion-winning side, defender Duncan Forbes was a colossal presence at the heart of the Norwich City defence during a Canary career that saw him make over 350 appearances for the club.

Forbes had been badly missed when injury ruled him out of a chunk of the 1971/72 campaign, but he returned to the side and scored two vital goals to help the Canaries make it over the finish line and on to promotion. With only five games remaining, he netted the only goal of the game to secure victory over Sheffield Wednesday at Carrow Road on 8 April 1972. He then repeated the trick a fortnight later to secure a 1-0 win over Swindon Town that left City on the brink of the big time.

A true Norwich City legend, the images of Forbes holding the Second Division trophy aloft at City Hall remain a wonderful record of an iconic moment in the club's rich history. As skipper of the 1974/75 team, Forbes missed just three league matches as City returned to the top flight at the first time of asking – ending the season in third place behind Manchester United and Aston Villa.

FORSTER, Fraser

Date of birth: 17 March 1988
Place of birth: Hexham
Position: Goalkeeper
Promotion campaign: 2009/10 League One champions
2009/10 League statistics: 38(-)-

Giant goalkeeper Fraser Forster joined Norwich City on a season-long loan from Newcastle United during the 2009/10 League One championship-winning season and his arrival swiftly put an end to the goalkeeping problems that had blighted the Canaries' start to the season.

An inspired signing by Paul Lambert, Forster performed outstandingly during his time at Carrow Road. His huge physical presence provided confidence for those in front of him while the player himself demonstrated the form that would see him win international recognition with England later in his career. The only blip on his Carrow Road copybook occurred in the 2-1 defeat at Leeds in October 2009 when a scuffed goal kick resulted in Jermaine Beckford's last-gasp winner for the hosts. However, Forster showed great mental strength to put the error behind him and go on to produce a number of match-winning saves throughout the remainder of the season.

During his time at Carrow Road, Forster became a firm favourite with the fans and was also voted the players' player of the season at the end of the League One campaign.

FOX, David

Date of birth: 13 December 1983
Place of birth: Leek
Position: Midfielder
Promotion campaign: 2010/11 Championship runners-up
2010/11 League statistics: 30(2)1

Midfield maestro David Fox joined Norwich City in the summer of 2010 from Colchester United and went on to play a major part in the Canaries' promotion to the Premier League.

City boss Paul Lambert knew all about Fox's excellent range of passing skills, having also signed him for Colchester 12 months earlier, and the player showed no signs of difficulty in stepping up to Championship level. Fox immediately formed a good central-midfield understanding with fellow summer recruit Andrew Crofts and netted his first goal in Canary colours to secure a valuable point from a tricky midweek trip to Millwall on 9 November 2010.

The architect of many successful passing moves throughout the season, Fox fittingly delivered the through ball that set up Simeon Jackson for the promotion-winning goal at Portsmouth in the penultimate game of the season.

FRANCIS, Damien
Date of birth: 27 February 1979
Place of birth: Wandsworth
Position: Midfielder
Promotion campaign: 2003/04 First Division champions
2003/04 League statistics: 39(2)7

Recruited from First Division rivals Wimbledon ahead of the 2003/04 campaign, all-action midfielder Damien Francis enjoyed a splendid debut season at Carrow Road as Norwich secured top spot and promotion to the Premier League.

A powerful and athletic midfielder, Francis had gained a growing reputation following a string of impressive performances for the Dons. Upon his arrival at Carrow Road, he soon had a new army of fans following a series of man-of-the-match performances in the opening months of the season.

Ironically, his first goal in Canary colours came against his former employers as City defeated Wimbledon 3-2 at Carrow Road on 26 August 2003. He also netted the only goal of the game to secure a vital 1-0 victory at home to Sunderland. With promotion assured, Francis was on target in consecutive victories over Watford and Preston North End as City closed in on the title.

FRANCOMB, George
Date of birth: 8 September 1991
Place of birth: Hackney
Position: Defender
Promotion campaign: 2009/10 League One champions
2009/10 League statistics: 2(-)-

Following his release from Tottenham Hotspur, tough-tackling full-back George Francomb progressed through the academy ranks at Colney to feature in the first team's League One title triumph of 2009/10. Handed a professional debut by Paul Lambert in the Football League Trophy victory over Gillingham on 6 October

2009, Francomb's league bow followed just four days later when he deputised for Jon Otsemobor in City's 1-0 victory over Carlisle United at Brunton Park. His second and final taste of first-team football in 2009/10 came in the hard-fought 1-0 Carrow Road success against Swindon Town on 24 October 2009.

Unable to cement a regular first team berth at Carrow Road, Francomb took in loan spells at Barnet, Hibernian and AFC Wimbledon before being released by Chris Hughton in May 2013 when he then agreed a permanent deal with the Dons.

GARRIDO, Javier
Date of birth: 15 March 1985
Place of birth: Irun, Spain
Position: Defender
Promotion campaign: 2014/15 Championship play-off winners
2014/15 League statistics: 3(4)-

Spanish left-back Javier Garrido completed a permanent move to Norwich City from Lazio in the summer of 2013 following an impressive season on loan from the Italian giants in 2012/13.

Garrido had played in 34 Premier League matches during the 2012/13 campaign, and displayed plenty of attacking flair to go with his defensive resolve. However, he totalled only ten appearances in all competitions in 2013/14 as Martin Olsson took control of the left-back position.

That once again proved the theme in City's 2014/15 promotion-winning season in the Championship when Garrido made just seven league appearances. Despite a lack of first-team opportunities, he remained a valued member of the City squad under both Neil Adams and Alex Neil. Whenever called upon, Garrido was always willing, ready and able to give his best for the Canary cause. His final game for City came on 14 February 2015 as City overcame Wolves 2-0 at Carrow Road. The Spaniard left the club at the end of the 2014/15 campaign when his contract expired.

GILL, Matt
Date of birth: 8 November 1980
Place of birth: Norwich
Position: Midfielder
Promotion campaigns: 2009/10 League One champions and 2010/11
    Championship runners-up

2009/10 League statistics: 5(3)-
2010/11 League statistics: -(4)-

Norwich-born midfielder Matt Gill joined the Canaries in the summer of 2009 following a number of successful seasons with Exeter City, where he had helped the St James Park club win promotion from non-league to League One.

Signed by Bryan Gunn, Gill had the misfortune of making his debut in the 7-1 defeat at home to Colchester United on the opening day of the 2009/10 campaign. Despite finding first-team football hard to come by under new manager Paul Lambert, Gill remained a popular and well-respected member of the City squad.

His final involvement in the League One success saw him play in the 3-0 win away to another of his former clubs, Bristol Rovers, in the Canaries' penultimate game of the season. He was limited to just four substitute appearances at Championship level in 2010/11 and took in a loan spell at Walsall before leaving Carrow Road following the club's promotion to the Premier League and the conclusion of his two-year contract.

GODFREY, Ben
Date of birth: 15 January 1998
Place of birth: York
Position: Midfielder
Promotion campaign: 2018/19 Championship champions
2018/19 League statistics: 26(5)4

A colossal performer in the heart of the City defence in the second-half of the 2018/19 season, Ben Godfrey stepped in to partner Christoph Zimmermann in central-defence, covering for the injured Timm Klose.

Initially recruited from York City in August 2016, Godfrey enjoyed an excellent 2017/18 season on loan at Shrewsbury Town, playing in a defensive midfield role as the Shrews reached the Football League Trophy Final and the League One play-offs.

He returned to Carrow Road in the summer of 2018 determined to make his mark at Championship level. Patience was the key for Godfrey as he was primarily limited to cup action in the opening months of the season. His ability to perform in either midfield or defence made him a valuable squad member and when his opportunity arose he certainly grabbed it with both hands. A vital winning goal away to Rotherham United, plus strikes against Bristol

City and Reading, all helped raise Godfrey's growing reputation, and his club form was rewarded with England under-20 involvement in March 2019.

GOODWIN, Steve

Date of birth: 23 February 1954
Place of birth: Chadderton
Position: Striker
Promotion campaign: 1974/75 third in Division Two
1974/75 League statistics: 2(-)-

Despite a lengthy Canary career that included over 100 reserve-team appearances, Steve Goodwin made just three league appearances for Norwich City, two of them coming during the 1974/75 season as John Bond guided City back to Division One at the first time of asking.

Under the management of Ron Saunders, Goodwin made his debut as a fresh-faced 17-year-old when he replaced Steve Grapes in City's 1-0 final-day-of-the-season defeat away to Hull City on 1 May 1971. He had to wait until 23 November 1974 for his next taste of Football League action, when he deputised for Phil Boyer in the 2-0 Carrow Road triumph over Bolton Wanderers.

After helping to secure both points against the Trotters, Goodwin remained in the starting line-up for the League Cup replay with Sheffield United at Carrow Road four days later, when his brace secured a 2-1 victory. He played in the following league game, a frustrating 1-0 defeat away to York City, before Boyer then returned to partner Ted MacDougall in the City attack.

GORDON, Dale

Date of birth: 9 January 1967
Place of birth: Great Yarmouth
Position: Midfielder
Promotion campaign: 1985/86 Division Two champions
1985/86 League statistics: 3(3)1

An outstanding performer for Norwich City across a number of top-flight campaigns, winger Dale Gordon featured fleetingly in the Canaries' 1985/86 Second Division title-winning campaign.

Having broken into the first team the previous season, Norfolk-born Gordon found senior opportunities hard to come by in his second season, mainly due to the excellent performances of Mark

Barham. After three substitute appearances, Gordon's first league start of the season came at home to Sunderland on 9 April 1986 as City closed in on promotion despite being held to a goalless draw by the Black Cats.

With promotion assured following a 2-0 win over Bradford City at the Odsal Stadium, Gordon started and scored in the 1-1 draw with Stoke City at Carrow Road. His goal cancelled out former Canary Keith Bertchin's opener, and the point won, coupled with results elsewhere, proved enough to guarantee the title was bound for Norfolk.

GOVIER, Steve
Date of birth: 6 April 1952
Place of birth: Watford
Position: Defender
Promotion campaign: 1971/72 Division Two champions
1971/72 League statistics: 3(-)1

A regular face for the second string during a lengthy Carrow Road career, central-defender Steve Govier had the unenviable task of trying to break the Duncan Forbes/Dave Stringer partnership in his pursuit of first-team football.

Primarily acting as cover for the two aforementioned Canary legends, Govier is always fondly remembered for his goal in the rearranged 1972/73 League Cup semi-final meeting with Chelsea. The 1971/72 campaign saw him limited to just three Second Division outings. With Forbes injured, Govier's first game of the season came in City's 2-1 win away to Hull City on 6 November 1971. A week later the big defender joined Peter Silvester on the scoresheet as City secured a 2-2 draw at home to Birmingham City. Govier's final contribution to the 1971/72 promotion success came on New Year's Day 1972 as Ron Saunders's side ran out 2-0 winners over Oxford United at the Manor Ground.

GRABBAN, Lewis
Date of birth: 12 January 1988
Place of birth: Croydon
Position: Striker
Promotion campaign: 2014/15 Championship play-off winners
2014/15 League statistics: 23(12)12 + play-offs −(1)-

Lewis Grabban became Neil Adams's first signing as City boss when the striker was recruited from AFC Bournemouth in the summer of 2014.

Upon his arrival in Norfolk, Grabban hit the ground running with goals in pre-season before winning the hearts of the Canary faithful by netting the only goal in the East Anglian derby triumph over arch rivals Ipswich Town at Portman Road in August 2014. A regular in the City side throughout his debut season, despite the arrival of fellow strikers Cameron Jerome and Kyle Lafferty, Grabban was highly rated by Adams and his successor Alex Neil.

The striker was also on target in the return fixture against Ipswich as City won 2-0 on 1 March 2015. Suspension ruled him out of the play-off semi-finals, but he tasted promotion glory when he replaced Jerome in the 74th minute of City's 2-0 Wembley victory over Middlesbrough in the play-off final.

GRAPES, Steve

Date of birth: 25 February 1953
Place of birth: Norwich
Position: Midfielder
Promotion campaigns: 1971/72 Division Two champions and 1974/75 third in Division Two
1971/72 League statistics: -(1)-
1974/75 League statistics: 6(2)2

Winger Steve Grapes made over 50 first-team appearances during a five-and-a-half year spell with Norwich City. The skilful wide-man also appeared 173 times for the club's reserve side.

Although unable to secure a regular starting place in the Canary first team, the Norwich-born winger proudly featured in both of the club's promotion successes in the 1970s. His sole involvement in the 1971/72 campaign came from the bench when he replaced Kenny Foggo in the 1-0 defeat away to Burnley on 29 January 1972.

Grapes's contribution to the 1974/75 league campaign consisted of eight appearances, six of which were starts. He also netted two goals in the opening fortnight of the season – grabbing the only goal of the game early in the second half to secure both points from a midweek triumph at home to Southampton on 21 August 1974, and ten days later he notched a second-half equaliser to secure a 1-1 draw with Sheffield Wednesday at Carrow Road.

GREEN, Robert

Date of birth: 18 January 1980
Place of birth: Chertsey
Position: Goalkeeper
Promotion campaign: 2003/04 First Division champions
2003/04 League statistics: 46(-)-

Robert Green became only the sixth Norwich City player to win a full England cap when he appeared as a substitute against Colombia in the United States in June 2005.

The home-grown keeper progressed through the youth and reserve teams at Colney before becoming ever-present in the 2003/04 First Division championship-winning season. An outstanding performer as City conquered all before them en route to the Premier League, it was early in 2004 that Green's exceptional club form won him his first call-up to the national squad. While Darren Huckerby grabbed the headlines with numerous match-winning performances and Craig Fleming collected the player of the season award, Green's contribution to the success of Nigel Worthington's side in 2003/04 should certainly not be underestimated.

His first-team debut came in the cut and thrust of an East Anglian derby in April 1999 with the youngster marking the occasion with a clean sheet, and 240 appearances later he had certainly added his name to Norwich City's long and proud list of top-class stoppers.

HAMMOND, Elvis

Date of birth: 6 October 1980
Place of birth: Accra, Ghana
Position: Striker
Promotion campaign: 2003/04 First Division champions
2003/04 League statistics: -(4)-

Blessed with a Christian name that made him a headline writer's dream, pacey forward Elvis Hammond joined the Canaries on a one-month loan deal from Fulham early in the 2003/04 season.

A quick but slightly built striker, Hammond had honed his attacking skills while progressing through the ranks at Craven Cottage but found first-team opportunities with the Londoners few and far between. His chances at Carrow Road were limited to just substitute appearances, the first coming when he replaced Paul McVeigh in the opening home game of the season as City recorded a 2-0 win over Rotherham United.

Three further outings from the bench came away to Sheffield United and at home to Wimbledon before Hammond's final game in a City shirt coincided with the 2-0 defeat against Nottingham Forest at the City Ground on 29 August 2003. Following the recurrence of a foot injury he then returned to Fulham a few days before the end of his loan period.

HANLEY, Grant

Date of birth: 20 November 1991
Place of birth: Dumfries
Position: Midfielder
Promotion campaign: 2018/19 Championship champions
2018/19 League statistics: 6(3)1

Scotland international defender Grant Hanley made an excellent impression at Carrow Road in 2017/18 following his switch from Newcastle United. It was therefore of little surprise that head coach Daniel Farke named Hanley as Norwich captain ahead of the 2018/19 campaign.

The reliable central-defender took his place in the starting line-up alongside Timm Klose for the curtain raiser away to Birmingham City. He was then on target a week later in City's first home game as West Bromwich Albion edged a seven-goal thriller 4-3.

Following the East Anglian derby at Portman Road in September and prior to the Canaries' next home match with Middlesbrough, it was announced that Hanley would be sidelined for at least six weeks with a thigh injury. With City having picked up just five points from a possible 18 this was seen as another blow to City's faltering start to the season.

However, Hanley's absence offered Christoph Zimmermann a chance to stake his claim and the German made the most of his opportunity, thus limiting Hanley to a place among the substitutes following his return to fitness.

HANSBURY, Roger

Date of birth: 26 January, 1955
Place of birth: Barnsley
Position: Goalkeeper
Promotion campaign: 1974/75 third in Division Two
1974/75 League statistics: 4(-)-

With the unenviable task of being understudy to legendary Canary keeper Kevin Keelan, Roger Hansbury certainly had to bide his time for a slice of first-team action at Carrow Road.

Hansbury deputised on four occasions for Keelan during the Canaries' 1974/75 promotion-winning campaign. He suffered something of a baptism of fire on his league debut as City were thumped 4-0 away to Fulham on 21 September 1974 but gave assured performances across a three-game spell later in the season.

He marked his home league debut with a clean sheet as a Johnny Miller brace secured both points from a 2-0 victory over Bolton Wanderers on 23 November 1974. A week later Hansbury featured in a frustrating 1-0 defeat away to York City before playing in his fourth and final league game of the season when John Bond's side began December with a 1-1 draw at home to Cardiff City.

HARPER, Kevin

Date of birth: 15 January 1976
Place of birth: Oldham
Position: Midfielder
Promotion campaign: 2003/04 Division One champions
2003/04 League statistics: 9(-)-

Kevin Harper was one of a trio of on-loan players who made their Canary debuts against Burnley in a 2-0 Carrow Road triumph on 11 September 2003, the other two being Peter Crouch and Darren Huckerby.

Harper joined City on loan from Portsmouth, initially arriving for one month as cover for the injured Mark Rivers. However, after making a good early impression his loan was extended for a further two months.

His direct approach won him many admirers before a combination of injury and suspension halted his progress. The Scot was sent off on the stroke of half-time against Derby County following a poorly judged two-footed tackle on Luciano Zavagno. His actions left his team-mates with an uphill task in the second half, but the ten men rose to the occasion and recorded a hard-fought 2-1 victory. Harper's final game in yellow and green came in the 3-1 win away to Walsall on 1 November 2003.

HART, Andrew
Date of birth: 14 January 1963
Place of birth: Great Yarmouth
Position: Defender
Promotion campaign: 1981/82 third in Division Two
1981/82 League statistics: -(1)-

Norfolk-born Andrew Hart's single taste of first-team football for the Canaries came in the 1981/82 season as Ken Brown's side won promotion back to Division One.

A versatile defender, Hart replaced Mark Nightingale in the 73rd minute of City's Carrow Road clash with Newcastle United on 19 September 1981. An eventful match had seen a young Chris Waddle give the visitors a 12th-minute lead before Dave Watson headed home an equaliser just six minutes later. After Mick McGuire failed to convert a second-half penalty, it appeared the points would be shared, but Hart was able to say his only appearance for the Canaries was a winning one as Ross Jack nodded home the winner ten minutes from time.

After leaving Carrow Road, Hart featured on the local non-league scene with spells at both Gorleston Town and Norwich United, despite suffering a lengthy spell sidelined by a knee injury.

HAYLOCK, Paul
Date of birth: 24 March 1963
Place of birth: Lowestoft
Position: Defender
Promotion campaigns: 1981/82 third in Division Two and 1985/86
   Second Division champions
1981/82 League statistics: 21(-)-
1985/86 League statistics: 12(-)1

During his four-and-a-half years as a professional at Carrow Road, right-back Paul Haylock featured in two promotion-winning seasons and sampled Wembley glory in the 1985 League Cup Final.

City's 1981/82 success saw Haylock make four league appearances in the first half of the season before finally dispossessing Richard Symonds of the right-back shirt in mid-February. After starting the 2-1 home win over Chelsea on 20 February 1982, Haylock remained in the side for the remaining 16 league fixtures as a Martin O'Neill-inspired City grabbed the third and final promotion place.

A first-team regular, Haylock amassed almost 200 games for the Canaries. He started the first 11 league games of the 1985/86 campaign and netted the final goal in a 4-0 rout of Sheffield United at Carrow Road in September 1985. A month later he played his penultimate league game for the club in a 2-1 defeat to Wimbledon in October 1985 as Ian Culverhouse arrived from Spurs and immediately established himself as City's first choice right-back. Haylock's final league outing for City arrived in the last away game of the season at Hull City once both promotion and the title had been secured.

HENDERSON, Ian
Date of birth: 24 January 1985
Place of birth: Thetford
Position: Striker
Promotion campaign: 2003/04 First Division champions
2003/04 League statistics: 14(5)4

A product of the Canaries' academy, forward Ian Henderson broke into the first team in 2002/03 before enjoying his most productive season at Carrow Road during the 2003/04 title-winning campaign.

With the ability to operate as an out-and-out forward or in an advanced wide position, Henderson chipped in with four goals for Nigel Worthington's team in 2003/04. He came off the bench to replace Kevin Harper with City trailing 1-0 away to Walsall in November 2003 and scored the equaliser as City produced a breathtaking salvo of three goals in 12 minutes to run out 3-1 winners.

Henderson was rewarded for his impressive introduction against the Saddlers with a start in the following home fixture against Millwall and he scored twice in a comfortable 3-1 win. His rich vein of scoring form then saw him grab his fourth goal in five games as Norwich drew 1-1 at home to Coventry City. The arrivals of Leon McKenzie and Mathias Svensson, and the permanent signing of Darren Huckerby, limited first-team opportunities for Henderson and fellow academy star Ryan Jarvis, but the youngster made 19 appearances and ended a memorable campaign with a First Division champions' medal.

HERNANDEZ, Onel

Date of birth: 1 February 1993
Place of birth: Moron, Cuba
Position: Midfielder
Promotion campaign: 2018/19 Championship champions
2018/19 League statistics: 34(6)8

Flying winger Onel Hernandez certainly set his stall out for an impactful 2018/19 season as he bagged a brace when City twice came from behind to secure a 2-2 draw from their opening day clash with Birmingham City at St Andrew's.

With electric pace and clever close control, the Cuban-born attacker produced a number of memorable performances in City's promotion-winning campaign. He also contributed some vital goals, most notably the incredible late equaliser against Nottingham Forest on Boxing Day 2018 as City came from 3-0 down to salvage a point on an unforgettable afternoon at Carrow Road. He also fired home the only goal of the game to seal a vital win away to Middlesbrough as City ended March 2019 with a seventh straight league victory.

Amusingly, Hernandez shot to national prominence early in 2019 when he declared his love of shopping at Argos in a Norwich City programme interview! The revelation resulted in him opening a new-look Argos store in Norwich as City fans flocked to meet their hero at an in-store signing event.

HILL, Jimmy

Date of birth: 31 October 1935
Place of birth: Co Antrim
Position: Midfielder
Promotion campaign: 1959/60 Division Three runners-up
1959/60 League statistics: 38(n/a)16

Jimmy Hill was ever-present throughout the Canaries' memorable 1958/59 FA Cup adventure, and like so many of the cup heroes he remained at the club the following season as City secured promotion to the Second Division.

Hill ended the 1959/60 campaign as joint leading scorer alongside Terry Allcock with 16 goals. The fact that he netted his 16 goals from 38 matches, versus Allcock's 44 outings, gave Hill the title of the team's best goals-to-games marksman come the conclusion of an incredible season.

The skilful Irishman was on target in City's opening day 2-2 draw at Southampton and he netted three league braces for Archie Macaulay's side en route to promotion. His first pair came in the 5-1 demolition of Port Vale at Carrow Road on 12 September 1959 and he was at the double again a month later to help secure a 3-2 victory over Colchester United at Carrow Road. A hat-trick of doubles was completed when Hill was twice on target in the 3-1 home victory over Wrexham on 6 February 1960.

HOADLEY, Phil

Date of birth: 6 February 1952
Place of birth: Battersea
Position: Defender
Promotion campaign: 1981/82 third in Division Two
1981/82 League statistics: 3(1)-

A fully committed and tough-tackling defender, Phil Hoadley played over 70 top-flight matches for the Canaries after joining the club from Orient ahead of the 1978/79 campaign.

In truth, his Carrow Road career was reaching its conclusion when he made four league appearances in the club's 1981/82 Second Division campaign. His first slice of action in 1981/82 came when he replaced goalscorer Ross Jack in City's 3-2 win at Wrexham in September 1981.

He played in the surprise 2-1 home defeat to Oldham Athletic on 3 October 1981 before making his final Carrow Road outing a fortnight later with a win as City overcame Shrewsbury Town 2-1.

Hoadley played his final game for Norwich on 24 October 1981 as Ken Brown's side suffered a 3-0 defeat away to Watford. He later played in Hong Kong before injury ended his career and he returned to Norfolk and began working for the club's Football in the Community scheme.

HOLT, Gary
Date of birth: 9 March 1973
Place of birth: Irvine
Position: Midfielder
Promotion campaign: 2003/04 First Division champions
2003/04 League statistics: 46(-)1

Energetic midfielder Gary Holt joined the Canaries on the eve of the 2001 transfer deadline from Kilmarnock for a reported fee of £100,000.

The Scot soon became the heartbeat of the Nigel Worthington side that reached the 2001/02 play-off final. An ever-present 2001/02 season saw him collect the Barry Butler Memorial Trophy after being voted the supporters' player of the season. Holt remained one of the first names on the manager's team-sheet for the next two campaigns as the Canaries eventually won promotion back to the top flight in 2003/04.

Once again the reliable Holt was ever-present throughout the 2003/04 season when he formed an excellent partnership with Damien Francis in the Canary engine room. His commitment to the team was further demonstrated in early November when he took up an unfamiliar role at right-back for three games to cover for the injured Marc Edworthy. A true box-to-box midfielder, Holt was never renowned for his goalscoring but did hit the target on Valentine's Day 2004 as City defeated Coventry City 2-0 at Highfield Road.

HOLT, Grant
Date of birth: 12 April 1981
Place of birth: Carlisle
Position: Striker
Promotion campaigns: 2009/10 League One champions and 2010/11 Championship runners-up
2009/10 League statistics: 39(-)24
2010/11 League statistics: 44(1)21

A goalscoring legend at Carrow Road who was absolutely adored by the Norwich fans during four memorable seasons at the club, Grant Holt was signed by Bryan Gunn from Shrewsbury Town in the summer of 2009.

Holt flourished under the management of Paul Lambert, who also made him City captain. He was the club's top scorer as City won the League One title in 2009/10 and promotion from the Championship in 2010/11.

The striker netted an unforgettable hat-trick against Ipswich Town as the Canaries hammered their local rivals 4-1 at Carrow Road on 28 November 2010, so enhancing further his reputation with the Canary faithful. Holt's 45 league goals across two seasons were the catalyst for the club's back-to-back promotion successes. He continued his impressive goalscoring tally in the Premier League and became the first player in the club's history to win the Barry Butler Memorial Trophy as player of the season on three occasions.

HOOIVELD, Jos
Date of birth: 22 April 1983
Place of birth: Zeijen
Position: Defender
Promotion campaign: 2014/15 Championship play-off winners
2014/15 League statistics: 6(-)-

Giant Dutch central-defender Jos Hooiveld joined the Canaries on a season-long loan from Premier League side Southampton ahead of the club's 2014/15 Championship campaign.

His Canary debut came on 13 September 2014 as Norwich produced a stirring comeback to turn a 2-0 half-time deficit into an heroic 4-2 victory away to Cardiff City. Hooiveld made a total of six appearances in the early part of the season under the management of Neil Adams and boasted an unbeaten record as a City player – the team registering three wins and three draws in the six matches he played.

His final outing for the Canaries came in the 3-3 draw at home to Brighton & Hove Albion on 22 November 2014. Following Adams's departure from Carrow Road in January 2015, it soon became clear that Hooiveld was not in new boss Alex Neil's plans. The player's loan deal was terminated with the experienced defender subsequently free to link-up with fellow Championship side Millwall.

HOOLAHAN, Wes

Date of birth: 20 May 1982
Place of birth: Dublin
Position: Midfielder
Promotion campaigns: 2009/10 League One champions, 2010/11 Championship runners-up and 2014/15 Championship play-off winners
2009/10 League statistics: 36(1)11
2010/11 League statistics: 36(5)10
2014/15 League statistics: 27(9)4 + play-offs 2(1)1

Wes Hoolahan is one of only a trio of Norwich City players to feature in three different post-war promotions for the club, the other two being Adam Drury and Russell Martin.

An extremely talented playmaker, Hoolahan was signed from Blackpool by then City boss Glenn Roeder in the summer of 2008. The Republic of Ireland international flourished under the management of Paul Lambert, playing at the tip of a diamond formation behind Grant Holt and Chris Martin and scoring 11 goals as City cantered to the 2009/10 League One title. The 2010/11 season saw Hoolahan again weigh in with double figures in the goals column, including a hat-trick as a substitute against Sheffield United in December 2010, while also laying on countless chances for team-mates.

Arguably the highlight of his Canary career was the Wembley play-off final triumph over Middlesbrough in May 2015, all of which was possible after City saw off arch rivals Ipswich Town in the second leg of the semi-final – a match that saw Hoolahan open the scoring from the penalty spot in front of a delighted Barclay.

HOOPER, Gary

Date of birth: 26 January 1988
Place of birth: Harlow
Position: Striker
Promotion campaign: 2014/15 Championship play-off winners
2014/15 League statistics: 16(14)12 + play-offs -(2)-

Gary Hooper was not often granted a starting place during the Canaries' successful 2014/15 play-off winning campaign. Despite regularly finding himself behind Lewis Grabban and Cameron Jerome in the quest for a striking role, Hooper still chipped in with a highly impressive 12 Championship goals.

The former Celtic man netted a brace in the 6-1 Boxing Day romp at home to Millwall and became the only City player to score a hat-trick in 2014/15 when he departed Carrow Road with the match ball following the Canaries' 4-0 victory over Blackpool on 7 February 2015.

In the latter stages of the campaign, as Alex Neil's men chased down Bournemouth and Watford, before finishing third, Hooper scored a vital last-gasp winner at Bolton and then let fly with a memorable volley to secure a point from the club's first visit to Rotherham United's New York Stadium on 25 April 2015. He appeared from the bench in both legs of the play-off semi-final but was an unused substitute in the Wembley final.

HOWARD, Trevor

Date of birth: 2 June 1948
Place of birth: King's Lynn
Position: Midfielder

Promotion campaign: 1971/72 Division Two champions
1971/72 League statistics: 8(12)5 -

Norfolk-born Trevor Howard featured in a number of roles for the Canaries throughout the late 60s and early 70s. His ability to play in various positions made him a valuable member of the City squad during his seven-season spell as a pro at Carrow Road.

Displaying such levels of flexibility resulted in Howard often appearing from the substitute's bench and hindered his attempts to cement a permanent position and place in the starting line-up.

The 1971/72 campaign saw Howard make 20 Second Division appearances but only eight were starts. Despite appearing in just eight league games from the off, Howard contributed five goals – three of which came from substitute appearances, which went some way to helping him earn the 'super sub' tag. He marked starts against Blackpool (away) and Oxford United (home) with goals in consecutive City victories. Two of his three strikes from the bench helped secure home victories over Luton Town and Hull City.

HOWSON, Jonny

Date of birth: 21 May 1988
Place of birth: Morley
Position: Midfielder
Promotion campaign: 2014/15 Championship play-off winners
2014/15 League statistics: 32(2)8 + play-offs 3(-)1

Signed from Leeds United in January 2012, Jonny Howson's arrival at Carrow Road was seen as a major coup for the Canaries and he went on to become a key player for City during his five-year spell in Norfolk.

With a great range of passing skills and eye for goal, Howson loved to get forward and support the attack. He scored a number of memorable goals, including the winner on the final day of the season at Manchester City in 2013 following a solo run and finish.

Generally viewed as a Rolls Royce performer during the 2014/15 season, Howson was sent off in Alex Neil's first match as City boss as the Canaries triumphed at Bournemouth on 10 January 2015. After serving his suspension he returned to the side and scored five vital league goals before also netting in the first leg of the play-off semi-final away to Ipswich Town.

HUBBARD, Phil

Date of birth: 25 January 1949
Place of birth: Lincoln
Position: Midfielder
Promotion campaign: 1971/72 Division Two champions
1971/72 League statistics: 6(2)1

Recruited from Lincoln City during the 1971/72 season, Phil Hubbard provided both cover and options in the Canary midfield as Ron Saunders's side went on to land the Second Division title and a place among English football's elite.

Tall, mobile and forceful – Hubbard certainly displayed all the attributes that Saunders craved from his midfield men. He debuted immediately after his arrival from Sincil Bank as City ended the calendar year of 1972 with a 3-0 victory over Charlton Athletic at Carrow Road on 27 December.

Hubbard netted his first and only goal for the Canaries in his third game as City ran out 2-1 winners at home to Fulham on 8 January 1972. Despite an impressive start to his Carrow Road career, Hubbard was unable to win a regular place in the side, but he did figure in the promotion celebrations at Brisbane Road on 24 April 1972 as he replaced Alan Black in City's promotion-sealing 2-1 victory.

HUCKERBY, Darren

Date of birth: 23 April 1976
Place of birth: Nottingham
Position: Striker
Promotion campaign: 2003/04
  First Division champions
2003/04 League statistics:
  36(-)14

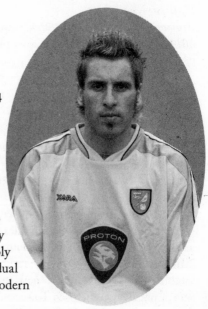

Darren Huckerby is unsurprisingly viewed by a large number of Norwich City fans as the best player to ever pull on a Norwich City shirt. He has unquestionably been the most exciting individual to represent the club in the modern era.

After joining the Canaries on a three-month loan deal from Manchester City in September 2003, the club confirmed his permanent arrival amidst unforgettable scenes prior to the game against Nottingham Forest on Boxing Day 2003. Huckerby's pace and skill terrorised rival defences throughout that season as City stormed to the title by eight clear points.

He produced countless match-winning performances during the 2004/05 campaign, including a memorable display against Cardiff City at Carrow Road in the final match of his loan spell. He weighed in with 14 goals and added the elusive element of extra quality that ensured Nigel Worthington's men finished top of the pile. Huckerby was twice voted player of the season and was also added to the club's Hall of Fame as he became a Norwich City legend during his four-and-a-half years at Carrow Road.

HUGHES, Stephen
Date of birth: 14 November 1982
Place of birth: Motherwell
Position: Midfielder
Promotion campaigns: 2009/10 League One champions and 2010/11
    Championship runners-up
2009/10 League statistics: 12(17)3
2010/11 League statistics: -(1)-

Scottish midfielder Stephen Hughes joined the Canaries in the summer of 2009 and enjoyed being part of a City squad that secured back-to-back promotion successes in 2009/10 and 2010/11.

Following spells with Glasgow Rangers, Leicester City and Motherwell, Hughes was signed by Bryan Gunn as a free agent in July 2009. He featured in 29 of City's 2009/10 League One fixtures and netted his first goal for the club in the 2-0 win at Hartlepool on 29 August 2009. In late November he came off the bench to grab a second-half equaliser in the 2-2 draw at Southampton.

Hughes's third and final goal for City came in the last away match of the League One title-winning campaign as Paul Lambert's men cruised to a 3-0 win at Bristol Rovers. Following the arrival of David Fox, Andrew Crofts and Andrew Surman, Hughes found opportunities hard to come by in 2010/11, with his last first-team action for the club coming in the 3-1 defeat away to Doncaster Rovers in September 2010.

HUSBAND, James
Date of birth: 3 January 1994
Place of birth: Leeds
Position: Defender
Promotion campaign: 2018/19 Championship champions
2018/19 League statistics: 1(-)-

As the Canaries' 2018/19 season kicked off away to Birmingham City, James Husband was the only name on the Norwich teamsheet that also started the previous season's opening-day draw at Fulham.

Signed from Championship rivals Middlesbrough in July 2017, the left-back agreed a three-year deal at Carrow Road. In the main, the 2017/18 season saw Husband share left-back duties with fellow summer signing Marco Stiepermann prior to the emergence of Jamal Lewis. An experienced player, Husband turned professional with Doncaster Rovers before joining Middlesbrough. His time at the Riverside saw him taking in loan spells with Fulham and Huddersfield Town.

Husband's place in the City line-up at St Andrew's was due to an injury to Lewis, who had missed the majority of the pre-season programme. He was withdrawn in the second half, with Moritz Leitner coming into midfield and Stiepermann dropping back to left-back. That proved to be his only involvement for City in 2018/19 as he then joined League One Fleetwood on a season-long loan deal.

JACK, Ross
Date of birth: 21 March 1959
Place of birth: Avoch, nr Inverness
Position: Striker
Promotion campaign: 1981/82 third in Division Two
1981/82 League statistics: 24(11)10

Signed from Everton for a bargain £20,000 in 1979, Ross Jack arrived at Carrow Road as a striker but was converted to more of an attacking midfielder by the Canary management team of Ken Brown and Mel Machin.

Jack hit a rich vein of form early in the 1981/82 season when he netted in six consecutive Second Division fixtures. His prolific spell began with a goal in the 1-1 Carrow Road draw with Barnsley on 5 September 1981. The Scot then scored in victories over Wrexham,

Newcastle United and Grimsby Town before netting consolation goals in 2-1 defeats against Chelsea and Oldham Athletic.

With Keith Bertschin and John Deehan spearheading the City attack in the second half of the 1981/82 campaign, Jack often found himself as City's twelfth man and appeared 11 times from the bench. He weighed in with ten league goals in total, his final strike coming in the 5-0 rout of Charlton Athletic at Carrow Road when he replaced Dave Bennett as City continued their ascent of the Second Division table.

JACKSON, Simeon

Date of birth: 28 March 1987
Place of birth: Kingston, Jamaica
Position: Striker
Promotion campaign: 2010/11 Championship runners-up
2010/11 League statistics: 20(19)13

Canadian international striker Simeon Jackson was a big hit at Carrow Road with vital goals in the 2010/11 Championship campaign, including the one that sealed promotion to the Premier League at Portsmouth.

His first Canary goal came against Swansea, and he then netted a useful brace in the 3-0 win over Bristol City with strikes either side of a Wes Hoolahan penalty at Ashton Gate in October 2010.

Jackson really came to the fore in the final weeks of the season as City secured the second automatic promotion spot. His crucial goals included two hat-tricks, the first against Scunthorpe United and a never-to-be-forgotten treble against Derby County at Carrow Road. During his time at Norwich, Jackson took the mantle of scoring the final competitive goal of the Paul Lambert era and the first of Chris Hughton's reign as City boss.

JARVIS, Ryan

Date of birth: 11 July 1986
Place of birth: Fakenham
Position: Striker
Promotion campaign: 2003/04 First Division champions
2003/04 League statistics: -(12)1

A skilful striker with quick feet and great awareness, Ryan Jarvis progressed through the Canaries' academy set-up and briefly held the title of being the club's youngest-ever player.

Jarvis made his first-team debut on 19 April 2003 in a goalless draw at Walsall and featured in a dozen of the Canaries' First Division fixtures the following season. All of his league involvement in 2003/04 came from the bench and his only goal of the campaign came in City's surprise 2-1 defeat at home to Watford on 15 November 2003 when Jarvis's late strike at the River End set up a grandstand finish before the visitors held out for all three points.

As the season progressed and Nigel Worthington strengthened his squad with the arrivals of Leon McKenzie and Mathias Svensson, and the permanent signing of Darren Huckerby, there were limited opportunities for Jarvis and fellow academy graduate Ian Henderson. Jarvis's final contribution for 2003/04 saw him replace Henderson for the final five minutes of a 3-0 home win against Gillingham on 16 March 2004.

JEROME, Cameron
Date of birth: 14 August 1986
Place of birth: Huddersfield
Position: Striker
Promotion campaign: 2014/15
2014/15 League statistics: 32(9)18 + play-offs 3(-)2

Powerful and much-travelled striker Cameron Jerome joined the Canaries in August 2014 from Stoke City. He marked his debut with a goal in a League Cup victory at home to Crawley Town and proved to be one of Neil Adams's best signings during his short reign as Norwich boss.

Jerome was a major asset in the 2014/15 promotion-winning campaign under Alex Neil and marked the Scot's first game in charge with a memorable and spectacular late winner away to Bournemouth in January 2015. The striker etched his name into Norwich

City folklore with the third and final goal in the play-off semi-final second leg against Ipswich Town as City secured an aggregate 4-2 victory and a first-ever trip to the new, redeveloped Wembley Stadium.

On an unforgettable afternoon in the proud history of Norwich City Football Club, Jerome opened the scoring in the play-off final victory over Middlesbrough. The striker netted from the tightest of angles before Nathan Redmond added the second in a 2-0 Wembley triumph.

JOHNSON, Bradley
Date of birth: 28 April 1987
Place of birth: Hackney
Position: Midfielder
Promotion campaign: 2014/15 Championship play-off winners
2014/15 League statistics: 40(1)15 + play-offs 3(-)-

Popular all-action midfielder Bradley Johnson was the inspirational driving force behind Norwich City's 2014/15 success as the Canaries sealed an immediate return to the Premier League following their end-of-season play-off victory.

Signed by Paul Lambert in 2011 from Leeds United, following the Canaries' promotion to the Premier League, Johnson was a regular face in the City side under Lambert, Chris Hughton, Neil Adams and Alex Neil.

The Londoner enjoyed an outstanding 2014/15 campaign and was rewarded with the Barry Butler Memorial Trophy after the supporters voted him the club's player of the season. Johnson scored an incredible 15 goals from midfield, a haul that was only bettered by leading scorer Cameron Jerome with 18. Among Johnson's goals were a number of spectacular efforts, including a memorable late winner away to Blackburn Rovers, which was followed five days later by another stunning strike to open the scoring in the 2-0 East Anglian derby victory over Ipswich Town on 1 March 2015.

JOHNSON, Oli
Date of birth: 6 November 1987
Place of birth: Wakefield
Position: Striker
Promotion campaigns: 2009/10 League One champions and 2010/11
   Championship runners-up

2009/10 League statistics: 4(13)4
2010/11 League statistics: -(4)-

Norwich City plucked striker Oli Johnson from Stockport County in January 2010 during the club's League One campaign. Prior to his arrival at Edgeley Park, Johnson was plying his trade on the non-league scene when County spotted his raw potential.

With a majority of the country covered in snow, Johnson made his Canary debut at home to Exeter City on 9 January 2010 on a weekend when very few League One fixtures beat the big freeze. Johnson replaced Wes Hoolahan in the latter stages of City's 3-1 victory over the Grecians and a week later he marked his second appearance from the bench with his first goal for the club when he netted City's fourth in the 5-0 thrashing of Colchester United.

Johnson will be fondly remembered by City fans for a late brace against Southend United at Carrow Road in February 2010, as the hosts came from behind to seal a vital 2-1 win. He formed part of the 2010/11 squad but was limited to just four substitute appearances – the final of which came in City's first-ever trip to the new Cardiff City stadium on 30 October 2010.

KEELAN, Kevin

Date of birth: 5 January 1941
Place of birth: Calcutta
Position: Goalkeeper
Promotion campaigns: 1971/72 Division Two champions and 1974/75 third in Division Two
1971/72 League statistics: 42(-)-
1974/75 League statistics: 38(-)-

Legendary keeper Kevin Keelan is Norwich City's record appearance maker, having appeared in a colossal 673 games for the club over a 17-year period from 1963 to 1980.

Keelan often wooed the Canary faithful by producing spectacular saves and displaying breathtaking reflexes to thwart the opposition. A top performer in the club's history-making 1971/72 season, Keelan was ever-present as the Canaries reached Division One for the first time.

As Ron Saunders's side maintained their top-flight status in 1972/73, Keelan's performances saw him collect the Barry Butler Memorial Trophy as the club's player of the season. The keeper played in both of City's League Cup finals at Wembley in 1973 and 1975. He then added a second promotion to his glowing Canary CV when he missed just four games of Norwich's 1974/75 promotion success. A member of the club's Hall of Fame and voted into City's 'Greatest Ever' line-up in 2008, Keelan remains an extremely popular guest when he returns to Carrow Road from his home in Florida.

KENNON, Sandy
Date of birth: 28 November 1933
Place of birth: Johannesburg
Date of death: 17 August 2015
Place of death: Norwich
Position: Goalkeeper
Promotion campaign: 1959/60 Division Three runners-up
1959/60 League statistics: 45(-)-

Goalkeeper Sandy Kennon replaced the injured Ken Nethercott during the club's gallant 1958/59 FA Cup adventure. Kennon's Canary debut came in the white-hot atmosphere of an FA Cup quarter-final replay with Sheffield United at Carrow Road. The 3-2 victory over the Blades saw City reach the semi-final for the first time as Kennon overcame a shaky start to star on the first of his 255 outings for the Canaries.

Kennon missed just one league game the following season as City backed up their FA Cup heroics by sealing the runners-up spot in the Third Division in 1959/60. Forced to sit out the 3-2 Carrow Road victory over Swindon Town on 7 November 1959, when Brian Ronson deputised, Kennon recorded a highly impressive 16 clean sheets from his 45 Third Division outings.

Ever-present in the club's 1961/62 League Cup triumph, Kennon later played for Colchester United and locally for Lowestoft Town before becoming a popular match-day host for corporate guests at Carrow Road. He died in August 2015, aged 81.

KLOSE, Timm
Date of birth: 9 May 1988
Place of birth: Frankfurt
Position: Defender
Promotion campaign: 2018/19 Championship champions
2018/19 League statistics: 23(8)4

Signed from Wolfsburg in January 2016, giant Swiss defender Timm

Klose chipped in with four vital goals in the Canaries' 2018/19 promotion-winning campaign.

Paired with skipper Grant Hanley for the opening game of the season away to Birmingham City, the Swiss international soon had to forge a new central-defensive understanding alongside Christoph Zimmermann after injury sidelined Hanley from first-team action. Klose struck up a solid partnership with Zimmermann and the Canaries' results swiftly began to improve.

The central-defender netted his first goal of the season when he headed City in front during a midweek trip to Derby County on 3 October 2018. His goal at Pride Park was cancelled out by a late Craig Bryson equaliser in a 1-1 draw and Klose was on target in the East Midlands again later in the month when he scored both goals in a 2-1 win at Nottingham Forest on 30 October 2018. A positive presence around the squad, Klose scored again to rescue City a vital point from their New Year's Day trip to Brentford.

KRUL, Tim
Date of birth: 3 April 1988
Place of birth: The Hague
Position: Goalkeeper
Promotion campaign: 2018/19 Championship champions
2018/19 League statistics: 46(-)-

Dutch international goalkeeper Tim Krul joined the Canaries in July 2018 after spending the previous season as back-up keeper at Premier League Brighton & Hove Albion.

A previous promotion winner at Championship level with Newcastle United, Krul's arrival brought vast experience and a confident personality to the changing room. After Angus Gunn had returned to his parent club, Manchester City, following a successful loan spell in the City goal throughout 2017/18, the Canaries' number-one shirt was very much up for grabs as the pre-season programme gathered pace.

Despite the efforts of Michael McGovern and Remi Matthews, there was little surprise when Krul emerged as Daniel Farke's first-choice stopper come the opening game of the season at St Andrew's. With a lack of first-team action prior to his arrival in Norfolk, Krul did appear a little rusty in the opening games of the season but soon went on to pull off a number of exceptional match-winning saves. His performance in the 2-2 draw away to Bristol City in

December was particularly impressive, as was the manner in which he continued to organise the young defensive unit that was in front of him throughout the season.

LAFFERTY, Kyle

Date of birth: 16 September 1987
Place of birth: Enniskillen
Position: Striker
Promotion campaign: 2014/15 Championship play-off winners
2014/15 League statistics: 11(7)1

Northern Ireland international striker Kyle Lafferty joined Norwich City in the summer of 2014 and agreed a three-year contract as boss Neil Adams began to rebuild the squad in pursuit of an immediate return to the Premier League.

Despite impressing at Championship level with Burnley earlier in his career, Lafferty proved to be a disappointing acquisition and struggled to make an impact at Carrow Road. Handed a debut from the bench in City's opening game of the season away to Wolves, Lafferty then started City's first home game of the 2014/15 campaign as Adams's men saw off Watford 3-0 on 16 August 2014. The big Irishman had to wait until January 2015 to finally score his first league goal in City colours as he netted in the 3-2 victory over Cardiff City in what was new boss Alex Neil's first home game as Canary boss.

With Cameron Jerome, Lewis Grabban and Gary Hooper all ahead of Lafferty in the pecking order for a place in Neil's starting line-up, the striker joined Turkish club Caykur Rizespor for the remainder of the 2014/15 campaign.

LANSBURY, Henri

Date of birth: 12 October 1990
Place of birth: Enfield
Position: Midfielder
Promotion campaign: 2010/11 Championship runners-up
2010/11 League statistics: 15(8)4

Talented Arsenal youngster Henri Lansbury initially joined the Canaries on a one-month loan deal from the Gunners in November 2010. He made his debut in the 4-1 local derby victory over Ipswich Town and made a great impression during his loan spell. Such was Lansbury's positive influence on the City side that the club swiftly moved to extend the loan deal for the remainder of the season. Lansbury made 23 league appearances and chipped in with some vital goals, including late strikes in midweek fixtures against Millwall and Bristol City at Carrow Road as City went on to seal promotion to the Premier League.

An England under-21 international, Lansbury featured in the final game of the season at home to Coventry City and took part in the civic celebrations that followed the Canaries' return to the big time. He then returned to his parent club, with many City fans hopeful that he would be back at Carrow Road again for the 2011/12 campaign. However, that outing against the Sky Blues proved to be his final game in Canary yellow.

LAPPIN, Simon

Date of birth: 25 January 1983
Place of birth: Glasgow
Position: Midfielder
Promotion campaigns: 2009/10 League One champions and 2010/11
  Championship runners-up
2009/10 League statistics: 42(2)-
2010/11 League statistics: 20(7)-

A popular left-sided player, who became affectionately known by the Norwich fans as the 'King of Spain', Simon Lappin originally joined City from St Mirren on 31 January 2007.

Lappin's Carrow Road career spanned six years and saw the former Scotland under-21 international figure heavily in the back-to-back promotion successes in 2009/10 and 2010/11 as the club enjoyed a meteoric rise under the inspirational management of fellow Scot Paul Lambert.

With the ability to operate at left-back or in a more advanced role on the left side of midfield, Lappin was City's most used player in the League One title-winning campaign – starting 42 of City's 46 fixtures and appearing as a substitute in two others. He was again a key member of the squad that sealed the runners-up spot in the Championship the following season and took great pride in his four Premier League appearances that followed in 2011/12.

LARKIN, Bernard (Bunny)

Date of birth: 11 January 1936
Place of birth: Birmingham

Position: Striker
Promotion campaign: 1959/60 Division Three runners-up
1959/60 League statistics: 9(n/a)3

Bunny Larkin made an instant impression in the Canaries' 1959/60 promotion campaign as he marked his debut with both goals in a 2-1 Third Division victory away to York City on 16 March 1960.

He joined Norwich from Birmingham City and after making a two-goal start to his Canary career he missed just two games as City went on to seal promotion. Along with Errol Crossan and Brian Whitehouse, Larkin was on target in the final game of the season as City wrapped up a successful campaign with a 3-0 victory over Chesterfield at Carrow Road.

Larkin also holds a special place in the Norwich City record books, having marked his debuts for the club in all three competitions with a goal. After netting the aforementioned brace against the Minstermen, he also scored on his FA Cup debut for City (also against York) and was on target when making his League Cup bow for the club against Oldham Athletic in the 1960/61 season.

LEITNER, Moritz
Date of birth: 8 December 1992
Place of birth: Munich
Position: Midfielder
Promotion campaign: 2018/19 Championship champions
2018/19 League statistics: 19(10)2

Deep-lying midfield playmaker Moritz Leitner joined the Canaries in the summer of 2018 following a loan spell at the club in the second-half of the 2017/18 campaign.

A great deal was expected of the one-time Borussia Dortmund midfielder following his permanent switch from FC Augsburg. However, Leitner began the campaign among the substitutes for the opening game of the season but soon worked his way into Daniel Farke's team. He was on target in the 1-1 East Anglian derby draw at Portman Road plus the thrilling 4-3 victory over Millwall on 10 November 2019.

Injured ahead of the hectic festive period, many feared Leitner's absence could disrupt the Canaries' progress, but the form of firstly Mario Vrancic and then Kenny McLean ensured the talented German was not missed as City enjoyed their best run of form and the promotion dream became reality. Once back to full fitness,

Leitner was limited to brief cameo roles from the bench in the final weeks of the season.

LEWIS, Jamal
Date of birth: 25 January 1998
Place of birth: Luton
Position: Defender
Promotion campaign: 2018/19 Championship champions
2018/19 League statistics: 42(-)-

Pacey left-back Jamal Lewis missed the Canaries' first two league games of the 2018/19 season due to injury. He made his first appearance of the campaign away to Sheffield United and from there on in remained an almost permanent feature of the team's defensive unit.

Recruited from the Luton Town youth system, Lewis joined the Norwich academy and was handed his first-team opportunity by Daniel Farke in December 2017. Lewis soon established himself as first-choice left-back and his emergence was, along with the performances of James Maddison and Angus Gunn, and the signing of Grant Hanley, seen as one of very few positives in a tough 2017/18 season at Carrow Road.

Extremely comfortable on the ball and with a burning desire to get forward and support attacking moves, Lewis enjoys his forays forward but has the ability to ensure they are not at the expense of his defensive duties. His full-back pairing with fellow academy graduate Max Aarons was undoubtedly a major factor in the Canaries' promotion success in 2018/19. The full-back's club form has already won him full international caps with Northern Ireland despite his tender years.

LIVERMORE, Doug
Date of birth: 27 December 1947
Place of birth: Liverpool
Position: Midfielder
Promotion campaigns: 1971/72 Division Two champions and 1974/75 third in Division Two
1971/72 League statistics: 41(-)-
1974/75 League statistics: 2(1)-

Gritty midfielder Doug Livermore played a vital role in Ron Saunders's 1971/72 title-winning side, missing just one match throughout an historic league campaign that ended with First Division football coming to Norfolk for the first time.

City boss Saunders recruited fellow Scouser Livermore from Liverpool in November 1970, and the hard-working midfielder swiftly became an integral part of the Norwich side. Sitting alongside midfield playmaker Graham Paddon, Livermore's grafting performances won him many admirers and phenomenal respect from his team-mates.

After suffering a knee injury during a League Cup tie with Southampton in November 1973, a setback which sidelined him for almost a year, he did return to the City side to make three appearances in the 1974/75 promotion-winning campaign. Later, during a highly successful coaching career, Livermore in fact celebrated a third promotion in Canary colours when he assisted Nigel Worthington in the club's 2003/04 First Division title triumph.

LOZA, Jamar
Date of birth: 10 May 1994
Place of birth: Kingston, Jamaica
Position: Striker
Promotion campaign: 2014/15 Championship play-off winners
2014/15 League statistics: -(2)1

Striker Jamar Loza progressed through the Canaries' academy to play Premier League football and win full international honours with Jamaica during his Carrow Road career.

Bizarrely, Loza was in fact released from Norwich in the summer of 2012 by Paul Lambert but recalled to the club by new boss Chris Hughton and subsequently handed a contract. A regular goalscorer at under-21 level, his performances as a mobile front man saw him take in a host of loan moves, which included stints at Coventry City, Leyton Orient and Southend United. His Norwich debut came under Neil Adams in the final game of the 2013/14 season at home to Arsenal, with City having already been relegated from the Premier League.

Loza made just two substitute appearances in the 2014/15 campaign, the first under Adams as City suffered a surprise 1-0 defeat at home to lowly Charlton Athletic in September 2014. The striker then marked his second league outing of the season with his only goal for the club as Alex Neil's Canaries rescued a point away to Huddersfield Town in March 2015 after Loza netted eight minutes into injury time to secure a 2-2 draw.

MacDOUGALL, Ted

Date of birth: 8 January 1947
Place of birth: Inverness
Position: Striker
Promotion campaign: 1974/75 Third in Division Two
1974/75 League statistics: 42(-)16

Leading goalscorer in each of his three seasons at Carrow Road, ace marksman Ted MacDougall netted 16 Second Division goals in an ever-present 1974/75 campaign as Norwich secured an instant return to the top flight.

MacDougall formed an outstanding strike partnership with Phil Boyer throughout his Canary career, and the two men scored an impressive 32 league goals between them in 1974/75. After scoring 11 goals in his debut season at the club, MacDougall began the 1974/75 campaign by heading home the winning goal against Blackpool as City marked opening day with a 2-1 Carrow Road triumph.

As a former Manchester United man, MacDougall took great delight in netting a brace against his table-topping former employers to seal a 2-0 home win on 28 September 1974. He netted a second brace of the season in a thrilling 3-2 victory over West Bromwich Albion as City twice came from behind to secure both points in front of over 34,000 fans at Carrow Road on 8 February 1975.

MACHIN, Mel

Date of birth: 16 April 1945
Place of birth: Newcastle-under-Lyme
Position: Defender
Promotion campaign: 1974/75 third in Division Two
1974/75 League statistics: 24(-)3

In similar fashion to team-mate Doug Livermore, Mel Machin tasted promotion glory with the Canaries as both a player and a coach.

Machin's playing career saw him take the well-trodden path from Dean Court to Carrow Road when he joined the Canaries in December 1973 from Bournemouth. Famed for his goal-preventing handball in the 1975 League Cup Final, Machin made 24 league appearances and netted a remarkable hat-trick at the City Ground as City triumphed 3-1 against Nottingham Forest on 12 October 1974.

After playing his part in City's promotion success in 1974/75, Machin starred once again the following season as City recorded a top-ten finish in the First Division. A deserved member of the club's Hall of Fame, Machin later served as Ken Brown's right-hand man as City secured promotions to the top flight in 1981/82 and 1985/86 plus League Cup glory at Wembley in 1985.

MACKAY, Malky
Date of birth: 19 February 1972
Place of birth: Bellshill
Position: Defender
Promotion campaign: 2003/04 First Division champions
2003/04 League statistics: 45(-)4

Alongside player-of-the-season Craig Fleming, giant Scottish centre-half Malky Mackay formed part of the central-defensive rock that underpinned the Canaries' First Division title triumph in 2003/04.

A member of the City side that suffered play-off heartbreak in 2001/02, Mackay missed just one league game in the 2003/04 success when suspension forced him to sit out the 4-1 Carrow Road victory over Cardiff City on 13 December 2003.

A strong, robust and powerful defender, Mackay was always a great threat from set-piece situations in the opposition's penalty area and scored four league goals en route to promotion. He headed home an 89th-minute winner to seal a 2-1 victory at home to Crystal Palace in September and was also on target as City ended 2003 in formidable fashion with a 4-0 win at Derby County. Mackay was very much the toast of Norfolk as he scored twice in the 3-1 East Anglian derby victory over Ipswich Town at Carrow Road on 7 March 2004.

MARSHALL, Ben
Date of birth: 29 March 1991
Place of birth: Salford
Position: Midfielder
Promotion campaign: 2018/19 Championship champions
2018/19 League statistics: 4(-)-

A vastly experienced campaigner at Championship level, Ben Marshall joined the Canary ranks from Wolverhampton Wanderers in June 2018 after agreeing a four-year deal at Carrow Road.

With the ability to operate comfortably at right-back or in a more advanced role on the right side of midfield, Marshall was expected to fit in perfectly to Daniel Farke's style of play with his proven track record as an attack-minded full-back. After Marshall had spent the second-half of the 2017/18 season on loan at Millwall, the Lions were also keen on his summer signature but the Canaries' ambitions saw Marshall opt for Norwich City.

He debuted in the opening-day draw at Birmingham City but really struggled to make a positive impact in the opening weeks of the season. His four league appearances all came in the opening month of the season for a City team that laboured to four points from five games. After then becoming limited to cup action, Marshall joined Millwall on loan following the Canaries' FA Cup exit to Portsmouth in January 2019.

MARTIN, Chris
Date of birth: 4 November 1988
Place of birth: Beccles
Position: Striker
Promotion campaigns: 2009/10 League One champions and 2010/11
    Championship runners-up
2009/10 League statistics: 36(6)17
2009/10 League statistics: 21(9)4

A product of the Canaries' academy, striker Chris Martin joined the club at the age of nine and featured in two promotion-winning campaigns during his 117-appearance and 34-goal Canary career.

After breaking through to the first team, Martin then took in a highly beneficial loan spell with Luton Town before returning to Carrow Road ahead of the 2009/10 League One campaign. Often forming part of a three-pronged attack with Grant Holt and Wes Hoolahan, Martin netted 17 times as City landed the League One title. His 17-goal haul included vital strikes to seal three points at home to Brentford and Leeds United plus a brace in the 5-0 revenge mission away to Colchester United.

The 2010/11 season saw first-team opportunities harder to come by following the summer signing of Simeon Jackson plus the arrival of Aaron Wilbraham and loan moves for strikers Sam Vokes and Danny Pacheco. However, Martin still made a valuable contribution with four goals from his 21 league starts as Norwich secured back-to-back promotions.

MARTIN, Russell
Date of birth: 4 January 1986
Place of birth: Brighton
Position: Defender
Promotion campaigns: 2009/10 League One champions, 2010/11 Championship runners-up and 2014/15 Championship play-off winners
2009/10 League statistics: 26(-)-
2010/11 League statistics: 46(-)5
2014/15 League statistics: 45(-)2 + play-offs 3(-)-

With over 300 first-team appearances for the club and three promotion-winning campaigns, defender Russell Martin fully deserves the label of 'Canary legend'.

Plucked from Peterborough United in November 2009 by Paul Lambert, who had previously managed him at Wycombe Wanderers, Martin swiftly made the right-back berth his own as City secured the League One title. Martin was then an instrumental figure in the back-to-back promotion success that followed in 2010/11. The ultra-reliable defender was ever-present and chipped in with vital goals at home to promotion rivals Queens Park Rangers and Cardiff City.

Surely the proudest moment of an outstanding Norwich City career came on 25 May 2015 when he captained City to promotion-winning glory via the Championship play-off final at Wembley. After skippering the team to a 2-0 victory over Middlesbrough, Martin led his team up the famous Wembley steps before hoisting aloft the trophy to the delight of over 40,000 Canary fans.

McCROHAN, Roy
Date of birth: 22 September 1930
Place of birth: Reading

Date of death: 3 March 2015
Place of death: Exmouth
Position: Defender
Promotion campaign: 1959/60 Division Three runners-up
1959/60 League statistics: 46(-)1

Only five men have made more first-team appearances for Norwich City than Roy McCrohan. A loyal club servant, McCrohan was ever-present throughout the famous 1958/59 FA Cup run and went on to savour promotion to the Second Division and League Cup glory during his Carrow Road career.

McCrohan featured in every single game of the Canaries' 1959/60 season as City sealed promotion from the Third Division as runners-up to champions Southampton. One of his 23 goals for the club also came during that season when he found himself on the scoresheet in a 1-1 draw at home to Grimsby Town on 16 April 1960.

After scoring against the Mariners, promotion was secured on home soil three games later when Southend United were defeated 4-3. Fittingly, McCrohan served City well at Second Division level and marked the end of his Canary carer with victory over Rochdale in the 1962 League Cup Final. He always remained a hugely popular character at reunion events before his death in 2015, aged 84.

McDONALD, Cody
Date of birth: 30 May 1986
Place of birth: Witham
Position: Striker
Promotion campaign: 2009/10 League One champions
2009/10 League statistics: 4(13)3

Spotted plying his trade at non-league Dartford by Bryan Gunn, striker Cody McDonald joined Norwich City in February 2009. He marked his City debut with a goal in true 'Roy of the Rovers' style as City defeated Cardiff City 2-0 at Carrow Road, but together with his new team-mates he was unable to help City prevent the drop to League One.

McDonald did score the Canaries' first goal of the 2009/10 League One title-winning season, but sadly it was somewhat overshadowed by Colchester United netting seven! As the 2009/10 campaign gathered pace under new boss Paul Lambert, McDonald featured regularly as a substitute and netted important goals in 2-1 wins against Walsall and Hartlepool in January 2010.

Despite finding league starts almost impossible to come by, due to the goalscoring form of Grant Holt and Chris Martin, McDonald remained a valued member of the City squad and was always a particularly popular figure with supporters. The following season saw him join League Two Gillingham on loan as part of the deal that brought Simeon Jackson to Carrow Road.

McGRANDLES, Conor
Date of birth: 24 September 1995
Place of birth: Falkirk
Position: Midfielder
Promotion campaign: 2014/15 Championship play-off winners
2014/15 League statistics: -(1)-

In similar vein to Leroy Fer, midfielder Conor McGrandles has just one 2014/15 substitute appearance to call upon to justify his inclusion in this publication.

A young Scottish midfielder, McGrandles was signed from Falkirk in the summer of 2014 on the recommendation of then City coach Gary Holt, who had managed the promising youngster during his time in charge at the Falkirk Stadium. McGrandles's services were acquired for a fee believed to have been in the region of £750,000 with the youngster viewed as a player of great potential for the future.

A series of injuries hampered him from making any kind of serious impact on the first-team scene at Carrow Road. His brief solo appearance came in the final stages of the 6-1 Boxing Day rout of Millwall at Carrow Road in 2014 when he replaced Bradley Johnson for his only slice of first-team action.

McGUIRE, Mick
Date of birth: 4 September 1952
Place of birth: Blackpool
Position: Midfielder
Promotion campaigns: 1974/75 third in Division Two and 1981/82 third in Division Two
1974/75 League statistics: 16(-)2
1981/82 League statistics: 39(-)2

Mick McGuire enjoyed two promotion-winning campaigns during a Norwich City career that spanned nine seasons and saw the versatile midfielder make over 200 appearances for the Canaries.

McGuire arrived in Norfolk in January 1975 following a £60,000 switch from Coventry City and made his debut on 18 January 1975 as Norwich suffered a shock 3-2 defeat at home to York City. Despite his Carrow Road bow ending in defeat, McGuire made a positive impression and even set up Dave Stinger for City's second goal. McGuire was then on the scoresheet in his next Carrow Road outing as City edged a five-goal thriller 3-2 against West Bromwich Albion. As the 1974/75 season reached its climax, McGuire headed home the opening goal of the game in a 3-0 win at Portsmouth to seal promotion on 26 April 1975. After arriving to help City win promotion under John Bond in 1975, McGuire then played in all bar three of City's 1981/82 Second Division fixtures as Ken Brown's Canaries ensured an immediate return to the top flight. The 1981/82 campaign saw McGuire net the winning goal in the club's first league meeting with nearby Cambridge United.

McKENZIE, Leon
Date of birth: 17 May 1978
Place of birth: Croydon
Position: Striker
Promotion campaign: 2003/04 First Division champions
2003/04 League statistics: 12(6)9

Striker Leon McKenzie became an instant hit with the Canary faithful after marking his Norwich City debut with both goals in a 2-0 victory in the East Anglian derby on 22 December 2003. Not only did McKenzie's two goals at Portman Road ensure local bragging rights for the Canaries, but the win shot City to the top of the First Division table.

Signed from Peterborough United, McKenzie followed up his memorable debut by scoring his third goal in as many games when he was on the scoresheet in City's 4-0 win at Derby County as Nigel Worthington's men ended 2003 in impressive style.

McKenzie netted an impressive nine goals from 18 appearances in the 2003/04 promotion-winning season, including vital strikes away to Rotherham United and Burnley. His goal against the Millers came in a pulsating 4-4 draw in January 2004 and he was on target in the nine-goal thriller at Turf Moor as City came out on top 5-3 on 3 April 2004. Always fondly remembered for his dream debut, McKenzie remains a popular guest whenever he returns to Carrow Road.

McLEAN, Kenny
Date of birth: 8 January 1992
Place of birth: Rutherglen
Position: Midfielder
Promotion campaign: 2018/19 Championship champions
2018/19 League statistics: 15(3)3

Despite joining the Canaries in the 2018 January transfer window from Aberdeen, attacking midfielder Kenny McLean saw his move to Norwich structured in such a way that he made an instant return to the Dons on loan for the remainder of the 2017/18 campaign.

The Scotland international finally arrived in Norfolk in the summer of 2018 in readiness for the 2018/19 Championship campaign and debuted from the bench in City's opening-day draw at Birmingham City. His Norwich career took an early blow after he suffered ankle ligament damage in the League Cup victory over Stevenage at Carrow Road on 14 August 2018. This required surgery and ruled him out for the remainder of the calendar year.

In the absence of Mario Vrancic, McLean was back in the team on 16 February 2019 as City won 4-0 away to Bolton Wanderers and his return to the first team fold coincided with the side's best run of form, winning eight consecutive games en route to promotion. McLean marked his return to full fitness and first-team action with an expertly taken brace in the 3-2 victory over in-form Bristol City at Carrow Road and also opened the scoring in a hard-fought 2-1 win away to Rotherham United in March.

McNAMEE, Anthony
Date of birth: 13 July 1984
Place of birth: Kensington
Position: Midfielder
Promotion campaigns: 2009/10 League One champions and 2010/11
     Championship runners-up
2009/10 League statistics: 7(10)1
2010/11 League statistics: 5(12)-

Tricky winger Anthony McNamee was signed from League One rivals Swindon Town during the 2009/10 season. He initially arrived at Carrow Road on loan before making the move permanent once the 2010 January transfer window opened for business.

He made his Norwich City debut in a 2-0 Carrow Road victory over Oldham Athletic on 5 December 2009 and went on to feature in 17 league games as City swiftly returned to the second tier. His only goal for the Canaries came on Easter Monday (5 April 2010) when he curled home a stunning strike to open the scoring in a 2-1 victory over Stockport County at Carrow Road.

Following City's promotion back to the Championship and the summer signings of Andrew Crofts, Andrew Surman and David Fox, McNamee found his opportunities limited in 2010/11. But he again made 17 appearances, including an impressive showing from the bench against Burnley at Carrow Road on 6 November 2010 to inspire City in coming back from 2-0 down to salvage a point.

McVEIGH, Paul

Date of birth: 6 December 1977
Place of birth: Belfast
Position: Striker
Promotion campaigns: 2003/04 First Division champions and 2009/10 League One champions
2003/04 League statistics: 36(8)5
2009/10 League statistics: 4(5)-

Paul McVeigh enjoyed two spells with Norwich City and was a promotion winner during both of his stints at Carrow Road. He first joined the Canaries from Tottenham Hotspur at the tail end of the 1999/2000 season and made his City debut in May 2000.

A small but very effective player, his creativity and eye for goal made him a real fans' favourite, as he made an important contribution to the team's transformation from second-tier strugglers to champions between 2001 and 2004. He started 36 league games in City's 2003/04 success and netted five goals – the first of which was a stunning late strike to defeat Reading 2-1 at Carrow Road on 30 September 2003.

Following his release from Luton Town in 2009, he came to train with the Canaries in the summer and impressed Bryan Gunn enough to earn a one-year deal with the club.

He made a total of nine league appearances during the 2009/10 League One title-winning campaign, with his final appearance in yellow and green coming in the penultimate game of the season as City cruised to a 3-0 victory away to Bristol Rovers on 1 May 2010.

MENDHAM, Peter

Date of birth: 9 April 1960
Place of birth: King's Lynn
Position: Midfielder
Promotion campaigns: 1981/82 third in Division Two and 1985/86
　Division Two champions
1981/82 League statistics: 25(4)6
1985/86 League statistics: 35(-)8

Another true Norwich City legend, Norfolk-born Peter Mendham sampled the highs of two promotion-winning seasons at Carrow Road and also cherished Wembley glory as a member of City's 1985 League Cup-winning team.

After breaking through to the City first team back in September 1978, Mendham produced a number of all-action displays as City secured promotion in 1981/82. He chipped in with six goals from midfield, including a last-gasp half-volley to ensure a 2-1 home victory over Shrewsbury Town on 17 October 1981.

After playing a starring role in the Canaries' League Cup success in 1985, Mendham then produced another memorable season in the Canary engine room to ensure his beloved Norwich City returned to the top flight at the first time of asking in 1985/86. Mendham reached double figures in the goalscoring column in 1985/86, eight of which came in the league, including the team's first goal of the campaign to ensure an opening-day 1-0 win at home to Oldham Athletic.

MILLER, John (Johnny)

Date of birth: 21 September 1950
Place of birth: Ipswich
Date of death: 18 February 2016
Place of death: Mansfield
Position: Midfielder
Promotion campaign: 1974/75 third in Division Two
1974/75 League statistics: 14(-)3

Unable to dislodge future Norwich manager Bryan Hamilton from the Ipswich Town side, Johnny Miller crossed the great Norfolk/ Suffolk divide when he left Portman Road to join the Canaries in October 1974.

He debuted in a City side brimming with confidence, so much so they were 3-0 up at the interval against Orient at Carrow Road on 26

October 1974. That victory over Orient represented a fifth straight Second Division victory for John Bond's side as they maintained second spot in the league table.

During his 14 league outings in 1974/75, Miller netted three goals including a brace in the 2-0 Carrow Road triumph over Bolton Wanderers on 23 November 1974. His final league goal of the season was scored after just 30 seconds of a 1-1 draw at home to Cardiff City in December 1974. However, his goals that really grabbed the headlines that season came when he returned to Portman Road and scored twice in Norwich's 2-1 League Cup quarter-final replay victory over their local rivals on 10 December 1974.

MORAN, James
Date of birth: 6 March 1935
Place of birth: Cleland, nr Motherwell
Position: Striker
Promotion campaign: 1959/60 Division Three runners-up
1959/60 League statistics: 6(n/a)5

The impressive form of Terry Bly and Terry Allcock throughout the Canaries' 1959/60 promotion-winning campaign resulted in first-team chances being thin on the ground for Scottish forward James Moran.

However, as a player whose Canary career saw him net a highly impressive 17 league goals in 36 games, he certainly delivered when called upon. Moran replaced the absent Bly on 17 October 1959 for his first taste of 1959/60 action and marked the occasion with a goal as City ran out 4-3 winners over Accrington Stanley at Carrow Road.

After netting against Stanley, Moran retained his place in the side for the next three games and scored a further three goals. On target in a 1-1 draw away to Grimsby Town, he then netted a brace in a 3-2 victory at home to Swindon Town on 7 November 1959. He marked his final game for City with a consolation goal in a 2-1 defeat at Chesterfield on 12 December 1959.

MORRIS, Carlton
Date of birth: 16 December 1995
Place of birth: Cambridge
Position: Striker
Promotion campaign: 2014/15 Championship play-off winners
2014/15 League statistics: -(1)-

Powerful frontman Carlton Morris progressed through the Canaries' academy and played a key role in the club's FA Youth Cup triumph in 2012/13.

His only first-team involvement to date came as a substitute when he replaced Nathan Redmond in City's surprise 1-0 defeat at home to Wigan Athletic on 4 March 2015. The midweek meeting with the struggling Latics came straight on the back of the euphoria of an East Anglian derby victory over Ipswich Town and proved to be a match that certainly fell into the 'after the Lord Mayor's show' category.

Morris's three goals en route to FA Youth Cup glory in 2012/13 have always seen him earmarked as a future first-team star. Although he has been unable to make his mark at Carrow Road, he has gained valuable experience with a host of loan moves including a successful spell with Shrewsbury Town in 2017/18 as the Shropshire club reached both the Football League Trophy and League One play-off finals.

MORRIS, Peter
Date of birth: 8 November 1943
Place of birth: Derbyshire
Position: Midfielder
Promotion campaign: 1974/75 third in Division Two
1974/75 League statistics: 40(-)-

When reflecting on the long and successful playing career of midfielder Peter Morris, it is difficult not to have him down as something of a promotion specialist, having sampled an elevation to a higher level with all three of his league clubs.

After enjoying promotion-winning campaigns with Mansfield Town and Ipswich Town, Morris completed the hat-trick when he joined the Canaries in June 1974 ahead of the club's 1974/75 season in the Second Division.

Despite his previous successes with City's arch rivals across the Norfolk/Suffolk border, Morris soon won over the Carrow Road faithful as he became a regular in John Bond's side. He debuted on the opening day of the season as City beat Blackpool 2-1 at Carrow Road and his consistency saw him miss just two league games as Norwich secured the third and final promotion berth behind Aston Villa and champions Manchester United. A highly successful maiden season with Norwich City saw Morris as both a promotion winner and a Wembley finalist as City reached the 1975 League Cup Final.

MOUNTFORD, Peter

Date of birth: 30 September 1960
Place of birth: Stoke-on-Trent
Position: Midfielder
Promotion campaign: 1981/82 third in Division Two
1981/82 League statistics: -(2)-

In a brief Norwich City career that consisted of one first-team start and three outings as substitute, 50 per cent of midfielder Peter Mountford's Canary career came in the club's successful Second Division promotion-winning season in 1981/82.

A promising youngster, Mountford made his debut on 20 February 1982 when he replaced Greig Shepherd in the latter stages of City's 2-1 victory over Chelsea at Carrow Road as first-half goals from Peter Mendham and Ross Jack, either side of a Clive Walker goal, sealed victory.

His final involvement in the 1981/82 campaign came a week later as once again he came off the bench in a Carrow Road fixture. However, on this occasion Mountford sampled the bitter taste of defeat as future Norwich City boss Glenn Roeder volleyed home the only goal of the game for Queens Park Rangers on 27 February 1982. The midfielder then twice tasted First Division football the following season before later playing league football for Charlton Athletic and Orient.

MULLETT, Joe

Date of birth: 2 October 1936
Place of birth: Birmingham
Date of death: 3 March 1995
Place of death: Sandwell, West Bromwich
Position: Defender
Promotion campaign: 1959/60 Division Three runners-up
1959/60 League statistics: 1(-)-

Defender Joe Mullett was recruited from Birmingham City in January 1959 with the city of Norwich in the midst of cup fever following the Canaries' high-profile triumphs over Manchester United and Cardiff City, resulting in a fifth-round match with the mighty Tottenham Hotspur appearing next on the agenda.

Patience was certainly the key for Mullett upon his arrival at Carrow Road. The defender would go on to amass almost 250 appearances for the club but was limited to four appearances in 1958/59 and just one single first-team outing the following season as Archie Macaulay's men won promotion from the Third Division.

Mullett's sole slice of action during that promotion-winning campaign came on Saturday, 24 October 1959 when he deputised for Matt Crowe in City's 1-0 home victory over Newport County. In front of a Carrow Road crowd of 24,138, a second-half goal from Errol Crossan proved enough to secure both points for the hosts and ensure that Mullett's match was a winning one.

MULRYNE, Philip

Date of birth: 1 January 1978
Place of birth: Belfast
Position: Midfielder
Promotion campaign: 2003/04 First Division champions
2003/04 League statistics: 14(20)3

Phil Mulryne joined the Canaries on transfer deadline day in March 1999 from Manchester United for a fee of £500,000. Signed by Bruce Rioch, Mulryne soon made a name for himself as a free-kick specialist, with his accurate right foot proving a potent weapon at set plays.

He played a major part in the club's journey to the play-off final in 2001/02, but the arrival of Damien Francis in 2003 forced Mulryne down the midfield pecking order, with the Northern Ireland international limited to 14 league starts in the Canaries' 2003/04 championship-winning season.

Despite a lack of full appearances, Mulryne was a vital squad member and also appeared on 20 occasions from the bench. Suffice to say, he certainly played his part in a memorable campaign, weighing in with three goals – two of them absolutely crucial. First he scored a late winner as ten-man City defeated Derby at Carrow Road on 21 October 2003 before an 'assist' from referee Neale Barry at Reading helped Mulryne volley the crucial goal in the 1-0 Easter Monday win, which all but sealed promotion.

MURPHY, Joshua
Date of birth: 24 February 1995
Place of birth: Wembley
Position: Midfielder
Promotion campaign: 2014/15 Championship play-off winners
2014/15 League statistics: 1(12)1

Together with twin brother Jacob, Josh Murphy progressed through the Norwich City Academy and was a member of the Canaries' 2012/13 FA Youth Cup-winning side.

Arguably the star performer and driving force behind the Youth Cup success, Murphy was blessed with electrifying pace and a good eye for goal. He soon stepped up to the first-team scene and served under City bosses Chris Hughton, Neil Adams, Alex Neil, Alan Irvine (caretaker) and Daniel Farke.

The majority of his involvement in City's 2014/15 campaign came in the first half of the season when Murphy's former youth-team boss Adams was in the manager's chair. A regular among the City substitutes, Murphy netted his first league goal for the club when he came off the bench to score in a 3-1 win away to Blackpool on 27 September 2014. His only league start came in the 1-1 draw at home to Leeds United in October 2014. With his first-team opportunities limited under new boss Neil, Murphy joined Wigan Athletic on loan in March 2015 but was unable to prevent the Latics' relegation from the Championship.

MUZINIC, Drazen
Date of birth: 25 January 1953
Place of birth: Yugoslavia
Position: Midfielder
Promotion campaign: 1981/82 third in Division Two
1981/82 League statistics: 6(1)-

Signed by John Bond, Yugoslavian international midfielder Drazen Muzinic joined the Canaries from Hajduk Split for a then club-record fee of £300,000 in September 1980.

However, the transfer proved to be something of an expensive failure as Muzinic went on to make just 23 appearances for City – six of which were as a substitute. He featured fleetingly under Ken Brown during the 1981/82 Second Division campaign. Selected in the starting line-up for the opening-day defeat at Rotherham United, Muzinic's Carrow Road career came to a close on 28 December 1981 when he made his final appearance for the club in a 3-1 festive defeat at home to league leaders Luton Town.

With promotion assured at the end of the 1981/82 campaign, Muzinic's contract was cancelled in the summer of 1982. His sizeable transfer fee remained a Norwich City record for over seven years until the Canaries completed the £580,000 signing of Robert Fleck from Glasgow Rangers in December 1987.

NELSON, Michael

Date of birth: 28 March 1980
Place of birth: Gateshead
Position: Defender
Promotion campaigns: 2009/10 League One champions and 2010/11
   Championship runners-up
2009/10 League statistics: 28(3)3
2010/11 League statistics: 7(1)2

Michael Nelson joined the Canaries from Hartlepool United in the summer of 2009 after being recommended to boss Bryan Gunn by his assistant Ian Butterworth, who had previously worked with Nelson at Victoria Park.

Despite enduring a 7-1 drubbing on his debut at home to Colchester United, Nelson enjoyed an impressive season in League One under Paul Lambert. A highly respected character in the dressing room, he popped up with vital goals as City ended the 2009/10 campaign as League One Champions. Nelson enjoyed a memorable return to Hartlepool in August 2009 when he opened the scoring for Norwich with an overhead kick in a 2-0 win. However, he will always be remembered for heading home the goal that sealed promotion back to the Championship at Charlton on 17 April 2010.

Nelson figured in eight Championship matches in 2010/11, scoring against Watford and Sheffield United, but found a regular place hard to nail down due to the competition provided by Elliott Ward, Zak Whitbread and Leon Barnett. With his contract due to expire at the end of the 2010/11 campaign, the club accepted an offer from Scunthorpe United in January 2011 and Nelson moved to Glanford Park.

NIELSEN, David

Date of birth: 1 December 1976
Place of birth: Skagen, Denmark
Position: Striker
Promotion campaign: 2003/04 First Division champions
2003/04 League statistics: 2(-)-

Pacey Danish striker David Nielsen joined the Canaries on loan from Wimbledon in December 2001 and made an instant impact at Carrow Road which resulted in a permanent move in January 2002.

His initial loan spell saw him actually play – and score! – for City against Wimbledon on 22 December 2001, despite still being registered as a Dons player. Nielsen was often effectively used as a substitute, when his pace and enthusiasm could alter the outcome of games in the latter stages.

His all-action style and willingness to run at defenders certainly made him popular with the City faithful. After appearing in the first two league games of 2003/04 away to Bradford City and at home to Rotherham United, it was announced that despite still having ten months remaining on his contract the player was returning to Denmark for 'family reasons'. His sudden departure, coupled with long-term injuries to Alex Notman and Zema Abbey, was a deciding factor in the club's bold, and ultimately successful, loan moves for Peter Crouch and Darren Huckerby.

NIGHTINGALE, Mark

Date of birth: 1 February 1957
Place of birth: Salisbury
Position: Midfielder
Promotion campaign: 1981/82 third in Division Two
1981/82 League statistics: 8(1)-

Former Bournemouth man Mark Nightingale served the Canaries in a number of positions across a four-year spell between 1977 and 1981. However, his flexibility ultimately counted against him as he was unable to cement a position of his own in the side under either John Bond or Ken Brown.

Having joined City in the summer of 1977, Nightingale started just 28 league games across his four years at Carrow Road. The club's 1981/82 season proved to be his final Canary campaign as he featured in nine Second Division fixtures across the opening weeks of the season.

Nightingale replaced Drazen Muzinic in the opening-day defeat at Rotherham United and then started the following eight fixtures in the right-back berth. He eventually lost the number-two shirt to Richard Symonds and his final appearance for the club came in a 2-0 defeat to Queens Park Rangers at Loftus Road on 10 October 1981.

NOTMAN, Alex
Date of birth: 10 December 1979
Place of birth: Dalkeith
Position: Striker
Promotion campaign: 2003/04 First Division champions
2003/04 League statistics: -(1)-

Scotland under-21 international striker Alex Notman joined the Canaries from Manchester United in November 2000 for a fee of £250,000 and proved to be Bryan Hamilton's last signing as Norwich City manager.

Despite his many impressive touches and neat link-up play, the diminutive Scot struggled for goals. He finally broke his scoring duck with his first and only goal for the club arriving in a 3-2 home defeat against Burnley on 16 April 2001.

Predominantly a fringe player, he sadly suffered a freak ankle injury in the East Anglian derby match away to Ipswich Town in September 2002 when he charged down a Mark Venus free-kick. After spending almost 12 months trying to regain his fitness, he made an attempted comeback with a brief substitute appearance against Burnley on 13 September 2003, which proved to be his final outing for the club. Notman's unfortunate retirement from the game was announced in November 2003 with the player aged just 23.

ODJIDJA-OFOE, Vadis
Date of birth: 21 February 1989
Place of birth: Ghent, Belgium
Position: Midfielder
Promotion campaign: 2014/15 Championship play-off winners
2014/15 League statistics: 1(4)-

Belgian international midfielder Vadis Odjidja-Ofoe was recruited from Club Brugge in the 2014 summer transfer window and viewed as a replacement for Leroy Fer, who had sealed a big-money move to Queens Park Rangers earlier in the window.

Despite a substantial transfer fee and a big reputation, the player was never able to make his mark in the Norwich first team. A number of niggling injuries and the form of others limited his opportunities under the management of both Neil Adams and Alex Neil during the 2014/15 promotion-winning campaign.

He debuted as a substitute, replacing Lewis Grabban, during the second half of City's comprehensive 3-0 win away to Brentford on 16 September 2014. The Belgian went on to make three further appearances from the bench and start one Championship match in 2014/15 – the goalless draw away to Sheffield Wednesday on 25 October 2014.

O'DONNELL, Neil

Date of birth: 21 December 1949
Place of birth: Glasgow
Position: Midfielder
Promotion campaign: 1971/72 Division Two champions
1971/72 League statistics: -(2)-

In and around the Norwich City squad for a six-and-a-half-year period between September 1967 to January 1974, versatile midfielder Neil O'Donnell made 64 first-team appearances and scored three goals for the Canaries.

He progressed through the youth ranks at Carrow Road, and after turning professional his adaptability saw him feature in a number of positions under City bosses Lol Morgan, Ron Saunders and John Bond, while also making over 175 appearances for the reserve side.

O'Donnell's involvement in the historic 1971/72 elevation to the top flight was limited to just two substitute appearances. He came off the bench to replace Malcolm Darling and play his part in a goalless midweek draw at home to Orient on 1 September 1971. His final involvement in the campaign came ten days later when he replaced goalscorer Kenny Foggo in the latter stages of City's 2-1 win away to Blackpool.

OLSSON, Martin

Date of birth: 17 May 1988
Place of birth: Gavle, Sweden

Position: Defender
Promotion campaign: 2014/15 Championship play-off winners
2014/15 League statistics: 42(-)1 + play-offs 3(-)-

Swedish international left-back Martin Olsson was signed from Blackburn Rovers by Chris Hughton in the summer of 2013.

Despite the Canaries' relegation from the Premier League at the end of Olsson's debut season with the club, he remained at Carrow Road and was a mainstay of the side during the 2014/15 promotion-winning campaign – even netting a rare goal in the team's thrilling 4-2 win at Cardiff City in September 2014.

For Olsson, the 2014/15 season began on a rather sour note when he was sent off as City suffered a 1-0 defeat in their first Championship fixture of the campaign away to Wolverhampton Wanderers. Dismissed by referee Simon Hooper for a second yellow-card offence following a challenge on Rajiv van La Para, he then appeared to shove the match official before departing the pitch. The incident left Olsson with a four-match ban, one match for the initial dismissal and a further three games for the fracas that followed. Once his suspension was served, Olsson immediately returned to the side and was ever-present for the remaining 41 league games plus the successful play-off campaign that followed.

O'NEIL, Gary
Date of birth: 18 May 1983
Place of birth: Beckenham
Position: Midfielder
Promotion campaign: 2014/15 Championship play-off winners
2014/15 League statistics: 10(11)- + play-offs -(1)-

A vastly experienced midfielder, Gary O'Neil was signed by Neil Adams in August 2014 and his arrival at Carrow Road certainly provided some additional nous and knowhow to the City squad.

He debuted in the Canaries' opening home game of 2014/15 when he replaced the goalscoring Alex Tettey towards the end of a comprehensive 3-0 victory over Watford. Predominantly used as a substitute by Adams, O'Neil started his first league game for City as they overcame Bolton Wanderers 2-1 in a televised Friday-night fixture at Carrow Road on 31 October 2014. He then proceeded to start seven of the next nine league games – sadly City won only three of them as the team began to slip down the table.

Following the mid-season change of manager, O'Neil started just two more league games under the management of Alex Neil. Often named among the substitutes and always a valued and well-respected member of the squad, he appeared briefly as a late substitute in the play-off final victory over Middlesbrough at Wembley when he replaced goalscorer Nathan Redmond.

O'NEILL, Martin
Date of birth: 1 March 1952
Place of birth: Kilrea
Position: Midfielder
Promotion campaign: 1981/82 third in Division Two
1981/82 League statistics: 20(-)6

The undisputed catalyst for the Canaries' late surge to promotion in 1981/82, midfield maestro Martin O'Neill had three spells with Norwich City – twice as a player and once in the manager's chair.

He initially joined City in February 1981 but made a move to Manchester City following Norwich's relegation at the end of the 1980/81 season. An unhappy time at Maine Road signalled his return to Norfolk in February 1982 with Ken Brown's side languishing in 11th in the Second Division table. O'Neill marked his second debut for the club with a goal against Sheffield Wednesday on 3 February 1982 and proceeded to score six goals in 20 games, which culminated in an incredible run of 10 wins from their last dozen fixtures to seal the third and final promotion place.

It was an O'Neill goal that began that memorable run of results across the final weeks of the season, the Northern Ireland international snapping up a dramatic winner five minutes from time to secure a vital 1-0 Carrow Road victory over Bolton Wanderers on 20 March 1982. Not until the 2003 signing of Darren Huckerby has one single player had such an impact on a Canary campaign.

OTSEMOBOR, Jon
Date of birth: 23 March 1983
Place of birth: Liverpool
Position: Defender
Promotion campaign: 2009/10 League One champions
2009/10 League statistics: 12(1)1

Signed for City by then boss Peter Grant, speedy right-back Jon Otsemobor joined the Canaries in the summer of 2007 on a free transfer from Crewe Alexandra, having begun his career with Liverpool.

Otsemobor played in the 2009/10 opening-day humiliation at the hands of Colchester United and found himself out of the starting line-up for the next three games. After impressing new boss Paul Lambert in training, he returned to the side for Lambert's Carrow Road bow at home to Wycombe Wanderers on 22 August 2009. On what was an impressive Canary performance, Otsemobor added his name to the scoresheet in a 5-2 victory. In the main, Otsemobor was seen as the team's first-choice right-back for the first half of the League One campaign, although minor injuries did hand occasional opportunities to Michael Spillane and George Francomb.

With his contract due to expire in the summer, plus Russell Martin arriving in December 2009 to take over right-back duties, Otsemobor opted to try his luck on the south coast and sealed a switch to Southampton in January 2010.

PACHECO, Dani
Date of birth: 5 January 1991
Place of birth: Pizarra, Spain
Position: Striker
Promotion campaign: 2010/11 Championship runners-up
2010/11 League statistics: 3(3)2

Spanish striker Dani Pacheco joined Norwich City at a particularly exciting time in the club's history. His arrival on loan from Liverpool towards the end of the 2010/11 season coincided with the team's bid to secure back-to-back promotions and a place in the Premier League.

A small and slight forward with quick feet and a great eye for a pass or shot, Pacheco made an impressive contribution with three starts, three substitute appearances and two goals as City landed the Championship runners-up spot.

Pacheco was thrust straight into the starting line-up as he was paired with Grant Holt for a debut in the 6-0 demolition of Scunthorpe United on 2 April 2010. After finding himself among the substitutes for the final four games of the season, the popular Spaniard came off the bench to net his first goal in Canary colours as he grabbed City's fifth goal in the 5-1 rout at Portman Road on 21 April 2010. With promotion assured, he then marked his last appearance with a goal in the 2-2 draw against Coventry City on the final day.

PADDON, Graham
Date of birth: 24 August 1950
Place of birth: Manchester
Date of death: 19 November 2007
Place of death: Norfolk
Position: Midfielder
Promotion campaigns: 1971/72 Division Two champions and 1981/82 third in Division Two
1971/72 League statistics: 40(-)8
1981/82 League statistics: 8(-)-

Blessed with extreme confidence and match-winning ability, ace midfielder Graham Paddon was an instrumental part of the Canaries' 1971/72 Second Division title-winning campaign. Paddon had two spells at Carrow Road and also featured in the opening weeks of the club's successful return to the top flight in 1981/82.

Paddon made 40 appearances and chipped in with eight Second Division goals for Ron Saunders's table toppers. His goalscoring form in 1971/72 began on the opening day when he netted the club's first goal of the season in a 1-1 draw with Luton Town at Kenilworth Road. He later blasted home a brace in the 5-1 victory over Blackpool at Carrow Road on 25 March 1972, as City began their promotion run-in. With Norwich 1-0 up in the promotion clincher at Orient, Paddon added the second goal from the penalty spot to ensure a 2-0 triumph and trigger the promotion party.

He enjoyed a successful spell with West Ham United, sandwiched between his two stints at Norwich, the latter ending with eight appearances under Ken Brown at the start of the 1981/82 promotion-winning campaign.

PASSLACK, Felix

Date of birth: 29 May 1998
Place of birth: Bottrop, Germany
Position: Defender
Promotion campaign: 2018/19 Championship champions
2018/19 League statistics: -(1)-

A German under-21 international, right-back Felix Passlack spent the 2018/19 season with the Canaries after agreeing a season-long loan deal from Borussia Dortmund.

With a glowing reputation in his home country, having progressed through the age groups at international level, Passlack's arrival at Carrow Road was seen as a real coup for the club and it was anticipated he would offer serious competition for Ivo Pinto at right-back.

However, the sudden emergence of Max Aarons resulted in both Passlack and Pinto being frozen out of the first team picture as Aarons made the right-back berth his own in City's promotion-winning campaign. Passlack gained useful experience of the English game by starting all five of the Canaries' cup ties in 2018/19, but his league involvement was limited to an occasional place on the substitutes' bench and a sole taste of the action came when he replaced Onel Hernandez for the final six minutes of City's 3-1 defeat at Preston on 13 February 2019.

PAYNE, Clive

Date of birth: 2 March 1950
Place of birth: Aylsham, Norfolk
Position: Defender
Promotion campaign: 1971/72 Division Two champions
1971/72 League statistics: 42(-)-

Together with goalkeeper Kevin Keelan and fellow defender Dave Stringer, right-back Clive Payne was an ever-present member of the Canaries' historic Second Division title-winning team in 1971/72.

Norfolk-born Payne made his initial breakthrough to the City first team back in September 1968 in a League Cup triumph away to Ipswich Town and patience was the key as he slowly but surely made the right-back berth his own. The 1970/71 season saw him establish himself as the club's first choice for the number-two shirt.

The fact that Payne, Stringer and Keelan were all ever-presents in 1971/72 reinforced the fact that boss Ron Saunders was keen to build his side on a solid defensive base. After helping City secure top-flight status for the first time, Payne featured regularly in the First Division in 1972/73 and also played at Wembley in City's 1973 League Cup final side. Very much a Saunders man, Payne was not to figure in new boss John Bond's plans and moved to AFC Bournemouth as a makeweight in Bond's efforts to recruit John Benson and Mel Machin from Dean Court.

PETERS, Martin

Date of birth: 8 November 1943
Place of birth: Plaistow
Position: Midfielder
Promotion campaign: 1974/75 third in Division Two
1974/75 League statistics: 10(-)2

Considered by many as Norwich City's finest player, England World Cup winner Martin Peters joined the Canaries in 1975 and provided invaluable experience and quality to a City side chasing promotion back to the First Division.

Peters's arrival at Norwich was certainly seen as a sensational coup by then boss John Bond, who parted with just £50,000 to lure the hero of 1966 from Tottenham Hotspur to Carrow Road.

With ten league fixtures remaining, Peters made his debut in a 1-1 draw away to league leaders Manchester United on 15 March 1975 and went on to score in a 3-0 Carrow Road triumph over Nottingham Forest and in the promotion-winning victory away to Portsmouth in April. Back in the big time, Peters then proceeded to show class, professionalism, goals and creativity over a five-year spell as Carrow Road witnessed some of the best displays of passing football in the club's history.

PHELAN, Mike

Date of birth: 24 September 1962
Place of birth: Nelson, Lancashire
Position: Midfielder
Promotion campaign: 1985/86 Division Two champions
1985/86 League statistics: 42(-)3

City boss Ken Brown pulled off yet another transfer master-stroke when he landed the services of midfielder Mike Phelan from Burnley in the summer of 1985 for a fee of just £60,000.

Blessed with strength and skill in equal measure, Phelan wasted little time in making his mark at Carrow Road and was ever-present in the Canary engine room as City, who had suffered relegation the previous season, returned to the top flight at the first attempt.

Phelan opened his goalscoring account for the season with arguably the pick of the bunch as City edged a seven-goal thriller at home to Crystal Palace on 18 September 1985. The midfield man was also on target in comprehensive victories away to Carlisle United (4-0) and against Millwall at home (6-1). A Second Division title winner inside his first 12 months in Norfolk, Phelan displayed no problems in stepping up to the rigours of First Division football the following season and became Canary captain following the sale of Steve Bruce to Manchester United in December 1987.

PINTO, Ivo

Date of birth: 7 January 1990
Place of birth: Lourosa, Portugal
Position: Defender
Promotion campaign: 2018/19 Championship champions
2018/19 League statistics: 3(-)-

A Portugal under-21 international, right-back Ivo Pinto joined the Canaries in the January 2016 transfer window from Dinamo Zagreb.

Thrust straight into a Premier League relegation battle, the defender suffered a real baptism of fire as City shipped five goals during his debut against Liverpool. Having led 3-1 in that first appearance against the Reds at Carrow Road, Pinto and his new team-mates contrived to lose the game 5-4 and were never able to recover from that crushing blow as relegation followed four months later.

At Championship level his pace and desire to get forward saw him become popular with supporters, and he was handed the captaincy when Russell Martin fell out of first-team contention under Daniel Farke. However, his forward play was often at the detriment of his defensive duties and after playing in three of City's opening five league games of 2018/19, when seven goals were conceded, Farke replaced Pinto with academy graduate Max Aarons. From late August onwards, Pinto did feature in League Cup games but was merely a spectator for Championship fixtures as Aarons made the right-back berth his own with a series of impressive performances. As widely anticipated, Pinto was released at the end of the title-winning season.

POWELL, Anthony (Tony)
Date of birth: 11 June 1947
Place of birth: Bristol
Position: Midfielder
Promotion campaign: 1974/75 third in Division Two
1974/75 League statistics: 40(-)2

One of many to take the well-trodden path from Bournemouth to Carrow Road in the 1970s, Tony Powell followed his manager John Bond to Norfolk and sampled promotion once again under Bond's leadership.

Powell formed part of the Cherries team that won promotion from the Fourth Division in 1970/71 and he tasted the promotion-winning champagne again come the end of his first season with the Canaries. Straight into the starting line-up for City's opening game of their 1974/75 Second Division campaign, Powell marked his Norwich debut against Blackpool with a goal. He opened the scoring at Carrow Road early in the second half in somewhat fortuitous circumstances as a 48th-minute clearance cannoned off his chest and past John Burridge. His goal set City on their way to a winning start as they ran out 2-1 winners on 17 August 1974.

Powell missed just two league games as his consistent performances saw him soon become one of the first names on Bond's teamsheet. He netted his second league goal of the season to set City on their way to a 2-0 victory at home to Millwall on 5 October 1974.

PUKKI, Teemu
Date of birth: 29 March 1990
Place of birth: Kotka, Finland
Position: Striker

Promotion campaign: 2018/19 Championship champions
2018/19 League statistics: 43(-)29

The 2018/19 season's surprise package, Finland international striker Teemu Pukki fired home an incredible 29 Championship goals in his debut campaign at Carrow Road as Norwich won promotion to the Premier League.

Pukki's 29-goal haul saw him etch his name into joint-second place in the list of top Canary league goalscorers in a season. At one stage it looked as though he might even overtake Ralph Hunt's record 31 goals from 1951/52, but in the end he had to settle for nestling behind Hunt and alongside Percy Varco, who plundered 29 Third Division (South) goals in 1927/28.

Among his plethora of goals were memorable late strikes in the Carrow Road triumphs over Millwall and Bolton Wanderers, plus an expertly taken brace in the 3-0 East Anglian derby victory over Ipswich Town on 10 February 2019. Voted the EFL's Championship player of the season, Pukki was unsurprisingly presented with the Barry Butler Memorial Trophy as City's player of the season prior to the promotion-clinching final home game with Blackburn Rovers. Pukki also ended the season with the Championship's Golden Boot after his 29 goals topped the league's scoring charts.

PUNTON, William (Bill)
Date of birth: 9 May 1934
Place of birth: Glenkinchie, East Lothian
Position: Midfielder
Promotion campaign: 1959/60 Division Three runners-up
1959/60 League statistics: 27(-)4

Flying winger Bill Punton began a 256-game Norwich City career by helping the Canaries to secure promotion to the Second Division in his first season at the club.

Punton joined a City side that had shot to national prominence following their exploits in the 1958/59 FA Cup the previous season. Without the distraction of a cup campaign and

with the pace and crossing ability of Punton in the team, boss Archie Macaulay's men improved on their fourth-place Third Division finish of the previous season by securing the runners-up spot behind champions Southampton.

The team improved their league finish by both two places and two points (57 in 1958/59 v 59 in 1959/60), which proved enough to secure a place in the Second Division. Punton chipped in with four goals from his 27 league appearances while also creating an abundance of chances for grateful team-mates. Punton's fourth and final goal of the campaign came in the thrilling 4-3 promotion-winning match at home to Southend United on 27 April 1960.

REDMOND, Nathan
Date of birth: 6 March 1994
Place of birth: Birmingham
Position: Midfielder
Promotion campaign: 2014/15
2014/15 League statistics: 33(10)4 + play-offs 3(-)2

Nathan Redmond played a starring role as Norwich City secured an instant return to the Premier League with Wembley glory in the 2014/15 play-offs.

Signed from Birmingham City, Redmond was an exciting right-winger who had already won England under-21 caps prior to joining the Canaries. Chris Hughton was the Norwich boss who signed him and, having managed the player during his time in charge at St Andrew's, Hughton clearly played a major part in Redmond's decision to move to Norwich.

Despite the club suffering relegation in his first season at Carrow Road, Redmond stayed loyal to the Canary cause and his blistering pace caused havoc among Championship defences. On the scoresheet in regulation matches at home to Huddersfield Town, Brentford, Blackpool and Fulham, Redmond saved his real match-winning form for the vital play-off campaign. On target in the 3-1 semi-final second-leg victory over Ipswich Town at Carrow Road, Redmond then picked the perfect moment to score his first away goal of the campaign as he ended a flowing team move with City's vital second goal in the 2-0 play-off final victory over Middlesbrough at Wembley.

RHODES, Jordan

Date of birth: 5 February 1990
Place of birth: Oldham
Position: Striker
Promotion campaign: 2018/19 Championship champions
2018/19 League statistics: 9(27)6

Experienced goal-getter Jordan Rhodes joined Norwich City in July 2018 after agreeing a season-long loan deal from Championship rivals Sheffield Wednesday.

Boasting a phenomenal goalscoring record with Huddersfield Town and Blackburn Rovers, Rhodes found goals less easy to come by during indifferent spells with Middlesbrough and Sheffield Wednesday. After falling down the pecking order at Hillsborough under Jos Luhukay, Rhodes jumped at the opportunity to rekindle his scoring form with the Canaries.

His arrival and pre-season performances gave the Carrow Road faithful reasons for optimism, and he scored his first Norwich goal in the opening home game of the season against West Bromwich Albion. After opening the scoring against the Baggies, Rhodes missed the opportunity of re-establishing the Canaries' lead when he saw a tame first-half penalty saved at the River End. The miss proved costly as City lost a seven-goal thriller 4-3. As the season progressed, Rhodes had to watch on from the bench as Teemu Pukki took centre stage in the scoring stakes. Rhodes, however, filled the injured Finn's boots perfectly when on 23 October 2018 he scored both goals in the 2-1 Carrow Road victory over Aston Villa.

RICHARDS, John

Date of birth: 14 June 1931
Place of birth: West Bromwich
Date of death: 20 November 2001
Place of death: Broxbourne
Position: Striker
Promotion campaign: 1959/60 Division Three runners-up
1959/60 League statistics: 5(-)2

With an impressive goal tally from his time at Swindon Town, striker John Richards joined Norwich City from the Wiltshire club in December 1959.

In a City side minus Terry Bly and Terry Allcock, Richards made his debut in attack alongside fellow debutant Rob Edwards as City suffered a 2-1 defeat away to Chesterfield on 12 December 1959. A Carrow Road bow followed a week later when Richards partnered the returning Allcock as City suffered a fourth game without a win as they went down 2-1 to high-flying Southampton.

It proved a case of third time lucky for Richards, who finally found himself in a winning Canary performance as City overcame Queens Park Rangers 1-0 at Carrow Road on 30 January 1960. He sampled another City triumph when he played in the 3-1 win at home to Wrexham in February. His final contribution to the 1959/60 success also proved to be his final outing for the Canaries as he signed off with a brace in a 4-0 victory over Accrington Stanley at Carrow Road on 5 March 1960.

RIVERS, Mark
Date of birth: 26 November 1975
Place of birth: Crewe
Position: Midfielder
Promotion campaign: 2003/04 First Division Champions
2003/04 League statistics: 7(5)4

Mark Rivers was a regular tormentor of the Canaries when plying his trade for Crewe Alexandra, so his arrival at Carrow Road in the summer of 2001 was therefore greeted with enthusiasm by the Canary faithful.

In his debut campaign he formed part of the City side that went close to Premier League promotion in 2001/02 – only being denied by a penalty shoot-out defeat in the play-off final against Birmingham City at Cardiff's Millennium Stadium.

Injuries and the form of others limited him to just seven starts in 2003/04. However, Rivers was certainly the man who got the promotion ball rolling – scoring the club's first goal of the season in blistering heat as City drew 2-2 at Bradford City on the opening day. Showing great form across the opening weeks of the season, Rivers netted three goals in the first two games at Carrow Road as City overcame Rotherham United 2-0 and Wimbledon 3-2.

His final outing came in the incident-packed 4-4 draw away to Rotherham United on 17 January 2004 when he replaced Marc Edworthy in the closing stages with City searching for an equaliser.

ROBERTS, Iwan

Date of birth: 26 June 1968
Place of birth: Bangor
Position: Striker
Promotion campaign: 2003/04 First Division Champions
2003/04 League statistics: 13(28)8

Legendary Welsh international striker Iwan Roberts made 306 appearances for the Canaries and netted 96 goals for the club. His seven-season Carrow Road career reached a fairytale ending as City won the First Division title and secured a return to the Premier League.

One of the club's all-time great players, Roberts was an inaugural member of the Norwich City Hall of Fame. Having carried the burden of being the go-to man for goals for so many seasons, Roberts certainly welcomed the support added by Darren Huckerby, Peter Crouch, Leon McKenzie and Mathias Svensson in the 2003/04 title-winning campaign.

A massive character in the Canary dressing room, Roberts contributed an impressive eight goals from 13 starts while also making a telling contribution from the bench with a further 28 appearances. His goal in the vital 1-0 victory over Sheffield United on 31 January 2004 was certainly one of his most important in Canary colours. With promotion assured, Roberts was given a memorable Carrow Road farewell as City defeated Preston North End 3-2 en route to the title.

RONSON, Brian

Date of birth: 7 August 1935
Place of birth: Durham
Date of death: June 2003
Place of death: Durham
Position: Goalkeeper

Promotion campaign: 1959/60 Division Three runners-up
1959/60 League statistics: 1(-)-

Goalkeeper Brian Ronson's single first-team appearance for Norwich City came in the Canaries' 1959/60 promotion-winning season.

Signed from Southend United by City boss Archie Macaulay in August 1959, Ronson arrived as cover for Sandy Kennon while Ken Nethercott continued his battle to try and regain full fitness following the shoulder injury he had sustained in the previous season's gallant FA Cup adventure.

Ronson's Canary debut saw him replace Kennon for the 3-2 Third Division victory over Swindon Town at Carrow Road on 7 November 1959. In front of a crowd of 22,494, a goal from Terry Allcock and a James Moran brace ensured that Ronson's big day ended on a happy, winning note. A regular in the City reserve side during his time at Norwich, he later played league football for Peterborough United.

ROSARIO, Robert
Date of birth: 4 March 1966
Place of birth: Hammersmith
Position: Striker
Promotion campaign: 1985/86 Division Two champions
1985/86 League statistics: 8(-)2

After first breaking through to the City first team at the tail end of the 1983/84 campaign, striker Robert Rosario partnered Kevin Drinkell for a seven-game spell in the 1985/86 Second Division title-winning season.

In the absence of John Deehan, Rosario was handed his first league start of the season in the 1-1 draw with Middlesbrough at Carrow Road on 14 September 1985. The big target man retained his place in the team over the next six league games and was on target in the 2-0 victory at home to Hull City and again in the comprehensive 4-0 rout of Carlisle United at Brunton Park.

Rosario's final involvement in the league programme saw him lead the line with summer-signing Wayne Biggins in a 1-1 draw at Brighton & Hove Albion on 2 November 1985. Biggins then cemented his place in the starting line-up as Drinkell's chosen strike partner and Rosario took in a loan move at Wolverhampton Wanderers before establishing himself as a first-team regular the following season.

ROSE, Michael

Date of birth: 28 July 1982
Place of birth: Salford
Position: Defender
Promotion campaign: 2009/10 League One champions
2009/10 League statistics: 11(1)1

Attack-minded left-back Michael Rose joined the Canaries on loan from Stockport County during the second half of the 2009/10 League One title-winning campaign. He became City's second signing from Edgeley Park that season, with the club having also signed Rose's former County team-mate Oli Johnson earlier in January 2010. The defender swiftly demonstrated his ability to get forward and support the attack when he marked his debut with City's second goal in the 2-1 Carrow Road victory over Hartlepool United on 30 January 2010.

Rose provided excellent cover for the injured Adam Drury and made a dozen appearances as Norwich secured promotion away to Charlton Athletic and then the title following a 2-0 victory over Gillingham a week later. Rose was strongly rumoured to be set to join the club at the end of the season but a permanent move to Carrow Road never happened and he joined Swindon Town in the summer of 2010.

ROYLE, Joe

Date of birth: 8 April 1949
Place of birth: Liverpool
Position: Striker
Promotion campaign: 1981/82 third in Division Two
1981/82 League statistics: 2(-)-

England international striker Joe Royle joined the Canaries in the twilight of a glittering playing career which saw him take in spells with Everton, Manchester City and Bristol City.

Signed in August 1980 from Bristol City, Royle made his debut on the opening day of the 1980/81 First Division season as a Justin Fashanu-inspired Norwich ran-out 5-1 winners against Stoke City at Carrow Road. Sadly, results like Stoke were few and far between and City suffered relegation at the end of Royle's first season with the club. However, the veteran frontman's performances made a positive impression on the Canary faithful, who voted him their player of the season.

Royle featured twice in City's 1981/82 promotion-winning campaign, his first appearance coming in a 2-1 victory over Cambridge United on 14 November 1981. On 5 December 1981 the curtain came down on his playing career when he was replaced by Peter Mendham in a goalless draw with Leicester City at Carrow Road. Forced to retire at the age of 33 with an on-going knee injury in 1982, Royle then began a highly successful managerial career when he took charge of Oldham Athletic.

RUDD, Declan

Date of birth: 16 January 1991
Place of birth: Diss
Position: Goalkeeper
Promotion campaigns: 2009/10 League One champions and 2010/11 Championship runners-up
2009/10 League statistics: 4(3)-
2010/11 League statistics: 1(-)-

Diss-born goalkeeper and lifelong Canary fan Declan Rudd progressed through the club's academy to play first-team football for his boyhood team.

Rudd was thrust straight into the action on his debut when he came off the bench to face a Simeon Jackson penalty following Fraser Forster's dismissal at Gillingham on 26 September 2009. His first job was to pick Jackson's spot-kick out of the net, but he went on to produce a number of smart stops before Darel Russell levelled late on.

His four starts in 2009/10 came when replacing the suspended Forster, who also saw red again in the Good Friday defeat at Tranmere Rovers.

Despite being a great shot stopper, in the main Rudd was unable to ever make a first-team place his own on a long-term basis. His opportunities tended to come from the bench, cup ties or covering for injuries and suspensions. Rudd's involvement in the 2010/11 promotion from the Championship saw him play in the 2-1 victory over Barnsley on 11 September 2010.

RUDDY, John

Date of birth: 24 October 1986
Place of birth: St Ives
Position: Goalkeeper

Promotion campaigns: 2010/11 Championship runners-up and 2014/15 Championship play-off winners
2010/11 League statistics: 45(-)-
2014/15 League statistics: 46(-)- + play-offs 3(-)-

Long-serving goalkeeper John Ruddy won an England cap and two promotions to the top-flight during a seven-year stint at Carrow Road.

Signed by Paul Lambert from Everton in the summer of 2010, the former Cambridge United keeper took a while to settle at Carrow Road, with many fans frustrated that the club were unable to secure the services of 2009/10 loanee Fraser Forster on a permanent basis. However, Ruddy certainly won over the fans with a series of commanding performances and missed just one league game during his debut season at Carrow Road in 2010/11, as Norwich secured back-to-back promotions. Ruddy then featured as City's first-choice keeper in the Premier League for the next three seasons.

The giant keeper was then an ever-present member of the 2014/15 City side that secured an instant return to the Premier League after their play-off success over Middlesbrough at Wembley.

RUSSELL, Darel
Date of birth: 22 October 1980
Place of birth: Mile End
Position: Midfielder
Promotion campaign: 2009/10 League One champions
2009/10 League statistics: 34(1)2

A product of the Canaries' youth system, midfielder Darel Russell progressed through the ranks and enjoyed two separate spells as a professional at Carrow Road.

A strong runner, his box-to-box style made him a firm favourite with the City fans. However, after breaking through to the first team in 1997, he struggled to maintain his early form and a combination of management changes, injuries and contract wrangles led to his inevitable departure from Carrow Road in August 2003, when he joined Stoke City.

Russell returned to Carrow Road for a second stint with Norwich in the summer of 2007. Following City's relegation in 2009, Russell was used in a slightly deeper role at the base of a successful diamond formation under Paul Lambert as City raced to the League One title. Russell scored twice in the 2009/10 League campaign, both goals coming against Gillingham. The first rescued a point at Priestfield in September 2009 and the second secured the title in City's penultimate home game.

SARGENT, Gary

Date of birth: 11 September 1952
Place of birth: Bedford
Position: Striker
Promotion campaign: 1971/72 Division Two champions
1971/72 League statistics: -(1)-

Striker Gary Sargent joined the Canaries as an apprentice in 1968 and his impressive goalscoring ratio saw him rewarded with a professional contract two years later.

A regular face in the second string, Sargent found opportunities to showcase his ability on the first-team scene rather hard to come by. His Canary debut arrived on 28 August 1971 when he replaced Malcolm Darling midway through the second half of a goalless Second Division match with Fulham at Craven Cottage.

That outing by the Thames proved to be Sargent's only slice of first-team action for City. He left Carrow Road in the summer of 1972 following the club's elevation to the top flight and sampled regular league football with Scunthorpe United, Peterborough United and Northampton Town. He had a brief Norwich career at first-team level, but timing makes him a promotion-winning Canary.

SAVINO, Ray

Date of birth: 16 November 1938
Place of birth: Norwich

Position: Midfielder
Promotion campaign: 1959/60 Division Three runners-up
1959/60 League statistics: 2(-)-

Norwich-born right-winger Ray Savino made two of his 27 first-team appearances for the Canaries during the club's 1959/60 Third Division promotion-winning campaign.

Having made his City debut back in 1957, Savino was a reserve-team regular and boss Archie Macaulay had no hesitation in asking him to step up to cover for Errol Crossan for a two-game spell in the vital latter stages of the 1959/60 season. He played his first game of the season in the 1-1 draw at home to Shrewsbury Town on Wednesday, 30 March 1960 and also started the next game three days later when a first-half Matt Crowe goal gave City both points from a 1-0 triumph over York City at Carrow Road.

With regular first-team football at Norwich never consistently coming his way, Savino moved on to Bristol City in 1963. He enjoyed a successful spell at Ashton Gate before returning to his Norfolk roots and touring the local non-league circuit.

SHACKELL, Jason

Date of birth: 27 September 1983
Place of birth: Stevenage
Position: Defender
Promotion campaign: 2003/04 First Division champions
2003/04 League statistics: 4(2)-

A product of the club's academy, defender Jason Shackell impressed at under-18 and reserve level before being handed his first-team debut away to Derby County in April 2003 when he covered at left-back for the injured Adam Drury.

With the ability to operate at left-back as well as his preferred role of centre-back, the following season saw Shackell continue to be involved with the first-team squad during the club's First Division championship-winning campaign.

He made four starts for Nigel Worthington's side in 2003/04 but only one in his chosen role in the centre of defence. He partnered the ever-present Craig Fleming when Malky Mackay was suspended for the visit of Cardiff City in December and slotted in at left-back in the absence of skipper Adam Drury for home victories over Reading and Gillingham. He also featured in the starting line-up for the 1-0 defeat at Crystal Palace in March 2004.

SHEPHERD, Greig

Date of birth: 29 September 1960
Place of birth: Edinburgh
Position: Striker
Promotion campaign: 1981/82 third in Division Two
1981/82 League statistics: 12(3)2

In a season when, at various stages, Norwich City named Keith Bertschin, Ross Jack, Joe Royle, John Deehan and John Fashanu among their striking options, Scottish centre-forward Greig Shepherd also managed to more than play his part in the 1981/82 promotion-winning success.

Shepherd featured in 15 Second Division fixtures, a dozen of them starts, as Norwich secured an instant return to the top flight. It was Shepherd, in fact, who scored their first goal of the promotion-winning season. The 1981/82 campaign was just seven minutes old when he struck to give City an opening-day lead over Rotherham United at Millmoor. Sadly, it was a short-lived advantage against a rampant Millers side who stormed back to win 4-1.

His second goal of the season came just two weeks later and this time set the tone for the Canaries' first away win of the season as Ken Brown's men triumphed 3-2 at Wrexham. Following the signing of John Deehan, Shepherd found a place in the City attack more difficult to come by and his final appearance of the season came in the Martin O'Neill-inspired victory at Bolton Wanderers on 20 March 1982.

SILVESTER, Peter

Date of birth: 19 February 1948
Place of birth: Wokingham

Position: Striker
Promotion campaign: 1971/72 Division Two champions
1971/72 League statistics: 26(-)12

Signed from Reading in September 1969, Peter Silvester spearheaded the Norwich City attack throughout the first six months of their 1971/72 Second Division title-winning season.

Silvester was on target in the Canaries' opening home game as Ron Saunders's men defeated Portsmouth 3-1 on 21 August 1971. In total he scored a dozen league goals before the turn of the year, which included a brace in the 3-2 Carrow Road victory over Oxford United and the only goal of the game to seal a vital success away at Swindon Town on 4 December 1971.

Sadly, what looked all set for a 20-goal-plus campaign for Silvester came to a shuddering halt when he suffered a season-ending knee injury in the 1-1 draw with Preston North End at Carrow Road on 22 January 1972. Despite that injury sidelining Silvester from action, he still ended the season as the club's second-highest scorer after Kenny Foggo pipped him to top spot by just one goal. Silvester's contribution to the Canaries' historic 1971/72 campaign is fondly remembered and he often forms part of modern-day Norwich City in his role as a match-day host for sponsors and guests at Carrow Road.

SMITH, Korey

Date of birth: 31 January 1991
Place of birth: Hatfield
Position: Midfielder
Promotion campaigns: 2009/10 League One champions and 2010/11
    Championship runners-up
2009/10 League statistics: 36(1)4
2010/11 League statistics: 19(9)-

Combative midfielder Korey Smith was a Norwich City youth-team captain who was handed his first-team debut under Bryan Gunn in April 2009 as Norwich fought against Championship relegation.

The all-action midfielder was a surprise name on Paul Lambert's first Norwich team-sheet but he grabbed his opportunity with both hands, scoring in City's 5-2 thumping of Wycombe Wanderers on 22 August 2009 in what was only his second start for the club and his first on home soil.

Smith's energy and ball-winning tenacity blossomed under Lambert and he played a key role in the League One title-winning triumph. His late winning goal at Wycombe on 2 January 2010 was one of many crucial contributions. Despite additional competition for places from new signings Andrew Crofts and Andrew Surman, Smith continued to feature at Championship level the following season and made 19 starts as City reached the Premier League.

SMITH, Steven
Date of birth: 30 August 1985
Place of birth: Bellshill
Position: Defender
Promotion campaign: 2010/11 Championship runners-up
2010/11 League statistics: 5(2)-

Hailing from Bellshill, just like 2003/04 promotion-winning hero Malky Mackay, left-back Steven Smith joined City on a free transfer from Glasgow Rangers.

The defender's time at Norwich was initially hampered by an Achilles injury he suffered in pre-season. Once fully fit, he made his Canary debut under the lights at Carrow Road as Norwich edged a thrilling Championship affair with Leicester City by running out 4-3 winners on 28 September 2010.

Smith's first start came the following Saturday at Ashton Gate. Adam Drury was withdrawn late on due to injury and Smith stepped into the left-back berth in a 3-0 away success. He then started four of the following five games before injury forced his withdrawal during the 2-2 draw at home to Burnley in November 2010. With Smith reportedly struggling to settle into life south of the border, he spent the second half of the 2010/11 season on loan with Aberdeen before making a permanent move to Preston North End in August 2011.

SPEARING, Tony
Date of birth: 7 October 1964
Place of birth: Romford
Position: Defender
Promotion campaign: 1985/86 Division Two champions
1985/86 League statistics: 7(1)-

An FA Youth Cup winner with the Canaries in 1983, tough-tackling left-back Tony Spearing became a popular member of the City squad for a four-year period following his Canary debut.

As with a host of home-grown players, patience was key for Spearing. Competition from others for the left-back position, coupled with a broken leg suffered shortly after establishing himself on the first-team scene, prevented Spearing from making the number-three shirt his own until the 1986/87 season.

However, he certainly played a part in the club's 1985/86 campaign as Ken Brown masterminded a second Norwich City promotion, and just as in 1981/82 it was at the first time of asking. Spearing covered for Dennis Van Wijk for seven league matches in the early part of the season with Norwich winning three, drawing two and losing twice as a new-look City side adjusted to facing new opponents. With promotion and the title assured, Spearing's final action of the season saw him appear from the bench in the penultimate game of the season at Hull.

SPILLANE, Michael
Date of birth: 23 March 1989
Place of birth: St Hellier
Position: Defender
Promotion campaign: 2009/10 League One champions
2009/10 League statistics: 10(3)1

A product of the Canaries youth academy, Michael Spillane had the ability to operate in midfield or in a defensive role either at centre-half or right-back.

After spending the 2008/09 season on loan at Luton Town, he returned to Carrow Road for the 2009/10 League One season and was battling with Jon Otsemobor for the right-back berth until he suffered a hamstring injury against Bristol Rovers on 3 October 2009.

The timing of Spillane's injury was particularly frustrating as he had netted his first goal of the season only five days earlier when City defeated Leyton Orient 4-0 at Carrow Road. By the time he had regained full fitness, Norwich had acquired the services of Russell Martin, who then became a regular feature in a winning team. Spillane had to wait until promotion was won before he found himself in the starting line-up again, his final two appearances of the season coming at home to Gillingham and away to Bristol Rovers. The latter proved to be his last game for the club.

SRBENY, Dennis
Date of birth: 5 May 1994
Place of birth: Berlin
Position: Striker

Promotion campaign: 2018/19 Championship champions
2018/19 League statistics: -(15)1

A January 2018 signing from SC Paderborn, striker Dennis Srbeny arrived at Norwich having carved out a growing reputation as a useful goalscorer in the lower divisions of German football.

After debuting as a substitute in the 1-1 draw at Derby County on 10 February 2018, he totalled 14 appearances for City in the second-half of the 2017/18 campaign, seven of which were starts. His first goal for the club came in a 2-1 victory over Aston Villa in April 2018. More often than not among the substitutes throughout the 2018/19 league season, Srbeny made 15 appearances from the bench and was on the scoresheet in the 4-0 rout of Sheffield Wednesday at Hillsborough on 3 November 2018. He also started all five of City's cup games in 2018/19, netting a memorable brace in the 3-1 League Cup triumph away to Cardiff City.

STEELE, William (Billy)
Date of birth: 16 June 1955
Place of birth: Kirkmuirhill, Lanark
Position: Midfielder
Promotion campaign: 1974/75 third in Division Two
1974/75 League statistics: 4(5)-

Despite being signed for Norwich City by Ron Saunders, it was John Bond who handed industrious Scottish midfielder Billy Steele his Canary debut in December 1973.

Steele was certainly thrown in at the deep end as Bond plunged him into the white-hot atmosphere of an East Anglian derby at Portman Road for his initial taste of first-team football on Boxing Day 1973.

After City suffered relegation from the First Division in 1974, Steele formed part of a City squad that was able to return to the top flight at the first given opportunity. Still making his mark on the first-team scene in 1974/75, Steele started four Second Division fixtures and also made five substitute appearances for Bond's promotion-winning troops. Remarkably, the side remained unbeaten in all four games that he started and suffered just one defeat in the five games in which he appeared from the bench. After really making his mark for the Canaries in the First Division in 1976/77, Steele's career was sadly ended by a knee injury suffered at Villa Park in April 1977.

STIEPERMANN, Marco

Date of birth: 9 February 1991
Place of birth: Dortmund
Position: Midfielder
Promotion campaigns: 2018/19 Championship champions
2018/19 League statistics: 39(4)9

After something of an indifferent first season at Carrow Road, Marco Stiepermann produced a host of match-winning performances during the Canaries' 2018/19 success.

Signed from VfL Bochum on a three-year contract in August 2017, Stiepermann was used mostly at left-back and occasionally in midfield during his initial campaign with the Canaries. The 2018/19 season then saw him operating in a more advanced midfield role and the German blossomed beyond belief. Linking up almost telepathically at times with summer signing Teemu Pukki, Stiepermann created countless chances for others and weighed in with nine Championship goals.

His goals included a wonderful curling effort to open the scoring away to Bristol City in December 2018 and he also found the net in the final two home games against Sheffield Wednesday and Blackburn Rovers as Norwich closed in on promotion.

STRINGER, David

Date of birth: 15 October 1944
Place of birth: Great Yarmouth
Position: Defender
Promotion campaigns: 1971/72 Division Two champions and 1974/75 third in Division Two
1971/72 League statistics: 42(-)4
1974/75 League statistics: 39(-)3

Norfolk-born defender Dave Stringer has served Norwich City Football Club in many capacities but is best remembered for an outstanding playing career and a successful spell as the club's manager.

Stringer turned professional at Carrow Road in May 1963 and made his first-team debut in April 1965. He was then virtually a permanent fixture in the City defence for the next decade.

Playing in all 42 league games in the 1971/72 promotion campaign, his four league goals that season included a header to clinch the Division Two Championship in a 1-1 draw away to

Watford on the final day of the season. His consistency alongside Duncan Forbes at the heart of the City defence saw him rewarded with the Barry Butler Memorial Trophy as the supporters' player of the season at the end of that classic campaign.

Stringer won a second promotion in 1974/75 as Norwich bounced back to Division One at the first attempt under John Bond. His total of 499 games for the club leaves him third in City's list of all-time appearance makers, with only Kevin Keelan (673) and Ron Ashman (662) above him.

SUGGETT, Colin

Date of birth: 30 December 1948
Place of birth: Chester-le-Street
Position: Midfielder
Promotion campaign: 1974/75 third in Division Two
1974/75 League statistics: 41(-)6

Skilful midfielder Colin Suggett was recruited from West Bromwich Albion by Ron Saunders for a then club record fee of £75,000 in February 1973. He played his part in helping the Canaries survive their debut season in the First Division but after suffering relegation in 1973/74, Suggett proved to be a vital ingredient in the John Bond side that bounced straight back to the top flight at the first attempt in 1974/75.

Suggett played in 41 league fixtures and chipped in with six goals, two of which were scored against Bristol City. He set the Canaries on their way to a 3-2 Carrow Road triumph over the Robins with a 17th-minute opener on 21 December 1974. Ironically, he also opened the scoring in the return fixture at Ashton Gate on 29 March 1975 – again in the 17th minute. That proved to be the only goal of the game and provided the Canaries with another vital victory en route to promotion. At the end of the 1974/75 season, Suggett was presented with the Barry Butler Memorial Trophy as City's player of the season.

SULLIVAN, Colin

Date of birth: 24 June 1951
Place of birth: Saltash
Position: Defender
Promotion campaign: 1974/75 third in Division Two
1974/75 League statistics: 35(1)1

Left-back Colin Sullivan joined the Canaries in 1974 from Plymouth Argyle for an initial fee of £50,000 and arrived in Norfolk just five days before his 23rd birthday.

Sullivan enjoyed a dream first season at Carrow Road. Debuting on the opening day of the season in a 2-1 victory over Blackpool, he scored his first goal in Canary colours as City defeated Notts County 3-0 at Carrow Road on 14 September 1974. He also played in every game of the club's League Cup campaign which ended with a Wembley date against Aston Villa.

In a season when many occupied the right-back position at various stages, Sullivan really made the left-back berth his own. After missing seven games towards the end of the season, Sullivan returned to the side for a tricky match away to struggling Millwall on 12 April 1974 and helped save City's blushes when he crossed for Geoff Butler to head home a last-minute equaliser. Sullivan swiftly adapted to First Division football following promotion and made a total of 182 appearances for the club.

SURMAN, Andrew
Date of birth: 20 August 1986
Place of birth: Johannesburg
Position: Midfielder
Promotion campaigns: 2010/11 Championship runners-up and 2014/15 Championship play-off winners
2010/11 League statistics: 19(3)3
2014/15 League statistics 1(-)

Midfielder Andrew Surman joined the Canaries in the summer of 2010 from Wolverhampton Wanderers and played an important role in the club's 2010/11 promotion-winning season. With the ability to operate on the left side of midfield or in a more central role, Surman's quality in possession often saw him creating chances for others with his neat passing skills and clever approach play.

In the closing stages of the 2010/11 campaign, Surman chipped in with three goals – his first coming late on against Bristol City to seal a 3-1 Carrow Road success on 14 March 2011. He then netted a vital winner at home to Nottingham Forest as City came from behind to win 2-1 on 15 April 2011. Surman also picked the perfect time to net his first away goal for the club, opening the scoring in City's memorable 5-1 triumph over arch-rivals Ipswich Town at Portman Road as Norwich closed in on promotion to the Premier League.

SVENSSON, Mathias

Date of birth: 24 September 1974
Place of birth: Boras, Sweden
Position: Striker
Promotion campaign: 2003/04 First Division champions
2003/04 League statistics: 16(4)7

Striker Mathias Svensson joined the Canaries from Charlton Athletic in December 2003 and played a vital part in the second half of the club's 2003/04 success.

A powerful yet skilful target man, Svensson made his first Norwich appearance alongside fellow debutant Leon McKenzie in the 2-0 East Anglian derby victory over Ipswich Town at Portman Road on 21 December 2003. Although McKenzie grabbed the headlines as his brace sent City top of the table, Svensson did not have to wait too long to find himself on the score-sheet for his new employers. Just five days after his debut, he marked his Carrow Road bow with the only goal of the game as City secured three points from their Boxing Day match with Nottingham Forest.

Despite City's host of attacking options, including the permanent arrival of Darren Huckerby, Svensson scored seven goals including vital efforts against Stoke City and Burnley plus a memorable strike in the Good Friday victory over promotion rivals Wigan Athletic at Carrow Road.

SYMONDS, Richard

Date of birth: 21 November 1959
Place of birth: Longham, Norfolk
Position: Defender
Promotion campaign: 1981/82 third in Division Two
1981/82 League statistics: 18(-)-

A home-grown player, versatile defender Richard Symonds was used sporadically by both John Bond and Ken Brown during his time at Carrow Road.

Widely regarded as an excellent man-to-man marker, Symonds was blessed with outstanding pace which helped him keep many a speedy winger in check during his Canary career.

With the ability to also operate in a midfield role, Symonds's flexibility saw him viewed very much as a utility player and that hindered his attempts to tie down a regular place of his own. However, the 1981/82 promotion-winning season proved to be Symonds's most

228

fruitful in terms of first-team action as manager Brown handed him 18 league outings and five cup appearances. Having covered for Greg Downs at left-back in the 3-2 win at Wrexham on 12 September 1981, he took over at right-back from Mark Nightingale for the 2-1 Carrow Road triumph over Shrewsbury in October 1981. Symonds then held the number-two shirt for a four-month spell until Paul Haylock emerged as the club's first-choice right-back.

TETTEY, Alexander

Date of birth: 4 April 1986
Place of birth: Accra, Ghana
Position: Midfielder
Promotion campaigns: 2014/15 Championship play-off winners and
   2018/19 Championship champions
2014/15 League statistics: 34(2)2 + play-offs 3(-)-
2018/19 League statistics: 26(4)1

A regular for the Canaries in their 2014/15 promotion via the end-of-season play-offs, Alex Tettey was the only member of the City squad with a Norwich City promotion on his CV as Daniel Farke's men sampled Championship success in 2018/19.

The tough-tackling Norwegian midfield international joined the Canaries back in August 2012. A popular player amongst the Carrow Road faithful, Tettey scored twice in the 2014/15 season in victories over Watford and Brentford, while being one of the first names on the City team-sheet under both Neil Adams and Alex Neil. Tettey is fondly remembered for his post-match celebratory jig at Wembley in 2015 and his winning goal the following season at Old Trafford.

Tettey's experience was certainly valued by Daniel Farke, with the City boss handing him the captain's armband following Grant Hanley's injury in the early part of the 2018/19 campaign. Tettey struck a memorable goal in the 2-0 win over Preston North End in August 2018 and made the defensive midfield role his own until he suffered an injury in the New Year's Day match at Brentford, which paved the way for Tom Trybull to return to the first-team picture.

THEOKLITOS, Michael

Date of birth: 11 February 1981
Place of birth: Melbourne
Position: Goalkeeper

Promotion campaign: 2009/10 League One champions
2009/10 League statistics: 1(-)-

Every player in this book has contributed in some way to a Norwich City promotion, however big or small their individual involvement may have been, and despite playing just one game for the Canaries, goalkeeper Michael Theoklitos certainly made an unforgettable mark on Carrow Road.

The Australian stopper was recruited by then City boss Bryan Gunn in the summer of 2009. He arrived at Carrow Road from Melbourne Victory, with his only experience of the English game being a brief spell with Blackpool.

He was installed as City's first-choice keeper ahead of the 2009/10 League One campaign and kept a clean sheet in a 1-0 pre-season victory over Crystal Palace on his City debut. In his first competitive match, on the opening day of the season, he conceded seven goals (five before half-time), a number of which he was at fault for as City crashed to a record 7-1 home defeat at the hands of Colchester United. Theoklitos never played first-team football again for City and his contract was cancelled by mutual consent in March 2010.

THOMPSON, Louis

Date of birth: 19 December 1994
Place of birth: Dover
Position: Midfielder
Promotion campaigns: 2018/19 Championship champions
2018/19 League statistics: 1(5)-

Clearly a player with great potential and an obvious desire to succeed with Norwich City, Welsh under-21 international midfielder Louis Thompson has seen his Canary career blighted by injury woes.

Signed from Swindon Town back in September 2014, Thompson remained at the County Ground on loan for the 2014/15 season and also spent his 2015/16 campaign with the Robins. He finally made his Norwich City debut in a League Cup tie at home to Coventry City in August 2016.

Two serious Achilles heel injuries prevented his progress, but the all-action midfielder certainly has a fan in City boss Daniel Farke, who handed him a new four-year contract in October 2018. Thompson started City's league match at home to Leeds United in August 2018 and also made five appearances from the bench in 2018/19, the last being the 2-1 Carrow Road triumph over Aston Villa on 23 October, when he unfortunately departed with a dislocated shoulder just moments after entering the fray.

THURLOW, Bryan

Date of birth: 6 June 1936
Place of birth: Loddon, Norwich
Date of death: 5 January 2002
Place of death: Norwich
Position: Defender
Promotion campaign: 1959/60 Division Three runners-up
1959/60 League statistics: 46(-)-

Ever-present in the Canaries' 1958/59 FA Cup adventure, right-back Bryan Thurlow was a highly dependable member of the City side that won promotion to the Second Division the following season.

Along with fellow cup heroes Ron Ashman, Roy McCrohan and Barry Butler, Thurlow played every game of City's 1959/60 season as Archie Macaulay's team ended a successful campaign as runners-up to Third Division champions Southampton.

One of few local players in the City team, Thurlow was blessed with the wonderful ability to sense danger and as a result was rarely caught out of position, with very few wingers getting the better of him in one-on-one situations. Thurlow was a true Norwich City great, playing 224 times for the club, and he was rightfully proud of all he achieved with his local team.

TIERNEY, Marc

Date of birth: 23 August 1985
Place of birth: Prestwich
Position: Defender
Promotion campaign: 2010/11 Championship runners-up
2010/11 League statistics: 14(2)-

Norwich boss Paul Lambert returned to former club Colchester United to sign left-back Marc Tierney during the 2011 January transfer window. With vast experience of the lower leagues, Tierney jumped at the chance of joining a Norwich City side that was harbouring realistic ambitions of promotion to the Premier League. He made his Canary debut as a substitute in a goalless draw with Crystal Palace at Selhurst Park on 29 January 2011. His first start came in the 2-1 victory over Millwall at Carrow Road three days later.

A tough-tackling full-back who loved to advance into the opposition's half, Tierney's game was tailor-made for the attacking brand of football that City played across their back-to-back promotion successes. He made the left-back berth his own in the final months of the 2011/12 season, making 16 appearances as Norwich secured the Championship runners-up spot, and his cart-wheeling antics during the promotion celebrations brought a smile to the faces of supporters and team-mates alike.

TRYBULL, Tom
Date of birth: 9 March 1993
Place of birth: Berlin
Position: Midfielder
Promotion campaigns: 2018/19 Championship champions
2018/19 League statistics: 22(9)1

Defensive midfielder Tom Trybull joined the Canaries in the summer of 2017 following Daniel Farke's appointment as head coach at Carrow Road.

After agreeing a one-year contract, the German's ability to operate in a holding role in front of the back four was expected to see him offer both cover and competition to Alex Tettey and Louis Thompson. After appearing regularly in Championship fixtures, his progress was rewarded with improved and extended terms before the 2017/18 season was out.

Trybull began 2018/19 in the starting line-up but the form of others then limited his involvement over the coming months. Come the turn of the year and he was back in the first-team picture. With both Marco Stiepermann and Alex Tettey forced off during the New Year's Day draw at Brentford, Trybull entered the fray at Griffin Park, and once the severity of Tettey's injury was confirmed he continued to cover for the sidelined Norwegian. Trybull headed home his first goal of the season in the 3-1 home win over Birmingham City in January as Norwich ended a run of five games without a win. His tenacity in midfield duels has won him many plaudits and he produced a number of gritty and determined performances as Norwich motored on to promotion.

TUDUR JONES, Owain
Date of birth: 15 October 1984
Place of birth: Bangor

Position: Midfielder
Promotion campaigns: 2009/10 League One champions and 2010/11
   Championship runners-up
2009/10 League statistics: 2(1)1
2010/11 League statistics: 1(1)-

Norwich City captured Welsh international midfielder Owain Tudur Jones in the summer of 2009 from Swansea City and his arrival was met with great enthusiasm by supporters.

A tall and imposing midfielder with an impressive range of passing skills, Tudur Jones's time at Swansea had been severely interrupted by injury. However, the view was that if Norwich could keep him fit then he would be a real asset in League One. Sadly he debuted in the 7-1 opening day mauling by Colchester United and that really set the tone for a tough time in Norfolk as he made just five league appearances in a two-year stay.

Tudur Jones failed to figure in new boss Paul Lambert's plans and his League One contribution of two starts, one substitute appearance and one goal all came under the watch of Bryan Gunn or caretaker Ian Butterworth. He was twice loaned to Yeovil Town but made a surprise return to the fold at Norwich late in 2010 and even started the first game of 2011 away to Middlesbrough. That 1-1 draw at the Riverside proved to be his final outing for City. He was subsequently loaned to Yeovil Town and Brentford before his contract was terminated by mutual consent in August 2011.

TURNER, Michael
Date of birth: 9 November 1983
Place of birth: Lewisham
Position: Defender
Promotion campaign: 2014/15 Championship play-off winners
2014/15 League statistics: 22(1)1

Experienced central-defender Michael Turner was signed from Sunderland by Chris Hughton in the summer of 2012. Turner had carved out a good reputation as a reliable centre-half at both Hull City and Sunderland, and he certainly never let anyone down at Carrow Road.

After suffering relegation from the Premier League, City's 2014/15 season was Turner's third at Carrow Road and he was a regular face in the starting line-up during Neil Adams's reign as City boss. Partnering skipper Russell Martin at the heart of the City defence, Turner netted a rare goal as City produced a memorable comeback to win 4-2 at Cardiff City in September 2014.

Despite the change of manager in January 2015, Turner was named in new manager Alex Neil's first City line-up as the Canaries triumphed 3-2 at home to Cardiff City. He then only made one further appearance before ending the campaign on loan to Championship rivals Fulham after Neil opted to recall the out-of-favour Seb Bassong to partner Martin for the remainder of the campaign.

VAN WIJK, Dennis
Date of birth: 16 December 1962
Place of birth: Oostzaan, Holland
Position: Defender
Promotion campaign: 1985/86 Divison Two champions
1985/86 League statistics: 27(2)1

Famed for his infamous handball that resulted in City conceding a penalty in the 1985 League Cup final, Dutch left-back Dennis Van Wijk enjoyed a four-year spell with Norwich City between 1982 and 1986.

Van Wijk was let off the hook at Wembley when Sunderland striker Clive Walker failed to convert the spot-kick opportunity that the Dutchman's handball had presented him. However, City's Wembley joy was short-lived as relegation to the second tier swiftly followed. Van Wijk, like many others, remained loyal to the Canary cause and played his part in ensuring an immediate return to the top flight.

The 1985/86 season saw Van Wijk come under pressure from Tony Spearing for the left-back role, but the experienced Dutchman remained the first choice when fit and started 27 of City's 42 league fixtures. Never renowned for his goalscoring, the 1985/86 season saw him net one of the four goals he scored during his Canary career. City were already one up when Van Wijk played a neat one-two with Mike Phelan before firing home City's second goal in a 3-0 victory over Blackburn Rovers at Carrow Road on 7 December 1985.

VOKES, Sam
Date of birth: 21 October 1989
Place of birth: Southampton
Position: Striker

Promotion campaign: 2010/11 Championship runners-up
2010/11 League statistics: 1(3)1

Welsh international striker Sam Vokes joined City on a 28-day emergency loan deal from Wolverhampton Wanderers in March 2011 to cover for the injured Aaron Wilbraham.

His Carrow Road debut coincided with two players netting hat-tricks – Grant Holt and Simeon Jackson – as Norwich thumped relegation-threatened Scunthorpe United 6-0 on Saturday, 6 April 2011. Vokes marked his first start for the club with a goal as he latched on to a pass from Holt to fire City in front at Watford after just 77 seconds of an eventful match that ended 2-2 at Vicarage Road on 12 April 2011.

Vokes's time with City was cut short when he was recalled to Molineux due to an injury crisis unfolding at his parent club. However, he certainly signed off from Norwich in some style – his final appearance for the club coming when he replaced Holt in the closing stages of the East Anglian derby at Portman Road on Thursday, 21 April 2011. With City leading 4-1, Vokes played a vital part in the approach to Dani Pacheco's goal that wrapped up a 5-1 thrashing of City's arch-rivals.

VRANCIC, Mario
Date of birth: 23 May 1989
Place of birth: Slavonski Brod
Position: Midfielder
Promotion campaigns: 2018/19 Championship champions
2018/19 League statistics: 14(22)10

Bosnian midfield maestro Mario Vrancic certainly made his mark on the Canaries' 2018/19 promotion-winning campaign as he contributed vital and spectacular goals in crucial fixtures in the final months of the season.

Signed from Darmstadt in June 2018, Vrancic made a good early impression upon his arrival with a number of sharp performances in City's pre-season friendly games. Once the season got under way for real, though, he failed to really show his quality in games and despite starting 29 Championship fixtures in 2017/18, he scored just once when he netted in a 3-2 victory over Reading in March 2018.

Vrancic's 2017/18 form was certainly in stark contrast to 2018/19 as he scored a remarkable ten Championship goals, despite starting just 14 games. He really was the star of the show in City's top-of-the-table clash with Leeds United at Elland Road on 2 February 2019. After opening the scoring with an early free-kick, he also added City's third and final goal in an impressive 3-1 win. Another stunning free-kick deep into injury-time saved City from a Carrow Road defeat to Sheffield Wednesday on Good Friday before he struck the promotion-winning goal against Blackburn Rovers in the penultimate game of the season. Fittingly, he also netted the final goal of the campaign to seal a 2-1 win away to Aston Villa.

WALFORD, Steve

Date of birth: 5 January 1958
Place of birth: Highgate
Position: Defender
Promotion campaign: 1981/82 third in Division Two
1981/82 League statistics: 42(-)1

Steve Walford's arrival at Carrow Road in March 1981 proved to be a case of too little too late as City fought in vain against the drop into Division Two.

Signed from Arsenal for a fee of £175,000, Walford very rarely missed a game throughout his Canary career and formed an excellent partnership with Dave Watson at the heart of the City defence across almost two-and-a-half seasons at Carrow Road. A left-footer and a good reader of the game, his presence added both balance and experience to the Norwich backline.

Along with goalkeeper Chris Woods, Walford was ever-present in the Norwich team that secured an immediate return to the top flight in 1981/82. In his 108 games for the club he scored only two goals, the first of which came in the 1981/82 campaign when he opened the scoring in a 2-1 victory over Cambridge United at Carrow Road on 14 November 1981.

WARD, Elliott

Date of birth: 19 January 1985
Place of birth: Harrow
Position: Defender
Promotion campaign: 2010/11 Championship runners-up
2010/11 League statistics: 39(-)1

Elliott Ward was one of a number of players brought to Carrow Road in the summer of 2010 as Paul Lambert looked to strengthen his group for the challenge of Championship football following their League One success in the previous campaign.

Ward debuted in the opening game of the season and played in 39 of City's 46 Championship fixtures. Recruited on a free transfer following his release from Coventry City, Ward was well-versed in what was needed at Championship level and already had one promotion from the second tier on his CV, dating back to his time at West Ham United.

It was an injury sustained in City's 2-1 win on Ward's return to Coventry in December that sidelined him for six of the seven league games he missed in 2010/11. However, he marked his return to the side with his first goal for the club to help secure a midweek 2-1 triumph over Millwall at Carrow Road on 1 February 2011.

WATSON, David

Date of birth: 20 November 1961
Place of birth: Liverpool
Position: Defender
Promotion campaigns: 1981/82 third in Division Two and 1985/86
   Division Two champions
1981/82 League statistics: 38(-)3
1985/86 League statistics: 42(-)3

A double promotion-winner with the Canaries, Dave Watson skippered the team to League Cup glory at Wembley in 1985 before then lifting the Second Division championship trophy the following season.

Plucked from Liverpool for a bargain £50,000 fee in December 1980, Watson jumped at the chance of first-team football with Norwich after becoming frustrated at the understandable lack of opportunities at Anfield. His fee doubled to £100,000 following 25 outings in yellow and green, and Watson went on to amass 256 appearances for

Norwich City as he became widely recognised as one of the club's best central-defenders of all time.

Always a dominant force in the air, Watson made 38 appearances in City's 1981/82 promotion triumph and headed home three goals. In 1985/86 he formed an ever-present central-defensive partnership alongside Steve Bruce as the club completed a hat-trick of promotions at the first attempt. There were many star performers as Ken Brown's side landed the 1985/86 Second Division title with a seven-point cushion but there was little doubt that Brown built his side on the solid defensive base that was provided by messrs Watson and Bruce.

WHALEY, Simon

Date of birth: 7 June 1985
Place of birth: Bolton
Position: Midfielder
Promotion campaign: 2009/10 League One champions
2009/10 League statistics: 3(-)-

A wave of enthusiasm surrounded the Canaries' signing of winger Simon Whaley from Preston North End in the summer of 2009.

Whaley's arrival offered City an exciting threat down the right and he was fully expected to be a class act in League One. He produced some excellent performances in pre-season and scored goals in victories away to Crystal Palace and at home to Wigan Athletic as Bryan Gunn's new-look side prepared for the big kick-off.

Named in the starting line-up for the opening-day massacre at home to Colchester United, Whaley's Canary career was almost over before it had started. Selected by caretaker boss Ian Butterworth for two games following Gunn's sacking, Whaley failed to impress new boss Paul Lambert. He was handed opportunities in League Cup and Football League Trophy fixtures before being loaned to Rochdale and Bradford City. He left Norwich City in February 2010 after his contract was cancelled by mutual consent.

WHITBREAD, Zak

Date of birth: 4 March 1984
Place of birth: Houston, Texas
Position: Defender
Promotion campaigns: 2009/10 League One champions and 2010/11
   Championship runners-up

2009/10 League statistics: 1(3)-
2010/11 League statistics: 20(2)1

One-time Liverpool central-defender Zak Whitbread was signed from League One rivals Millwall during the Canaries' 2009/10 League One title-winning campaign.

A classy defender who was particularly comfortable in bringing the ball out of defence, Whitbread was also blessed with good pace and had all the attributes to make the perfect defender. However, he struggled with a number of injuries throughout his career, which prevented him from enjoying sustained spells of first-team action. A popular character in the dressing room, there was never any doubt throughout his Carrow Road career that a fit Zak Whitbread was a major asset.

Whitbread figured briefly in the Canaries' League One title success, debuting in the 5-0 victory away to Colchester United. However, it was the 2010/11 promotion from the Championship that really saw him come to the fore at Carrow Road. Playing alongside Michael Nelson, Leon Barnett or, most regularly, Elliott Ward, Whitbread made 22 league appearances and was on the score-sheet in the 1-1 draw at Hull City on 19 March 2011.

WHITEHOUSE, Brian
Date of birth: 8 September 1935
Place of birth: West Bromwich
Date of death: 16 January 2017
Place of death: Sutton Coldfield
Position: Striker
Promotion campaign: 1959/60 Third Division runners-up
1959/60 League statistics: 10(-)4

Signed from West Bromwich Albion for a fee of £7,000 in March 1960, striker Brian Whitehouse chipped in with four goals from ten games to help City secure promotion to the Second Division in 1959/60.

Just two days after putting pen to paper on his Norwich City contract, Whitehouse made his Canary debut at Somerton Park in a 1-1 draw with Newport County on 12 March 1960. He netted his first goal for the club on his fifth appearance as City drew 1-1 at home to Shrewsbury Town.

The striker was also on target in the thrilling 4-3 victory over Southend United at Carrow Road as promotion was secured on

Wednesday, 27 April 1960. His fourth and final goal of the campaign came on the final day of the season as City wrapped up a successful campaign with a 3-0 win at home to Chesterfield. Whitehouse ended his Norwich City career with an impressive goals-to-game ratio after scoring 18 goals in 49 matches. He was also the first player to score a League Cup goal for the club.

WHITTAKER, Steven

Date of birth: 16 June 1984
Place of birth: Edinburgh
Position: Defender
Promotion campaign: 2014/15 Championship play-off winners
2014/15 League statistics: 37(-)2 + play-offs 3(-)-

Steven Whittaker became Chris Hughton's first signing as Norwich boss when he joined City from Glasgow Rangers in the summer of 2012. A full Scottish international, Whittaker was a model professional and a popular member of the Colney dressing room, where his consistent professionalism won a great level of respect.

He had the ability to operate at right-back, centre-back or in midfield but played most of his Norwich career in the right-back role. He was often an unfair target for the Carrow Road boo boys in testing times, but he never shied away from the ball or a tackle and was a key member of City's 2014/15 promotion-winning team. Featuring under both Neil Adams and Alex Neil, Whittaker played in 37 league games and netted an important late equaliser to salvage a draw at Derby County in December 2014. He started all three matches in the end-of-season play-off campaign and played a vital role in the build-up to Nathan Redmond's goal in the play-off final victory over Middlesbrough at Wembley.

WILBRAHAM, Aaron

Date of birth: 21 October 1979
Place of birth: Knutsford
Position: Striker
Promotion campaign: 2010/11 Championship runners-up
2010/11 League statistics: 5(7)1

After impressing Norwich manager Paul Lambert with his displays for MK Dons against the Canaries during the 2009/10 League One campaign, striker Aaron Wilbraham initially joined City on an emergency loan deal from Stadium MK in December 2010.

The loan allowed Wilbraham to make his City debut on 1 January 2011 as Norwich won a crucial top-of-the-table clash with Queens Park Rangers 1-0 at Carrow Road. A permanent deal was then completed once the January transfer window opened for business.

Signed as back-up cover for Grant Holt, Wilbraham chipped in with a vital goal in a 3-2 win at Leicester City on 8 March 2011 before a back injury ended his season. An excellent professional whose commitment won him cult status among the Norwich fans, Wilbraham also featured in the club's Premier League campaign in 2011/12 and netted his 100th career goal in City's 2-1 defeat at Fulham on 31 March 2012.

WILLIAMS, David
Date of birth: 11 March 1955
Place of birth: Cardiff
Position: Midfielder
Promotion campaign: 1985/86 Division Two champions
1985/86 League statistics: 37(2)8

Cultured midfielder Dave Williams joined Norwich City in 1985 and proved to be a key component in the club's 1985/86 Second Division title-winning team.

Debuting in the opening-day victory over Oldham Athletic at Carrow Road, Williams featured in all bar three matches in his maiden season at Carrow Road. He chipped in with vital goals too as Ken Brown's men stormed back to the First Division in style. The Welshman netted his first goal in Canary yellow in October as City won 2-0 at Roker Park in their first meeting with Sunderland since the League Cup Final at Wembley seven months earlier.

Williams notched a brace in the pre-Christmas 6-1 thrashing of Millwall at Carrow Road and then scored both goals to ensure City overcame a dogged Carlisle United at home in March 1986. He stepped up to a coaching role under Dave Stringer later in his Canary career and played an influential role in the Canaries' 1988/89 season when they mounted a serious push for a league and cup double.

WOODS, Chris
Date of birth: 14 November 1959
Place of birth: Swineshead, Lincolnshire
Position: Goalkeeper

Promotion campaigns: 1981/82 third in Division Two and 1985/86
   Division Two champions
1981/82 League statistics: 42(-)-
1985/86 League statistics: 42(-)-

Another well-recognised name from the
Norwich City goalkeeping dynasty,
Chris Woods was ever-present
in two promotion-winning
campaigns for the Canaries as
well as being a Wembley winner
in the 1985 League Cup Final.

Blessed with a natural
calm assurance and lightning
reflexes, Woods had an ability
to make the most difficult of
saves with the minimum of
fuss. In some quarters Woods
is regarded as the club's finest
keeper and he won his first
England cap while at Carrow
Road before travelling to the
1986 World Cup finals in Mexico
as understudy to England number one
Peter Shilton.

Consistency was the key to Woods's
success at Carrow Road after he missed just five games from a
potential 272 following his £225,000 arrival from Queens Park
Rangers in 1981. He certainly provided those operating in front of
him with a feeling of confidence. Another shrewd signing by Ken
Brown, Woods was voted City's player of the season in 1983/84.

WOODS, Clive

Date of birth: 18 December 1947
Place of birth: Norwich
Position: Midfielder
Promotion campaign: 1981/82 third in Division Two
1981/82 League statistics: 8(-)1

Very much 'the one that got away', Norwich-born Clive Woods
played the majority of his professional career at local rivals Ipswich
Town and enjoyed FA Cup success with Town in 1978.

With his position on the left wing at Portman Road likely to come under stiff competition from recent signing Kevin O'Callaghan, Woods leapt at the chance of signing for the team he supported as a boy as John Bond lured him to Carrow Road in March 1980.

Woods featured regularly for City upon his arrival, but following John Bond's decision to move on to Manchester City later in the year he found first-team opportunities less frequent under new boss Ken Brown. Still, he contributed briefly in the early stages of City's 1981/82 promotion and started in eight of the club's first 11 matches. Woods struck the winner in the Canaries' 2-1 midweek triumph away to Grimsby Town on 22 September 1981. His final game for the club came the following month as City succumbed to a 3-0 reverse at Watford on 24 October 1981.

ZIMMERMANN, Christoph
Date of birth: 12 January 1993
Place of birth: Dusseldorf
Position: Defender
Promotion campaigns: 2018/19 Championship champions
2018/19 League statistics: 39(1)2

Giant central-defender Christoph Zimmermann followed head coach Daniel Farke from the Borussia Dortmund reserve side to Carrow Road in the summer of 2017.

Zimmermann played regularly throughout his first season at the club, partnering both Grant Hanley and Timm Klose at various stages of the campaign. His performance in the League Cup tie away to Arsenal won him reported plaudits from Arsene Wenger, but it was during the 2018/19 season that Zimmermann really came to the fore.

Despite being named among the City substitutes on the opening day of the season at Birmingham City, Zimmermann went on to feature in 40 of City's 46 league games and captained the team throughout 2019 following the injury sustained by Alex Tettey at Brentford on New Year's Day. Zimmermann proved to be an inspirational leader and his performances were rewarded with the runners-up spot in the player-of-the-season poll.

APPENDIX

Results, Appearances and Final League Tables

Norwich City's score is always
listed first in the table of results.

In the player statistics the
first figure relates to the number
of league matches they started,
the figures in brackets relate to
substitute appearances and the third
column relates to goals scored.

1959/60 Third Division

Date	Opponent	Result
Sat, Aug 22	Southampton	2-2
Wed, Aug 26	**Tranmere Rovers**	**3-0**
Sat, Aug 29	**Reading**	**4-2**
Mon, Aug 31	Tranmere Rovers	0-0
Sat, Sep 5	Shrewsbury Town	3-1
Wed, Sep 9	**Barnsley**	**0-0**
Sat, Sep 12	**Port Vale**	**5-1**
Wed, Sep 16	Barnsley	0-2
Sat, Sep 19	Wrexham	2-1
Wed, Sep 23	**Bury**	**2-0**
Sat, Sep 26	Brentford	4-3
Tue, Sept 29	Bury	0-1
Sat, Oct 3	**Colchester United**	**3-2**
Mon, Oct 5	Southend United	0-1
Sat, Oct 10	**Bournemouth**	**2-3**
Sat, Oct 17	Accrington Stanley	4-3
Sat, Oct, 24	**Newport County**	**1-0**
Sat, Oct, 31	Grimsby Town	1-1
Sat, Nov 7	**Swindon Town**	**3-2**
Sat, Nov 21	**Coventry City**	**1-4**
Sat, Nov 28	Bradford City	1-1
Sat, Dec 12	Chesterfield	1-2
Sat, Dec 19	**Southampton**	**1-2**
Sat, Dec 26	Mansfield Town	2-3
Mon, Dec 28	**Mansfield Town**	**5-1**
Sat, Jan 2	Reading	2-0
Sat, Jan 9	Halifax Town	1-0
Sat, Jan 23	Port Vale	1-2
Sat, Jan 30	**Queens Park Rangers**	**1-0**
Sat, Feb 6	**Wrexham**	**3-1**
Sat, Feb 13	**Brentford**	**2-1**
Sat, Feb 20	Colchester United	0-3
Sat, Feb 27	Bournemouth	0-0
Sat, Mar 5	**Accrington Stanley**	**4-0**
Sat, Mar 12	Newport County	1-1
Wed, Mar 16	York City	2-1
Sat, Mar 19	**Bradford City**	**0-0**
Sat, Mar 26	Swindon Town	1-0
Wed, Mar 30	**Shrewsbury Town**	**1-1**
Sat, Apr 2	**York City**	**1-0**
Sat, Apr 9	Coventry City	1-2
Sat, Apr 16	**Grimsby Town**	**1-1**
Mon, Apr 18	**Halifax Town**	**3-0**
Sat, Apr 23	Queens Park Rangers	0-0
Wed, Apr 27	**Southend United**	**4-3**
Sat, Apr 30	**Chesterfield**	**3-0**

Player Name	Starts (subs) goals
ASHMAN, Ron	46(n/a)**2**
BUTLER, Barry	46(n/a)**1**
McCROHAN, Roy	46(n/a)**1**
THURLOW, Bryan	46(n/a)-
CROWE, Matt	45(n/a)**4**
KENNON, Sandy	45(n/a)-
ALLCOCK, Terry	44(n/a)**16**
CROSSAN, Errol	43(n/a)**13**
HILL, Jimmy	38(n/a)**16**
PUNTON, Bill	27(n/a)**4**
BLY, Terry	25(n/a)**7**
BRENNAN, Bobby	20(n/a)**4**
WHITEHOUSE, Brian	10(n/a)**4**
LARKIN, Bunny	9(n/a)**3**
MORAN, James	6(n/a)**5**
RICHARDS, John	5(n/a)**2**
SAVINO, Ray	2(n/a)-
EDWARDS, Rob	1(n/a)-
MULLETT, Joe	1(n/a)-
RONSON, Brian	1(n/a)-
OWN GOALS	-

	P	W	D	L	F	A	Pts
Southampton	46	26	9	11	106	75	61
Norwich City	**46**	**24**	**11**	**11**	**82**	**54**	**59**
Shrewsbury Town	46	18	16	12	97	75	52
Grimsby Town	46	18	16	12	87	70	52
Coventry City	46	21	10	15	78	63	52
Brentford	46	21	9	16	78	61	51
Bury	46	21	9	16	64	51	51
Queens Park Rangers	46	18	13	15	73	54	49
Colchester United	46	18	11	17	83	74	47
Bournemouth	46	17	13	16	72	72	47
Reading	46	18	10	18	84	77	46
Southend United	46	19	8	19	76	74	46
Newport County	46	20	6	20	80	79	46
Port Vale	46	19	8	19	80	79	46
Halifax Town	46	18	10	18	70	72	46
Swindon Town	46	19	8	19	69	78	46
Barnsley	46	15	14	17	65	66	44
Chesterfield	46	18	7	21	71	84	43
Bradford City	46	15	12	19	66	74	42
Tranmere Rovers	46	14	13	19	72	75	41
York City	46	13	12	21	57	73	38
Mansfield Town	46	15	6	25	81	112	36
Wrexham	46	14	8	24	68	101	36
Accrington Stanley	46	11	5	30	57	123	27

1971/72 Second Division

Date	Opponent	Result
Sat, Aug 14	Luton Town	1-1
Sat, Aug 21	Portsmouth	3-1
Sat, Aug 28	Fulham	0-0
Wed, Sep 1	Orient	0-0
Sat, Sep 4	Carlisle United	1-0
Sat, Sep 11	Blackpool	2-1
Sat, Sep 18	Oxford United	3-2
Sat, Sep 25	Bristol City	1-0
Tue, Sept 28	Preston North End	2-0
Sat, Oct 2	Queens Park Rangers	0-0
Sat, Oct 9	Sunderland	1-1
Wed, Oct 13	Burnley	3-0
Sat, Oct 16	Luton Town	3-1
Sat, Oct 23	Millwall	1-2
Sat, Oct 30	Cardiff City	2-1
Sat, Nov 6	Hull City	2-1
Sat, Nov 13	Birmingham City	2-2
Sat, Nov 20	Sheffield Wednesday	1-1
Sat, Nov 27	Middlesbrough	2-0
Sat, Dec 4	Swindon Town	1-0
Sat, Dec 11	Watford	1-1
Sat, Dec 18	Carlisle United	0-3
Mon, Dec 27	Charlton Athletic	3-0
Sat, Jan 1	Oxford United	2-0
Sat, Jan 8	Fulham	2-1
Sat, Jan 22	Preston North End	1-1
Sat, Jan 29	Burnley	0-1
Sat, Feb 12	Millwall	2-2
Sat, Feb 19	Cardiff City	0-0
Sat, Mar 4	Birmingham City	0-4
Sat, Mar 11	Sunderland	1-1
Wed, Mar 15	Hull City	2-0
Sat, Mar 18	Portsmouth	1-2
Sat, Mar 25	Blackpool	5-1
Sat, Apr 1	Charlton Athletic	2-0
Mon, Apr 3	Queens Park Rangers	0-0
Tue, Apr 4	Bristol City	2-2
Sat, Apr 8	Sheffield Wednesday	1-0
Sat, Apr 15	Middlesbrough	0-0
Sat, Apr 22	Swindon Town	1-0
Mon, Apr 24	Orient	2-1
Sat, Apr 29	Watford	1-1

Player Name	Starts (subs) goals
KEELAN, Kevin	42(-)-
PAYNE, Clive	42(-)-
STRINGER, Dave	42(-)4
LIVERMORE, Doug	41(-)-
PADDON, Graham	40(-)8
FOGGO, Ken	38(2)13
ANDERSON, Terry	32(2)-
CROSS, David	32(-)8
FORBES, Duncan	27(-)2
SILVESTER, Peter	26(-)12
BUTLER, Geoff	23(-)-
BRIGGS, Max	21(6)-
BLACK, Alan	19(1)-
BONE, Jimmy	13(-)4
HOWARD, Trevor	8(12)5
HUBBARD, Phil	6(2)1
DARLING, Malcolm	4(-)1
BELL, Bobby	3(-)-
GOVIER, Steve	3(-)1
O'DONNELL, Neil	0(2)-
GRAPES, Steve	0(1)-
SARGENT, Gary	0(1)-
OWN GOALS	1

	P	W	D	L	F	A	Pts
Norwich City	42	21	15	6	60	36	57
Birmingham City	42	19	18	5	60	31	56
Millwall	42	19	17	6	64	46	55
Queens Park Rangers	42	20	14	8	57	28	54
Sunderland	42	17	16	9	67	57	50
Blackpool	42	20	7	15	70	50	47
Burnley	42	20	6	16	70	55	46
Bristol City	42	18	10	14	61	49	46
Middlesbrough	42	19	8	15	50	48	46
Carlisle United	42	17	9	16	61	57	43
Swindon Town	42	15	12	15	47	47	42
Hull City	42	14	10	18	49	53	38
Luton Town	42	10	18	14	43	48	38
Sheffield Wednesday	42	13	12	17	51	58	38
Oxford United	42	12	14	16	43	55	38
Portsmouth	42	12	13	17	59	68	37
Orient	42	14	9	19	50	61	37
Preston North End	42	12	12	18	52	58	36
Cardiff City	42	10	14	18	56	69	34
Fulham	42	12	10	20	45	68	34
Charlton Athletic	42	12	9	21	55	77	33
Watford	42	5	9	28	24	75	19

1974/75 Second Division

Date	Opponent	Result
Sat, Aug 17	**Blackpool**	2-1
Wed, Aug 21	**Southampton**	1-0
Sat, Aug 24	Aston Villa	1-1
Tue, Aug 27	Southampton	1-1
Sat, Aug 31	**Sheffield Wednesday**	1-1
Sat, Sep 7	Hull City	0-0
Sat, Sep 14	**Notts County**	3-0
Sat, Sep 21	Fulham	0-4
Tue, Sept 24	Sunderland	0-0
Sat, Sep 28	**Manchester United**	2-0
Sat, Oct 5	**Millwall**	2-0
Sat, Oct 12	Nottingham Forest	3-1
Sat, Oct 19	**Portsmouth**	2-0
Sat, Oct 26	Orient	3-0
Sat, Nov 2	West Bromwich Albion	1-1
Sat, Nov 9	**Bristol Rovers**	0-1
Sat, Nov 16	Oldham Athletic	2-2
Sat, Nov 23	**Bolton Wanderers**	2-0
Sat, Nov 30	York City	0-1
Sat, Dec 7	**Cardiff City**	1-1
Sat, Dec 14	Blackpool	1-2
Sat, Dec 21	**Bristol City**	3-2
Thu, Dec 26	Notts County	1-1
Sat, Dec 28	**Oxford United**	1-0
Sat, Jan 11	Cardiff City	1-2
Sat, Jan 18	**York City**	2-3
Sat, Jan 25	Oxford United	1-2
Sat, Feb 1	Bristol Rovers	2-0
Sat, Feb 8	**West Bromwich Albion**	3-2
Sat, Feb 15	Bolton Wanderers	0-0
Sat, Feb 22	**Oldham Athletic**	1-0
Sat, Mar 8	**Sunderland**	0-0
Sat, Mar 15	Manchester United	1-1
Sat, Mar 22	**Hull City**	1-0
Sat, Mar 29	Bristol City	1-0
Mon, Mar 31	**Fulham**	1-2
Sat, Apr 5	**Orient**	2-0
Tue, Apr 8	Sheffield Wednesday	1-0
Sat, Apr 12	Millwall	1-1
Sat, Apr 19	**Nottingham Forest**	3-0
Sat, Apr 26	Portsmouth	3-0
Wed, Apr 30	**Aston Villa**	1-4

Player Name	Starts (subs) goals
MacDOUGALL, Ted	42(-)**16**
SUGGETT, Colin	41(-)**6**
BOYER, Phil	40(-)**16**
MORRIS, Peter	40(-)-
POWELL, Tony	40(-)2
FORBES, Duncan	39(-)1
STRINGER, Dave	39(-)3
KEELAN, Kevin	38(-)-
SULLIVAN, Colin	35(1)1
MACHIN, Mel	24(-)3
BUTLER, Geoff	17(1)1
McGUIRE, Mick	16(-)2
MILLER, John	14(-)3
PETERS, Martin	10(-)2
BENSON, John	9(1)-
GRAPES, Steve	6(2)**2**
HANSBURY, Roger	4(-)-
STEELE, Billy	4(5)-
LIVERMORE, Doug	2(1)-
GOODWIN, Steve	2(-)-
OWN GOALS	-

	P	W	D	L	F	A	Pts
Manchester United	42	26	9	7	66	30	61
Aston Villa	42	25	8	9	79	32	58
Norwich City	**42**	**20**	**13**	**9**	**58**	**37**	**53**
Sunderland	42	19	13	10	65	35	51
Bristol City	42	21	8	13	47	33	50
West Bromwich Albion	42	18	9	15	54	42	45
Blackpool	42	14	17	11	38	33	45
Hull City	42	15	14	13	40	53	44
Fulham	42	13	16	13	44	39	42
Bolton Wanderers	42	15	12	15	45	41	42
Oxford United	42	15	12	15	41	51	42
Orient	42	11	20	11	28	39	42
Southampton	42	15	11	16	53	54	41
Notts County	42	12	16	14	49	59	40
York City	42	14	10	18	51	55	38
Nottingham Forest	42	12	14	16	43	55	38
Portsmouth	42	12	13	17	44	54	37
Oldham Athletic	42	10	15	17	40	48	35
Bristol Rovers	42	12	11	19	42	64	35
Millwall	42	10	12	20	44	56	32
Cardiff City	42	9	14	19	36	62	32
Sheffield Wednesday	42	5	11	26	29	64	21

1981/82 Second Division

Date	Opponent	Result
Sat, Aug 29	Rotherham United	1-4
Wed, Sep 2	**Crystal Palace**	**1-0**
Sat, Sep 5	**Barnsley**	**1-1**
Sat, Sep 12	Wrexham	3-2
Sat, Sep 19	**Newcastle United**	**2-1**
Tue, Sep 22	Grimsby Town	2-1
Sat, Sep 26	Chelsea	1-2
Sat, Oct 3	**Oldham Athletic**	**1-2**
Sat, Oct 10	Queens Park Rangers	0-2
Sat, Oct 17	**Shrewsbury Town**	**2-1**
Sat, Oct 24	Watford	0-3
Sat, Oct 31	**Bolton Wanderers**	**0-0**
Sat, Nov 7	Cardiff City	0-1
Sat, Nov 14	**Cambridge United**	**2-1**
Sat, Nov 21	**Derby County**	**4-1**
Tue, Nov 24	Crystal Palace	1-2
Sat, Nov 28	Blackburn Rovers	0-3
Sat, Dec 5	**Leicester City**	**0-0**
Mon, Dec 28	**Luton Town**	**1-3**
Wed, Dec 30	Charlton Athletic	0-0
Sat, Jan 16	**Rotherham United**	**2-0**
Sat, Jan 30	Newcastle United	1-2
Wed, Feb 3	**Sheffield Wednesday**	**2-3**
Sat, Feb 6	**Wrexham**	**4-0**
Tue, Feb 16	Oldham Athletic	0-2
Sat, Feb 20	**Chelsea**	**2-1**
Wed, Feb 24	Barnsley	1-0
Sat, Feb 27	**Queens Park Rangers**	**0-1**
Sat, Mar 13	**Watford**	**4-2**
Tue, Mar 16	Orient	1-1
Sat, Mar 20	Bolton Wanderers	1-0
Sat, Mar 27	**Cardiff City**	**2-1**
Sat, Apr 3	Cambridge United	2-1
Sat, Apr 10	**Charlton Athletic**	**5-0**
Mon, Apr 12	Luton Town	0-2
Sat, Apr 17	Derby County	2-0
Tue, Apr 20	Shrewsbury Town	2-0
Sat, Apr 24	**Blackburn Rovers**	**2-0**
Sat, May 1	Leicester City	4-1
Wed, May 5	**Grimsby Town**	**2-1**
Sat, May 8	**Orient**	**2-0**
Sat, May 15	Sheffield Wednesday	1-2

Player Name	Starts (subs) goals
WALFORD, Steve	42(-)**1**
WOODS, Chris	42(-)-
McGUIRE, Mick	39(-)**2**
WATSON, Dave	38(-)**3**
BERTSCHIN, Keith	35(1)**12**
DOWNS, Greg	28(-)**1**
MENDHAM, Peter	25(4)**6**
BARHAM, Mark	25(2)**4**
JACK, Ross	24(11)**10**
DEEHAN, John	22(-)**10**
BENNETT, Dave	21(1)**3**
HAYLOCK, PAUL	21(-)-
O'NEILL, Martin	20(-)**6**
SYMONDS, Richard	18(-)-
SHEPHERD, Greig	12(3)**2**
DONACHIE, Willie	11(-)-
NIGHTINGALE, Mark	8(1)-
PADDON, Graham	8(-)-
WOODS, Clive	8(-)**1**
MUZINIC, Drazen	6(1)-
FASHANU, John	4(1)**1**
HOADLEY, Phil	3(1)-
ROYLE, Joe	2(-)-
MOUNTFORD, Peter	0(2)-
HART, Andrew	0(1)-
OWN GOALS	**2**

	P	W	D	L	F	A	Pts
Luton Town	42	25	13	4	86	46	88
Watford	42	23	11	8	76	42	80
Norwich City	**42**	**22**	**5**	**15**	**64**	**50**	**71**
Sheffield Wednesday	42	20	10	12	55	51	70
Queens Park Rangers	42	21	6	15	65	43	69
Barnsley	42	19	10	13	59	41	67
Rotherham United	42	20	7	15	66	54	67
Leicester City	42	18	12	12	56	48	66
Newcastle United	42	18	8	16	52	50	62
Blackburn Rovers	42	16	11	15	47	43	59
Oldham Athletic	42	15	14	13	50	51	59
Chelsea	42	15	12	15	60	60	57
Charlton Athletic	42	13	12	17	50	65	51
Cambridge United	42	13	9	20	48	53	48
Crystal Palace	42	13	9	20	34	45	48
Derby County	42	12	12	18	53	68	48
Grimsby Town	42	11	13	18	53	65	46
Shrewsbury Town	42	11	13	18	37	57	46
Bolton Wanderers	42	13	7	22	39	61	46
Cardiff City	42	12	8	22	45	61	44
Wrexham	42	11	11	20	40	56	44
Orient	42	10	9	23	36	61	39

1985/86 Second Division

Date	Opponent	Result
Sat, Aug 17	Oldham Athletic	1-0
Tue, Aug 20	Blackburn Rovers	1-2
Sat, Aug 24	Millwall	2-4
Mon, Aug 26	Barnsley	1-1
Sat, Aug 31	Portsmouth	0-2
Sat, Sep 7	Sheffield United	4-0
Sat, Sep 14	Middlesbrough	1-1
Wed, Sep 18	Crystal Palace	4-3
Sat, Sep 21	Huddersfield Town	0-0
Sat, Sep 28	Hull City	2-0
Sat, Oct 5	Wimbledon	1-2
Sat, Oct 12	Carlisle United	4-0
Sat, Oct 19	Shrewsbury Town	3-1
Sat, Oct 26	Sunderland	2-0
Sat, Nov 2	Brighton & Hove Albion	1-1
Sat, Nov 9	Bradford City	0-0
Sat, Nov 16	Stoke City	1-1
Sat, Nov 23	Grimsby Town	3-2
Sat, Nov 30	Leeds United	2-0
Sat, Dec 7	Blackburn Rovers	3-0
Sat, Dec 14	Oldham Athletic	3-1
Sat, Dec 21	Millwall	6-1
Thu, Dec 26	Charlton Athletic	3-1
Wed, Jan 1	Fulham	1-0
Sat, Jan 11	Middlesbrough	2-0
Sat, Jan 18	Portsmouth	2-0
Sat, Jan 25	Crystal Palace	2-1
Sat, Feb 1	Barnsley	2-2
Sat, Feb 8	Shrewsbury Town	3-0
Sat, Mar 8	Wimbledon	1-2
Wed, Mar 12	Huddersfield Town	4-1
Sat, Mar 15	Carlisle United	2-1
Sat, Mar 22	Sheffield United	5-2
Sat, Mar 29	Fulham	2-1
Mon, Mar 31	Charlton Athletic	0-1
Sat, Apr 5	Brighton & Hove Albion	3-0
Wed, Apr 9	Sunderland	0-0
Sat, Apr 12	Bradford City	2-0
Sat, Apr 19	Stoke City	1-1
Sat, Apr 26	Grimsby Town	0-1
Tue, Apr 29	Hull City	0-1
Sat, May 3	Leeds United	4-0

Player Name	Starts (subs) goals
BRUCE, Steve	42(-)8
PHELAN, Mike	42(-)3
WATSON, Dave	42(-)3
WOODS, Chris	42(-)-
DRINKELL, Kevin	41(-)22
WILLIAMS, David	37(2)8
BARHAM, Mark	35(-)9
MENDHAM, Peter	35(-)8
CULVERHOUSE, Ian	30(-)-
BIGGINS, Wayne	28(-)7
VAN WIJK, Dennis	27(2)1
DEEHAN, John	22(4)4
HAYLOCK, Paul	12(-)1
BROOKE, Garry	8(5)2
ROSARIO, Robert	8(-)2
SPEARING, Tony	7(1)-
GORDON, Dale	3(3)1
CLAYTON, Paul	1(-)-
DONOWA, Louie	0(2)-
OWN GOALS	**5**

	P	W	D	L	F	A	Pts
Norwich City	42	25	9	8	84	37	84
Charlton Athletic	42	22	11	9	78	45	77
Wimbledon	42	21	13	8	58	37	76
Portsmouth	42	22	7	13	69	41	73
Crystal Palace	42	19	9	14	57	52	66
Hull City	42	17	13	12	65	55	64
Sheffield United	42	17	11	14	64	63	62
Oldham Athletic	42	17	9	16	62	61	60
Millwall	42	17	8	17	64	65	59
Stoke City	42	14	15	13	48	50	57
Brighton & Hove Albion	42	16	8	18	64	64	56
Barnsley	42	14	14	14	47	50	56
Bradford City	42	16	6	20	51	63	54
Leeds United	42	15	8	19	56	72	53
Grimsby Town	42	14	10	18	58	62	52
Huddersfield Town	42	14	10	18	51	67	52
Shrewsbury Town	42	14	9	19	52	64	51
Sunderland	42	13	11	18	47	61	50
Blackburn Rovers	42	12	13	17	53	62	49
Carlisle United	42	13	7	22	47	71	46
Middlesbrough	42	12	9	21	44	53	45
Fulham	42	10	6	26	45	69	36

2003/04 First Division

Date	Team	Result
Sat, Aug 9	Bradford City	2-2
Sat, Aug 16	**Rotherham United**	**2-0**
Sat, Aug 23	Sheffield United	0-1
Tue, Aug 26	**Wimbledon**	**3-2**
Sat, Aug 30	Nottingham Forest	0-2
Sat, Sep 13	**Burnley**	**2-0**
Tue, Sep 16	Gillingham	2-1
Sat, Sep 20	Stoke City	1-1
Sat, Sep 27	**Crystal Palace**	**2-1**
Tue, Sep 30	**Reading**	**2-1**
Sat, Oct 4	Wigan Athletic	1-1
Wed, Oct 15	West Ham United	1-1
Sat, Oct 18	West Bromwich Albion	0-1
Tue, Oct 21	**Derby County**	**2-1**
Sat, Oct 25	**Sunderland**	**1-0**
Sat, Nov 1	Walsall	3-1
Sat, Nov 8	**Millwall**	**3-1**
Sat, Nov 15	**Watford**	**1-2**
Sat, Nov 22	Preston North End	0-0
Tue, Nov 25	**Coventry City**	**1-1**
Sat, Nov 29	**Crewe Alexandra**	**1-0**
Sat, Dec 6	Millwall	0-0
Sat, Dec 13	**Cardiff City**	**4-1**
Sun, Dec 21	Ipswich Town	2-0
Fri, Dec 26	**Nottingham Forest**	**1-0**
Sun, Dec 28	Derby County	4-0
Sat, Jan 10	**Bradford City**	**0-1**
Sat, Jan 17	Rotherham United	4-4
Sat, Jan 31	**Sheffield United**	**1-0**
Sat, Feb 7	Wimbledon	1-0
Sat, Feb 14	Coventry City	2-0
Sat, Feb 21	**West Ham United**	**1-1**
Tue, Mar 2	**West Bromwich Albion**	**0-0**
Sun, Mar 7	**Ipswich Town**	**3-1**
Sat, Mar 13	Cardiff City	1-2
Tue, Mar 16	**Gillingham**	**3-0**
Sat, Mar 20	Crystal Palace	0-1
Sat, Mar 27	**Stoke City**	**1-0**
Sat, Apr 3	Burnley	5-3
Fri, Apr 9	**Wigan Athletic**	**2-0**
Mon, Apr 12	Reading	1-0
Sat, Apr 17	**Walsall**	**5-0**
Sat, Apr 24	Watford	2-1
Sat, May 1	**Preston North End**	**3-2**
Tue, May 4	Sunderland	0-1
Sun, May 9	Crewe Alexandra	3-1

Player Name	Starts(subs)sgoals
FLEMING, Craig	46(-)3
GREEN, Robert	46(-)-
HOLT, Gary	46(-)1
MACKAY, Malky	45(-)4
EDWORTHY, Marc	42(1)-
DRURY, Adam	42(-)-
FRANCIS, Damien	39(2)7
McVEIGH, Paul	36(8)5
HUCKERBY, Darren	36(-)14
SVENSSON, Mathias	16(4)7
MULRYNE, Philip	14(20)3
HENDERSON, Ian	14(5)4
CROUCH, Peter	14(1)4
ROBERTS, Iwan	13(28)8
McKENZIE, Leon	12(6)9
HARPER, Kevin	9(-)-
EASTON, Clint	8(2)2
BRENNAN, Jim	7(8)1
RIVERS, Marc	7(5)4
COOPER, Kevin	6(4)-
SHACKELL, Jason	4(2)-
NIELSEN, David	2(-)-
BRIGGS, Keith	1(2)-
ABBEY, Zema	1(2)-
JARVIS, Ryan	0(12)1
HAMMOND, Elvis	0(4)-
NOTMAN, Alex	0(1)-
OWN GOALS	**2**

	P	W	D	L	F	A	Pts
Norwich City	46	28	10	8	79	39	94
West Bromwich Albion	46	25	11	10	64	42	86
Sunderland	46	22	13	11	62	45	79
West Ham United	46	19	17	10	67	45	74
Ipswich Town	46	21	10	15	84	72	73
Crystal Palace	46	21	10	15	72	61	73
Wigan Athletic	46	18	17	11	60	45	71
Sheffield United	46	20	11	15	65	56	71
Reading	46	20	10	16	55	57	70
Millwall	46	18	15	13	55	48	69
Stoke City	46	18	12	16	58	55	66
Coventry City	46	17	14	15	67	54	65
Cardiff City	46	17	14	15	68	58	65
Nottingham Forest	46	15	15	16	61	58	60
Preston North End	46	15	14	17	69	71	59
Watford	46	15	12	19	54	68	57
Rotherham United	46	13	15	18	53	61	54
Crewe Alexandra	46	14	11	21	57	66	53
Burnley	46	13	14	19	60	77	53
Derby County	46	13	13	20	53	67	52
Gillingham	46	14	9	23	48	67	51
Walsall	46	13	12	21	45	65	51
Bradford City	46	10	6	30	38	69	36
Wimbledon	46	8	5	33	41	89	29

2009/10 League One

Date	Team	Result
Sat, Aug 8	**Colchester United**	1-7
Sat, Aug 15	Exeter City	1-1
Tue, Aug 18	Brentford	1-2
Sat, Aug 22	**Wycombe Wanderers**	5-2
Sat, Aug 29	Hartlepool United	2-0
Sat, Sept 5	**Walsall**	0-0
Mon, Sept 14	MK Dons	1-2
Sat, Sept 19	**Charlton Athletic**	2-2
Sat, Sept 26	Gillingham	1-1
Tue, Sep 29	**Leyton Orient**	4-0
Sat, Oct 3	**Bristol Rovers**	5-1
Sat, Oct 10	Carlisle United	1-0
Mon, Oct 19	Leeds United	1-2
Sat, Oct 24	**Swindon Town**	1-0
Sat, Oct 31	Stockport County	3-1
Sat, Nov 14	**Tranmere Rovers**	2-0
Sat, Nov 21	Southampton	2-2
Tue, Nov 24	**Brighton & Hove Albion**	4-1
Tue, Dec 1	Southend United	3-0
Sat, Dec 5	**Oldham Athletic**	2-0
Sat, Dec 12	Yeovil Town	3-3
Sat, Dec 19	**Huddersfield Town**	3-0
Sat, Dec 26	**Millwall**	2-0
Sat, Jan 2	Wycombe Wanderers	1-0
Sat, Jan 9	**Exeter City**	3-1
Sat, Jan 16	Colchester United	5-0
Sat, Jan 23	**Brentford**	1-0
Tue, Jan 26	Walsall	2-1
Sat, Jan 30	**Hartlepool United**	2-1
Sat, Feb 6	Millwall	1-2
Sat, Feb 13	Brighton & Hove Albion	2-1
Sat, Feb 20	**Southampton**	0-2
Tue, Feb 23	**Southend United**	2-1
Sat, Feb 27	Oldham Athletic	1-0
Sat, Mar 6	**Yeovil Town**	3-0
Sat, Mar 13	Huddersfield Town	3-1
Sat, Mar 20	Swindon Town	1-1
Sat, Mar 27	**Leeds United**	1-0
Fri, Apr 2	Tranmere Rovers	1-3
Mon, Apr 5	**Stockport County**	2-1
Sat, Apr 10	**MK Dons**	1-1
Tue, Apr 13	Leyton Orient	1-2
Sat, Apr 17	Charlton Athletic	1-0
Sat, Apr 24	**Gillingham**	2-0
Sat, May 1	Bristol Rovers	3-0
Sat, May 8	**Carlisle United**	0-2

Player Name	Starts(subs)goals
LAPPIN, Simon	42(2)-
HOLT, Grant	39(-)**24**
DOHERTY, Gary	38(-)**6**
FORSTER, Fraser	38(-)-
MARTIN, Chris	36(6)**17**
HOOLAHAN, Wes	36(1)**11**
SMITH, Korey	36(1)**4**
DRURY, Adam	35(-)-
RUSSELL, Darel	34(1)**2**
NELSON, Michael	28(3)**3**
MARTIN, Russell	26(-)-
BERTHEL ASKOU, Jens	21(1)**2**
HUGHES, Stephen	12(17)**3**
OTSEMOBOR, Jon	12(1)**1**
ROSE, Michael	11(1)**1**
SPILLANE, Michael	10(3)**1**
McNAMEE, Anthony	7(10)**1**
GILL, Matt	5(3)-
JOHNSON, Oli	4(13)**4**
McDONALD, Cody	4(13)**3**
ELLIOTT, Stephen	4(6)**2**
McVEIGH, Paul	4(5)-
RUDD, Declan	4(3)-
CURETON, Jamie	3(3)**2**
DALEY, Luke	3(4)-
ALNWICK, Ben	3(-)-
WHALEY, Simon	3(-)-
ADEYEMI, Tom	2(9)-
TUDUR JONES, Owain	2(1)**1**
FRANCOMB, George	2(-)-
WHITBREAD, Zak	1(3)-
THEOKLITOS, Michael	1(-)-
OWN GOALS	**1**

	P	W	D	L	F	A	Pts
Norwich City	46	29	8	9	89	47	95
Leeds United	46	25	11	10	77	44	86
Millwall	46	24	13	9	76	44	85
Charlton Athletic	46	23	15	8	71	48	84
Swindon Town	46	22	16	8	73	57	82
Huddersfield Town	46	23	11	12	82	56	80
Southampton	46	23	14	9	85	47	73
Colchester United	46	20	12	14	64	52	72
Brentford	46	14	20	12	55	52	62
Walsall	46	16	14	16	60	63	62
Bristol Rovers	46	19	5	22	59	70	62
Milton Keynes Dons	46	17	9	20	60	68	60
Brighton & Hove Albion	46	15	14	17	56	60	59
Carlisle United	46	15	13	18	63	66	58
Yeovil Town	46	13	14	19	55	59	53
Oldham Athletic	46	13	13	20	39	57	52
Leyton Orient	46	13	12	21	53	63	51
Exeter City	46	11	18	17	48	60	51
Tranmere Rovers	46	14	9	23	45	72	51
Hartlepool United	46	14	11	21	59	67	50
Gillingham	46	12	14	20	48	64	50
Wycombe Wanderers	46	10	15	21	56	76	45
Southend United	46	10	13	23	51	72	43
Stockport County	46	5	10	31	35	95	25

2010/11 Championship

Date	Team	Result
Fri, Aug 6	**Watford**	2-3
Sat, Aug 14	Scunthorpe United	1-0
Sat, Aug 21	**Swansea City**	**2-0**
Sat, Aug 28	Nottingham Forest	1-1
Sat, Sep 11	**Barnsley**	**2-1**
Tue, Sept 14	Doncaster Rovers	1-3
Sat, Sept 18	Preston North End	1-0
Sat, Sept 25	**Hull City**	**0-2**
Tue, Sep 28	**Leicester City**	**4-3**
Sat, Oct 2	Bristol City	3-0
Sat, Oct 16	Queens Park Rangers	0-0
Tue, Oct 19	**Crystal Palace**	**1-2**
Sat, Oct 23	**Middlesbrough**	**1-0**
Sat, Oct 30	Cardiff City	1-3
Sat, Nov 6	**Burnley**	**2-2**
Tue, Wed 9	Millwall	1-1
Sat, Nov 13	Reading	3-3
Sat, Nov 20	**Leeds United**	**1-1**
Sun, Nov 28	**Ipswich Town**	**4-1**
Sat, Dec 4	Derby County	2-1
Sat, Dec 11	**Portsmouth**	**0-2**
Sat, Dec 18	Coventry City	2-1
Tue, Dec 28	**Sheffield United**	**4-2**
Sat, Jan 1	**Queens Park Rangers**	**1-0**
Mon, Jan 3	Middlesbrough	1-1
Sat, Jan 15	**Cardiff City**	**1-1**
Sat, Jan 22	Sheffield United	2-1
Sat, Jan 29	Crystal Palace	0-0
Tue, Feb 1	**Millwall**	**2-1**
Sat, Feb 5	Burnley	1-2
Sat, Feb 12	**Reading**	**2-1**
Sat, Feb 19	Leeds United	2-2
Tue, Feb 22	**Doncaster Rovers**	**1-1**
Sat, Feb 26	Barnsley	2-0
Sat, Mar 5	**Preston North End**	**1-1**
Tue, Mar 8	Leicester City	3-2
Mon, Mar 14	**Bristol City**	**3-1**
Sat, Mar 19	Hull City	1-1
Sat, Apr 2	**Scunthorpe United**	**6-0**
Sat, Apr 9	Swansea City	0-3
Tue, Apr 12	Watford	2-2
Fri, Apr 15	**Nottingham Forest**	**2-1**
Thu, Apr 21	Ipswich Town	5-1
Mon, Apr 25	**Derby County**	**3-2**
Mon, May 2	Portsmouth	1-0
Sat, May 7	**Coventry City**	**2-2**

Player Name	Starts(subs)goals
MARTIN, Russell	46(-)5
RUDDY, John	45(-)-
HOLT, Grant	44(1)21
CROFTS, Andrew	44(-)8
WARD, Elliott	39(-)1
HOOLAHAN, Wes	36(5)10
FOX, David	30(2)1
BARNETT, Leon	25(-)1
MARTIN, Chris	21(9)4
JACKSON, Simeon	20(19)13
LAPPIN, Simon	20(7)-
WHITBREAD, Zak	20(2)1
SMITH, Korey	19(9)-
SURMAN, Andrew	19(3)3
DRURY, Adam	19(1)1
LANSBURY, Henri	15(8)4
TIERNEY, Marc	14(2)-
NELSON, Michael	7(1)2
McNAMEE, Anthony	5(12)-
WILBRAHAM, Aaron	5(7)1
SMITH, Steven	5(2)-
PACHECO, Dani	3(3)2
BERTHEL ASKOU, Jens	2(3)-
VOKES, Sam	1(3)1
TUDUR JONES, Owain	1(1)-
RUDD, Declan	1(-)-
GILL, Matt	0(4)-
JOHNSON, Oli	0(4)-
EDWARDS, Rob	0(3)-
DALEY, Luke	0(1)-
HUGHES, Stephen	0(1)-
OWN GOALS	**4**

	P	W	D	L	F	A	Pts
Queens Park Rangers	46	24	16	6	71	32	88
Norwich City	**46**	**23**	**15**	**8**	**83**	**58**	**84**
Swansea City	46	24	8	14	69	42	80
Cardiff City	46	23	11	12	76	54	80
Reading	46	20	17	9	77	51	77
Nottingham Forest	46	20	15	11	69	50	75
Leeds United	46	19	15	12	81	70	72
Burnley	46	18	14	14	65	61	68
Millwall	46	18	13	15	62	48	67
Leicester City	46	19	10	17	76	71	67
Hull City	46	16	17	13	52	51	65
Middlesbrough	46	17	11	18	68	68	62
Ipswich Town	46	18	8	20	62	68	62
Watford	46	16	13	17	77	71	61
Bristol City	46	17	9	20	62	65	60
Portsmouth	46	15	13	18	53	60	58
Barnsley	46	14	14	18	55	66	56
Coventry City	46	14	13	19	54	58	55
Derby County	46	13	10	23	58	71	49
Crystal Palace	46	12	12	22	44	69	48
Doncaster Rovers	46	11	15	20	55	81	48
Preston North End	46	10	12	24	54	79	42
Sheffield United	46	11	9	26	44	79	42
Scunthorpe United	46	12	6	28	43	87	42

2014/15 Championship

Date	Team	Result
Sun, Aug 10	Wolverhampton Wanderers	0-1
Sat, Aug 16	Watford	3-0
Tue, Aug 19	Blackburn Rovers	3-1
Sat, Aug 23	Ipswich Town	1-0
Sat, Aug 30	AFC Bournemouth	1-1
Sat, Sept 13	Cardiff City	4-2
Tue, Sept 16	Brentford	3-0
Sat, Sept 20	Birmingham City	2-2
Sat, Sept 27	Blackpool	3-1
Tue, Sept 30	Charlton Athletic	0-1
Sat, Oct 4	Rotherham United	1-1
Sat, Oct 18	Fulham	0-1
Tue, Oct 21	Leeds United	1-1
Sat, Oct 25	Sheffield Wednesday	0-0
Fri, Oct 31	Bolton Wanderers	2-1
Tue, Nov 4	Middlesbrough	0-4
Sat, Nov 8	Nottingham Forest	1-2
Sat, Nov 22	Brighton & Hove Albion	3-3
Sat, Nov 29	Reading	1-2
Sat, Dec 6	Wigan Athletic	1-0
Sat, Dec 13	Huddersfield Town	5-0
Sat, Dec 20	Derby County	2-2
Fri, Dec 26	Millwall	6-1
Sun, Dec 28	Reading	1-2
Sat, Jan 10	AFC Bournemouth	2-1
Sat, Jan 17	Cardiff City	3-2
Sat, Jan 24	Brentford	1-2
Sat, Jan 31	Birmingham City	0-0
Sat, Feb 7	Blackpool	4-0
Tue, Feb 10	Charlton Athletic	3-2
Sat, Feb 14	Wolverhampton Wanderers	2-0
Sat, Feb 21	Watford	3-0
Tue, Feb 24	Blackburn Rovers	2-1
Sun, Mar 1	Ipswich Town	2-0
Wed, Mar 4	Wigan Athletic	0-1
Sat, Mar 7	Millwall	4-1
Sat, Mar14	Derby County	1-1
Tue, Mar 17	Huddersfield Town	2-2
Sat, Mar 21	Nottingham Forest	3-1
Fri, Apr 3	Brighton & Hove Albion	1-0
Mon, Apr 6	Sheffield Wednesday	2-0
Sat, Apr 11	Bolton Wanderers	2-1
Sat, Apr 14	Leeds United	2-0
Fri, Apr 17	Middlesbrough	0-1
Sat, Apr 25	Rotherham United	1-1
Sat, May 2	Fulham	4-2

2014/15 PLAY-OFFS

Sat, May 9	Ipswich Town (Play-off S/F First Leg)	1-1
Sat, May 16	Ipswich Town (Play-off S/F Second Leg)	3-1
Mon, May 25	Middlesbrough (Play-off Final)	2-0

Player Name	League starts(subs) goals	Play-offs starts(subs)goals
RUDDY, John	46(-)-	3(-)-
MARTIN, Russell	45(-)2	3(-)-
OLSSON, Martin	42(-)1	3(-)-
JOHNSON, Bradley	40(1)15	3(-)-
WHITTAKER, Steven	37(-)2	3(-)-
TETTEY, Alexander	34(2)2	3(-)-
REDMOND, Nathan	33(10)4	3(-)2
JEROME, Cameron	32(9)18	3(-)2
HOWSON, Jonny	32(2)8	3(-)1
HOOLAHAN, Wes	27(9)4	2(1)1
GRABBAN, Lewis	23(12)12	0(1)-
TURNER, Michael	22(1)1	-
BASSONG, Sebastien	18(-)-	3(-)-
HOOPER, Gary	16(14)12	0(2)-
DORRANS, Graham	12(3)3	1(2)-
LAFFERTY, Kyle	11(7)1	-
O'NEIL, Gary	10(11)-	0(1)-
CUELLAR, Carlos	8(-)-	-
HOOIVELD, Jos	6(-)-	-
BENNETT, Elliott	3(6)-	0(1)-
BENNETT, Ryan	3(4)-	-
GARRIDO, Javier	3(4)-	-
MURPHY, Josh	1(12)1	-
ODJIDJA OFOE, Vadis	1(4)-	-
SURMAN, Andrew	1(-)-	-
ANDREU, Tony	0(6)-	-
LOZA, Jamar	0(2)1	-
FER, Leroy	0(1)-	-
McGRANDLES, Conor	0(1)-	-
MORRIS, Carlton	0(1)-	-
OWN GOALS	1	-

	P	W	D	L	F	A	Pts
Bournemouth	46	26	12	8	98	45	90
Watford	46	27	8	11	91	50	89
Norwich City	**46**	**25**	**11**	**10**	**88**	**48**	**86**
Middlesbrough	46	25	10	11	68	37	85
Brentford	46	23	9	14	78	59	78
Ipswich Town	46	22	12	12	72	54	78
Wolverhampton W.	46	22	12	12	70	56	78
Derby County	46	21	14	11	85	56	77
Blackburn Rovers	46	17	16	13	66	59	67
Birmingham City	46	16	15	15	54	64	63
Cardiff City	46	16	14	16	57	61	62
Charlton Athletic	46	14	18	14	54	60	60
Sheffield Wednesday	46	14	18	14	43	49	60
Nottingham Forest	46	15	14	17	71	69	59
Leeds United	46	15	11	20	50	61	56
Huddersfield Town	46	13	16	17	58	75	55
Fulham	46	14	10	22	62	83	52
Bolton Wanderers	46	13	12	21	54	67	51
Reading	46	13	11	22	48	69	50
Brighton & Hove Albion	46	10	17	19	44	54	47
Rotherham United	46	11	16	19	46	67	46
Millwall	46	9	14	23	42	76	41
Wigan Athletic	46	9	12	25	39	64	39
Blackpool	46	4	14	28	36	91	26

2018/19 Championship

Date	Team	Result
Sat, Aug 4	Birmingham City	2-2
Sat, Aug 11	**West Bromwich Albion**	3-4
Sat, Aug 18	Sheffield United	1-2
Wed, Aug 22	**Preston North End**	2-0
Sat, Aug 25	**Leeds United**	0-3
Sun, Sept 2	Ipswich Town	1-1
Sat, Sept 15	**Middlesbrough**	1-0
Wed, Sept 19	Reading	2-1
Sat, Sept 22	Queens Park Rangers	1-0
Sat, Sept 29	**Wigan Athletic**	1-0
Wed, Oct 3	Derby County	1-1
Sat, Oct 6	**Stoke City**	0-1
Sat, Oct 20	Nottingham Forest	2-1
Tue, Oct 23	**Aston Villa**	2-1
Sat, Oct 27	**Brentford**	1-0
Sat, Nov 3	Sheffield Wednesday	4-0
Sat, Nov 10	**Millwall**	4-3
Sat, Nov 24	Swansea City	4-1
Tue, Nov 27	Hull City	0-0
Sat, Dec 1	**Rotherham United**	3-1
Sat, Dec 8	**Bolton Wanderers**	3-2
Sat, Dec 15	Bristol City	2-2
Sat, Dec 22	Blackburn Rovers	1-0
Wed, Dec 26	**Nottingham Forest**	3-3
Sat, Dec 29	**Derby County**	3-4
Tue, Jan 1	Brentford	1-1
Sat, Jan 12	West Bromwich Albion	1-1
Fri, Jan 18	**Birmingham City**	3-1
Sat, Jan 26	**Sheffield United**	2-2
Sat, Feb 2	Leeds United	3-1
Sun, Feb 10	**Ipswich Town**	3-0
Wed, Feb 13	Preston North End	1-3
Sat, Feb 16	Bolton Wanderers	4-0
Sat, Feb 23	**Bristol City**	3-2
Sat, Mar 2	Millwall	3-1
Fri, Mar 8	**Swansea City**	1-0
Wed, Mar 13	**Hull City**	3-2
Sat, Mar 16	Rotherham United	2-1
Sat, Mar 30	Middlesbrough	1-0
Sat, Apr 6	**Queens Park Rangers**	4-0
Wed, Apr 10	**Reading**	2-2
Sun, Apr 14	Wigan Athletic	1-1
Fri, Apr 19	**Sheffield Wednesday**	2-2
Mon, Apr 22	Stoke City	2-2
Sat, April 27	**Blackburn Rovers**	2-1
Sun, May 5	Aston Villa	2-1

Player Name	Starts (subs) goals
KRUL, Tim	46(-)-
PUKKI, Teemu	43(-)**29**
LEWIS, Jamal	42(-)-
AARONS, Max	41(-)**2**
STIPERMAN, Marco	39(4)**9**
ZIMMERMANN, Christoph	39(1)**2**
BUENDIA, Emiliano	35(3)**8**
HERNANDEZ, Onel	34(6)**8**
GODFREY, Ben	26(5)**4**
TETTEY, Alex	26(4)**1**
KLOSE, Timm	23(8)**4**
TRYBULL, Tom	22(9)**1**
LEITNER, Moritz	19(10)**2**
CANWELL, Todd	18(6)**1**
McLEAN, Kenny	15(5)**3**
VRANCIC, Mario	14(22)**10**
RHODES, Jordan	9(27)**6**
HANLEY, Grant	6(3)**1**
MARSHALL, Ben	4(-)-
PINTO, Ivo	3(-)-
THOMPSON, Louis	1(5)-
HUSBAND, James	1(-)-
SRBENY, Dennis	0(15)**1**
PASSLACK, Felix	0(1)-
OWN GOALS	**1**

	P	W	D	L	F	A	Pts
Norwich City	46	27	13	6	93	57	**94**
Sheffield United	46	26	11	9	78	41	89
Leeds United	46	25	8	13	73	50	83
West Bromwich Albion	46	23	11	12	87	62	80
Aston Villa	46	20	16	10	82	61	76
Derby County	46	20	14	12	69	54	74
Middlesbrough	46	20	13	13	49	41	73
Bristol City	46	19	13	14	59	53	70
Nottingham Forest	46	17	15	14	61	54	66
Swansea City	46	18	11	17	65	62	65
Brentford	46	17	13	16	73	59	64
Sheffield Wednesday	46	16	16	14	60	62	64
Hull City	46	17	11	18	66	68	62
Preston North End	46	16	13	17	67	67	61
Blackburn Rovers	46	16	12	18	64	69	60
Stoke City	46	11	22	13	45	52	55
Birmingham City	46	14	19	13	64	58	52
Wigan Athletic	46	13	13	20	51	64	52
Queens Park Rangers	46	14	9	23	53	71	51
Reading	46	10	17	19	49	66	47
Millwall	46	10	14	22	48	64	44
Rotherham United	46	8	16	22	52	83	40
Bolton Wanderers	46	8	8	30	29	78	32
Ipswich Town	46	5	16	25	36	77	31